Small Wonder

Small Wonder

Global Power and Its Discontents

Fred Dallmayr

ROWMAN & LITTLEFIELD PUBLISHERS, INC.
Lanham • Boulder • New York • Toronto • Oxford

ROWMAN & LITTLEFIELD PUBLISHERS, INC.

Published in the United States of America
by Rowman & Littlefield Publishers, Inc.
A wholly owned subsidiary of The Rowman & Littlefield Publishing Group, Inc.
4501 Forbes Boulevard, Suite 200, Lanham, Maryland 20706
www.rowmanlittlefield.com

PO Box 317
Oxford
OX2 9RU, UK

British Library Cataloguing in Publication Information Available

Library of Congress Cataloging-in-Publication Data

Dallmayr, Fred R. (Fred Reinhard), 1928–
Small wonder : global power and its discontents / by Fred Dallmayr.
    p. cm. — (New critical theory)
    Includes bibliographical references and index.
    ISBN 0-7425-4967-4 (cloth : alk. paper) — ISBN 0-7425-4968-2 (pbk. : alk. paper)
1. Sociology—Philosophy. 2. Critical theory. 3. Culture—Philosophy.
4. Civilization—Philosophy. I. Title. II. Series.
    HM461.D34 2005
    301'.01—dc22   2005009618

Printed in the United States of America

∞™ The paper used in this publication meets the minimum requirements of American
National Standard for Information Sciences—Permanence of Paper for Printed Library
Materials, ANSI/NISO Z39.48–1992.

To all people trampled down by bigness

All good things start small—
and get smaller.

Daniel Berrigan

Our country is different from his. His is the
military, money, power, a Ferrari. Ours is
the men and women who give their lives for
it, the Plaza, life, the earth.

Hebe de Bonafini

. . . he has put the mighty from their thrones,
and exalted those of low degree;
he has filled the hungry with good things,
and sent the rich away empty.

Luke 1:52–53

Table of Contents

Preface

This book is a sequel to my earlier collection of essays titled *Peace Talks—Who Will Listen?* That earlier book was written in the aftermath of September 11 and during the fury of violence surrounding the war against Iraq. Borrowing a leaf from Erasmus, I had allowed "peace" to speak directly, addressing humankind with the plea to relinquish warfare in favor of the superior path of peace and justice. The subtitle "Who Will Listen?" was not meant as a rhetorical ploy, but as a summons or exhortation.

In the meantime, this summons remains still largely unheeded. In many parts of the world, violence and mayhem are still the order of the day. Instead of bringing people closer together in a shared world, globalization (so-called) has unleashed a mad scramble for global political, military, and economic power or supremacy. Desires and ambitions which, in previous ages, were more or less geographically contained, have now been unleashed to encompass the entire globe and even extend into planetary space. Unsurprisingly, such globalized ambitions spawn the result of global violence and global "terror." In a steadily militarized world, the fate of grassroots democracy and the lives of ordinary people are placed at risk everywhere. In a globe placed under the tutelage of "military-industrial complexes," the emphasis is bound to be put on domination and "terror wars"—in lieu of the cultivation of cross-cultural learning, cooperation, and peace.

Like *Peace Talks*, the present book is written "against the grain" or against ruling "self-images of the age." One of these ruling images—especially in the West—is that progress means growth, that bigger is better, and that the biggest is the best. Against this image—which I would not hesitate to call idolatry—this book directs attention to "smallness" and the care for smallness—where that term does not denote pettiness or small-mindedness, but rather something like reticence, shyness, modesty, and self-limitation. It is this kind of reticent modesty which is at the heart of the great philosophical teachings of the past, as well as at the core of the great world religions East and West. When Plato placed the beginning of philosophy in "wondering" (*thaumazein*), he clearly alerted us to the needed openness to the recessed "wonder" of the world—away from fixed doctrines and ideological formulas. More than two thousand years later, his words were still echoed by the philosopher Edmund Husserl who, in his old age and having reached great fame, stated that now at last he was able to be a "true beginner." Without exception, all the great world religions likewise remind us of the need for modesty and patient self-overcoming, a need deriving from our mortal finitude in the face of infinity. Memorable for Christians in this regard are the so-called beatitudes which, among other things, extend blessings to the meek, the hungry, and the peacemakers. Memorable too is the response given by Prophet Muhammad when asked to pinpoint the nature of faith: "gentleness and self-restraint." Not much needs to be added to these words.

In straining against the dominant "grain," this book seeks to draw attention to this submerged and today almost apocryphal alternative of reticence. In pointing to this alternative, the book does not mean to be seditious—although its outlook will no doubt be perceived as troublesome by people firmly wedded to power politics and the entanglements of worldly bigness. Placing itself in the Socratic tradition, the book in a way seeks to "speak truth to power"—an effort never readily appreciated by the powerful (as the Socratic example indicates). More specifically, my intent is to draw attention to the "discontents" of global power—discontents evident in the price exacted by big power on the side of justice and peace. Although perhaps troubling to some, the tenor of the book is not aggressive or belligerent (and in fact shuns belligerence altogether). Without condoning injustice or exploitation, the tenor rubs against the grain peaceably—reminding people enamored with worldly power and prestige of their own recessed potential for justice, non-exploitation, and wondering.

In pursuing my alternative path I am fully aware of my indebtedness to a number of mentors and friends. The theme of "small wonder" draws inspiration from Walter Benjamin's "Angelus Novus," from Theodor Adorno's "negative dialectics," from Maurice Merleau-Ponty's entwinement of "the visible and the invisible," and from Jacques Derrida's adumbration of a "messianism" without (messianic) power. Inspiration also derives from Martin Heidegger's notions of revealment/concealment and the sheltering withdrawal of the divine, as well as from Gianni Vattimo's formulations of "*pensiero debole*" and divine "*kenosis*." Among contemporary philosophers with whom I had the pleasure of interacting over a period of time I should signal my indebtedness especially to Calvin Schrag, Hans-Georg Gadamer, Thomas McCarthy, and (in a more indirect way) Charles Taylor and Alasdair MacIntyre. Among colleagues in political theory my gratitude extends especially to Hwa Yal Jung (to whom one of the chapters is dedicated), Stephen White, Tracy Strong, Peter Euben, and Iris Marion Young. My reflections on globalization and global power are indebted in major ways to such colleagues as Richard Falk, Robert Johansen, Franke Wilmer, and Chandra Muzaffer. None of them, of course, is responsible for whatever errors of judgment may be found in these pages.

As always, the major debt of gratitude is owed to my wife, Ilse, and our children Dominique and Philip, without whose loving support and encouragement not a single line could have been written.

F.D.
April 2005

Introduction

The title of this book, *Small Wonder*, is meant as a kind of password or entry code to the diverse pathways pursued in its pages. In many ways, the password may be startling. Our age is not known as an age of wonder or wonderment, but rather as an age of science, an age of steadily accumulating knowledge and information about everything there is. Major analysts of modernity, including Max Weber, have stipulated that modernization or societal advancement inevitably signals a process of "disenchantment" and secularization, a process banishing wonder into the domain of fantasy or human pathologies. At a time when everything in this word is subject to calculation and rational control, wonder and wondering acquire the connotation of backwardness and idiosyncratic obstinacy. In choosing the title *Small Wonder* I fully realize its "untimely" character; the choice is one of my ways of challenging or calling into question some of the "self-images of the age."[1] As will become clearer in subsequent chapters, I actually use the term "wonder" in two different, though related, senses. The first sense is ironic and perhaps satirical, the second sense more serious and engaging. The first sense prompts us to wonder and even marvel at some of the self-images of our time; the second sense elicits wonder on a more recessed level.

As indicated before, our time prides itself as an age of science and rationality. Among other things, rationality involves acceptance of the law of causality, that is, a willingness to trace effects back to underlying causes and even to anticipate certain effects in the presence of certain causal factors. What is startling and even amazing about our time, however, is the irrationality pervading the prevailing rationality: the widespread readiness to disconnect causes and effects, actions and reactions under the impulse of ideological preferences or strategic objectives. Political disasters or violent upheavals that might have been anticipated and even prevented are often blithely ascribed to happenstance or spontaneous malice. It is here that the first sense of my title comes into play. If a person consumes too much liquor and ends up in the gutter, we realize the cause and say, "small wonder." If someone touches a boiling pot of water and sustains painful burns, our response again is "small wonder." However, if political leaders abuse their power by aggrandizing and enriching themselves at the expense of the common people, we seem ready to suspend causal laws and be mystified by likely effects. If people's lands are unlawfully confiscated, their homes demolished, and friends or relatives imprisoned, tortured, and perhaps killed, can we be baffled by adverse reactions? Are we assumed to ascribe the latter to "evil" dispositions or perhaps "original sin"? Would it not be more plausible and more rational to say in these cases too: "small wonder"? And indeed, it is small wonder if abuse causes resentment, the infliction of injustice a desire to redress the injury, and the violation of human dignity an urge to avenge the violence.

My point here is not that all events on earth can be calculated and anticipated. Individuals as well as societies are often the victims of natural disasters that cannot be fully predicted or controlled. However, a good part—I would claim: the preponderant part—of human misfortunes is self-inflicted or the result of human causes. The major causes of human misfortune and misery are injustice and the abuse of power by the powerful. This is why, throughout the ages and in all civilizations, ethical thinkers have counseled against tyranny and the accumulation of political, economic, and military power in the hands of unaccountable (or barely accountable) elites. This is also why they have insisted on ethical and character training for all those aspiring to leadership positions.[2] The reason is obvious: the more powerful elites are, and the more unchecked their power, the more opportunity is there for injustice and oppression. On the other hand, the more limited rulers are—the more restrained by public and ethical norms—the more beneficial the regime will be and the more likely it is that common people will prosper. The town hall of the Italian city of Siena contains a series of medieval frescoes that are beautiful and pertinent. The frescoes depict respectively "The Allegory of Bad Government," "The Effects of Bad Government in Town and Country," "The Allegory of Good Government," and "The Effects of Good Government in Town and Country." The allegorical depiction of bad government portrays rulers obsessed with power lust and greed; the effects are shown to be strife, violence, and mayhem. The allegorical image of good government depicts rulers dedicated to justice and the observance of cardinal virtues; the effects of this regime are happiness and flourishing people in city and country. In line with these good effects the room is appropriately also called "Peace Hall."

As it seems to me, political leaders in East and West today ought to be sent to Siena to view these frescoes—and to ponder the cause-effect relation captured in them. Unfortunately, most contemporary rulers—including so-called world leaders—are completely unaware of, or unconcerned with, this relation. Many of them abandon themselves headlong to power lust and greed, without any concern for consequences—or rather they ascribe adverse consequences to ill fortune or the ill will of adversaries. Some of them gamble and blunder blindly, hoping that bad rulership will lead to happiness and peace—which, of course, is impossible. A good number are openly disdainful of the relation depicted in Siena, proclaiming brazenly that politics and political rulership have nothing to do with ethics (even while admonishing common people to be morally well-behaved and good-natured). With these attitudes and dispositions on the part of "leaders," what can common people, what can humanity expect? The past hundred years have been the scene of incredible sufferings for people: world wars, holocaust, genocides, and ethnic cleansings. And the end of these calamities is not in sight. Plans are already afoot to intensify the arms race among powerful nations and even to build new arsenals of nuclear bombs (so-called "smart" nuclear weapons). Unconstrained by any ethical rules, some governments today resemble gangster bands by openly inciting wanton slayings, while other adepts of violence boldly propagate global apocalypse or the advent of a nuclear Armageddon. In the face of such misconduct, what can any halfway sane person expect but grim and disastrous consequences? Small wonder.

There is another sense of "wonder," however, to which my title cautiously refers. Behind the drama of large-scale catastrophes—induced by grandiose political schemes and their mystifications—something else is at work, but quietly and unobtrusively. Behind the enormity of accumulated power, wealth, and technology in our world, something else lies sheltered which escapes accumulation. This is what gives sense to life and rescues it from utter futility. It is "small," but only in the sense that it requires diligence and disdains flagrant display. Traditional philosophy teaches that "wonder" (*thaumazein*) is at the beginning of all learning and insight—wonder that anything at all exists (which requires that we are released at least in some fashion from the powerful grip of accumulated things). In his "Letter on Humanism," Martin Heidegger relates a story about Heraclitus, which was initially recorded by Aristotle in one of his writings. At the time the story takes place (which was roughly 500 BC), Heraclitus was a famous philosopher whose reputation had spread through the length and breadth of ancient Greece. At one point, a group of strangers (we would call them "tourists" or sightseers) traveled to the place where he was staying. The basic motive of their visit was curiosity: the expectation of experiencing something spectacular, like a famous thinker uttering deep thoughts. As it happened, however, on their arrival Heraclitus was standing near a stove warming himself—a very ordinary and unspectacular sight. As Heidegger continues the story:

> The vision of a shivering thinker offers little of interest. At this disappointing sight the curious quickly lose their desire to come closer. What are they supposed to do here? Such an everyday and unexciting occurrence—somebody who is chilled warming himself at a stove—anyone can find any time at home . . . As the visitors are on the verge of departing, Heraclitus reads the frustrated curiosity in their faces. Hence, seeking to encourage them he invites them explicitly to come closer with the words: "Here too gods are present" [or: Here too the divine is present].[3]

That the gods or the divine are present also—or rather principally—in ordinary and inconspicuous surroundings is what the title of this book suggests. The suggestion is bound to be disturbing for many; in fact, it militates against the "self-image" of vast stretches of human history. For too long, I fear, the divine has been usurped and co-opted by powerful elites for their own purposes. In many different variations, the alliance of "throne and altar" has been the preferred model of governments all over the world, with the "altar" (or religious leaders) being reduced to acolytes of the powerful, providing the needed incense of legitimation. Differently and more sharply phrased: for too long in human history the divine has been nailed to the cross of worldly power. However, in recent times, there are signs that the old alliance may be ending and that religious faith may begin to liberate itself from the chains of worldly manipulation. Exiting from the palaces and mansions of the powerful, faith—joined by philosophical wisdom—is beginning to take shelter in inconspicuous smallness, in those recesses of ordinary life unavailable to co-optation. In the "Letter on Humanism" quoted before, Heidegger in the end ponders the prospect of philosophical reflection in our time. "The thinking that is to come," he writes, "can no longer, as Hegel demanded, abandon the name 'wisdom' and claim for itself absolute knowledge." Rather, "thinking is on the descent into the poverty of its provisional language"; it "gathers language into a simple saying" that lays "inconspicuous furrows in language"—akin to the furrows a farmer draws in a field. In a different vein and from a different angle, Walter Benjamin spoke of a descent into smallness beyond the reach of manipulation. Debunking the triumphalism of historical progress by pointing to its steadily accumulating debris, he reminded readers of the possibility of an inconspicuous event: the fact that "every second of time is the narrow gate through which the Messiah might enter."[4]

The successive chapters in this book explore the different senses of wonder outlined above, showing sometimes their contrast, sometimes their correlation and mutual interpenetration. The opening chapter sets the tone of the book by dealing with the term's more hopeful or recuperative meaning. The presentation begins with a rough sketch of the development of cultural and intellectual perspectives in Western civilization since ancient times. As the presentation tries to show, the development can be read as a movement away from grand metaphysical and theological panoramas—formulated *"sub specie aeternitatis"*—in the direction of more modest vistas and a growing recognition of the role of human finitude. Major way stations along this route were the rise of "nominalism" in the late Middle Ages, the Cartesian and Kantian intellectual revolutions, and finally the massive assaults on metaphysical systems launched by Nietzsche and Søren Kierkegaard. As a consequence of this gathering momentum, philosophers at long last accepted their own humanity by turning to the practical "life-world" undergirding rational arguments—a turn prominently articulated by leading "phenomenologists" (from Husserl and Heidegger to Merleau-Ponty) and seconded by members of the early Frankfurt School. It is at this point that a major worry arises: whether the accent on finitude is at all compatible with transcendent truth and also with religious faith (or the "rumor of angels")? Here the notion of "small wonder" comes into play by stressing the nexus of transcendence and immanence: the fact that infinity only makes sense today as horizon of the finite. As a corollary, the chapter pleads in favor of an ordinary "life-world" politics at odds with grand political agendas exploiting "higher values" as ideological tools.

The next several chapters turn to the nether side of the notion of small wonder: the gathering perils to humanity's survival spawned (unsurprisingly) by the "great power" politics of the late modern age. Staying on the philosophical or intellectual plane, chapter 2 discusses the dark "underside of modernity" as perceived by such prominent late modern thinkers as Theodor Adorno, Martin Heidegger, and the Latin American Enrique Dussel. Although undeniably launched as an engine of human emancipation and self-legislation, modernity in their view has steadily revealed darker features attributable to its intrinsic complicity with mastery and domination. In the case of Adorno, this realization surfaced first during his years in exile, under the shadow of fascist totalitarianism. In *Dialectic of Enlightenment*, a work jointly written with Max Horkheimer, the darkening of horizons was traced to the rise of a calculative and instrumental rationality bent on streamlining everything in sight, trampling underfoot both marginalized "others" and disenchanted nature. His later *Negative Dialectics* deepened this analysis, expanding it into a critique of all "totalizing" systems of thought from Plato to Hegel; as an antidote or corrective the study proposed the rigorous emphasis on non-totality, on the inescapable "nonidentity" between reason and experience, between concepts and the lived world (or life-world). Roughly during the same period, Heidegger in a series of writings formulated his own critique of the perils looming in modernity, ascribing these perils mainly to the fascination with instrumental fabrication (what he called *"Machenschaft"*), while simultaneously urging a reflective turn canceling the addiction to totalizing power and violence. With the demise of fascist totalitarianism, the dangers perceived by Adorno and Heidegger seem to have vanished; but this is far from being the case. Under the aegis of globalization, totalizing ambitions now operate on a planetary scale: evident in the opposition between hegemonic "North" and dominated "South." Speaking no longer from the European center of modernity but from its non-Western periphery, Enrique Dussel continues the critique of modernity's "underside" by advocating a transformative "transmodernity" extending the initial liberating promise to people everywhere.

Chapter 3 directly follows up on this discussion but moves the accent to the concrete political plane. Under contemporary auspices of globalization, great power politics and its totalizing ambitions surface chiefly in the form of a new imperialism or the emergence of a global empire (politely labeled *"pax Americana"*). The chapter traces the formation of this new imperial structure, accentuating its conflictual relations both with domestic democracy and the prospect of a broader "cosmopolitan" democracy. A chief objective of the chapter is to sort out the arguments typically advanced in support of empire or else in opposition to it. To profile contemporary arguments more sharply, the chapter presents a comparison with the argumentative strategies surrounding the early-modern Spanish Empire (as articulated famously in the disputations held at Valladolid in 1550). As the comparison shows, the most prominent strategy employed by apologists of empire is the claim of civilizational benevolence—sometimes called "white man's burden" or *"mission civilisatrice"*—a claim backed up by the asserted need to control or coerce barbarians and infidels, if necessary by military means. What differentiates the contemporary situation from the earlier Spanish example are mainly the immense advances in technological sophistication, especially relating to weapons of mass destruction. In addition, new theoretical resources have become available to apologists (out of reach to the Spaniards) including the resources of Machiavellian power politics, Hobbesian formulas of a Leviathan state, and Nietzschean visions of a "grand (planetary) politics." After recounting chief arguments of empire's opponents (from Bartolomé de Las Casas to Dussel) the chapter concludes with a plea for a more interdependent global commonwealth or cosmopolis—though not a blandly unified or homogeneous commonwealth but rather one where interdependence is nurtured by a variety of local and regional centers of public agency.[5]

The next two chapters shift the focus to two prominent critics of empire: the Indian novelist Arundhati Roy and the literary critic Edward Said. In intriguing ways, Arundhati Roy's writings illustrate the different senses of this book's title. As author of the prize-winning novel *The God of Small Things*, Roy draws attention to the mystery and "small wonder" inconspicuously sheltered in ordinary lives; but at the same time and for the same reason she lashes out at the sham counterfeits of wonder. In writings like *Power Politics, The Cost of Living*, and *War Talk*, she indefatigably pokes holes into the arrogant conceit of worldly bigness: big governments, big military-industrial complexes, big dams, and big bombs. As she hopefully remarks at one point: "Perhaps that's what the twenty-first century has in store for us: the dismantling of the Big." To be sure, developments in our time seem to run counter to this hope, in a manner disheartening to sensitive observers. Although not immune to bouts of despair, Roy at crucial junctures fortunately recalls another potential or possibility: that of "a small god up in heaven readying herself for us."[6] A similar kind of beacon—namely, the promise of truth and justice—has also been the lodestar of the late Edward Said (who passed away in September of 2003). Chapter 5 examines Said's lifework, paying special attention to his own conception of the role of public intellectuals in our time. Relying on his famous Reith Lectures (of 1993), the chapter shows how—in opposition to propagandists and detached mandarins—intellectuals for Said serve the task of critical gadflies willing to "speak truth to power." In a prominent way, Said himself exemplified the role of public intellectual in his critical interventions in the Near East situation, and more broadly in his analyses of "Orientalism" and of the widespread collusion of Orientalist discourses with Western colonialism and imperialist power politics. By way of conclusion, the chapter draws a parallel between Said's perspective and the gadfly role of Socrates—who, in Maurice Merleau-Ponty's famous portrayal, needs to seen both as a loyal Athenian and an engaged critic of Athenian conventions.

As the examples of Said, Roy, and Merleau-Ponty indicate, the role of critical public intellectuals is crucial in our time as a counterweight—however fragile—to the accumulation of increasingly unaccountable forms of power and wealth in the world. To be sure, in our globalizing age, this counterweight cannot be limited to, or monopolized by, European or Western theorists, but must expand to embrace intellectuals from all parts of the globe. In this respect, there is an urgent need to cultivate an arena, or rather several networks, of global intellectual interactions—in anticipation of the development of a global public sphere (capable of holding global rulers accountable). As it happens, networks of this kind can already be found—in embryonic or more developed form—in many areas of the globe. Chapter 6 offers an overview of some of these arenas, starting from a discussion of main forms of critical theorizing endemic to Europe (such as "Frankfurt-School" critical theory, "Freiburg-School" phenomenology and hermeneutics, and French post-structuralism and deconstruction). As this discussion shows, most European perspectives—despite obvious divergences—are linked through a shared opposition to hegemonic "scientism" and a commitment to preserve the nexus of theory and praxis. Turning first to India, the chapter discovers numerous parallels to European orientations—although parallels formulated independently and without any subservience to European models. The chief Indian counterparts are the Delhi Center for the Study of Developing Societies and the project of "Subaltern Studies." Moving to East and Southeast Asia, attention is drawn to the Japanese Kyoto School (mediating Zen Buddhism and European phenomenology) and to the far-flung networks of "engaged Buddhism" (aiming at the critical transformation of both self and society). Following brief references to the Islamic context as well as to Africa and Latin America, the chapter concludes by endorsing Ulrich Beck's important call for "a new critical theory with a cosmopolitan intent."[7]

The remaining chapters are all in one way or another directed against dominant self-images of the age. Chapter 7 is meant as a tribute or "homage" to Merleau-Ponty. The chosen topic in this chapter is the issue of individual and social identity and of the process of identity formation. In this domain, contemporary literature is dominated by two diametrically opposed conceptions: on the one side, the conception of a stable or "essential" identity (frequently portrayed as a universal "human nature"); and on the other, the conception of radical malleability and arbitrary identity "construction." In some radical "postmodern" formulations, identity construction is portrayed as an utterly contingent fabrication, a creation ex nihilo through the exercise of arbitrary decision. Predicated on the traditional freedom-necessity bifurcation, these different views are shown to be radically flawed and misleading. The conception of an "essential" identity is challenged because of its neglect of differentiation and its frequent complicity with hegemonic or imperial forms of universalism. Still more forcefully, the constructivist model is criticized for its arbitrary "decisionism," its revival of subject-object dichotomies, and—above all—for its subservience to the central modern project of mastery and fabrication (what Heidegger called *Machenschaft*). As an antidote the chapter turns to approaches linking social identity formation with creatively interactive "praxis," a perspective adumbrated in Charles Taylor's notion of a "politics of recognition" and deepened in Merleau-Ponty's discussion of an existential engagement or embroilment where self and other are (as he says) "like two *nearly* concentric circles which can be distinguished only by a slight and mysterious slippage."[8]

Continuing this line of criticism, chapter 8 takes aim centrally at the modern fascination with construction or technical-instrumental fabrication. Wedded to the control and exploitation of nature, modern science and technology are completely unable to respect "nature's ways," that is, to "let nature be" in its unfolding and regenerative modalities outside the purview of technical control. This inability is illustrated in the field of modern medicine that—despite its impressive and largely beneficial advances in combating diseases—is incapable on its own to promote and safeguard human health and well-being. Elaborating on this point the chapter turns to the writings of Hans-Georg Gadamer, and especially his book *The Enigma of Health*. As Gadamer points out in this study, modern medical science has indeed made enormous strides toward containing and sometimes even eradicating major illnesses; however, none of these strides removes the "enigma" or mysterious character of human health which operates "naturally" or by itself sustaining our way of being. Especially semi- or unconscious processes of life—like breathing, digesting, and sleeping—testify to our insertion into a "nature," which, resisting fabrication, preserves its own rhythm and unregimented balance. The chapter draws a parallel between *The Enigma of Health* and Gadamer's magnum opus, *Truth and Method*. Without rejecting scientific methods, "truth" in that work designates the self-disclosure of a mode of being, an unplanned happening not reducible to methodological formulas. The same work also asserts an affinity between "nature's way" and the "mimetic" playfulness of works of art, an affinity predicated on the intrinsic self-directedness of both domains not subservient to external goals or standards. Exploring broader social and political connotations, Gadamer's work makes room for a notion like "natural rightness" or appropriateness of conduct as a counterpoise to political streamlining and ideological manipulation.

Chapter 9 delves more deeply into the relation between "truth" and "method," by examining (or rather reexamining) a celebrated debate during the later part of the last century: the debate between Gadamer and Jürgen Habermas. In this debate—again without dismissing methodology—Gadamer took the side of "truth" seen as the ongoing disclosure of modes of being, a disclosure which can never be grasped cognitively from an external (meta-) perspective, but can only be explored through concrete engagement and the labor of "hermeneutical" understanding (which continuously transforms the interpreter). On the other hand, denouncing the broad sweep of hermeneutical engagement, Habermas at the time insisted on the formulation of a metatheoretical perspective from whose angle different forms of knowledge can be separated and objectively validated through proper scientific methods. The chapter traces Habermas's efforts at boundary drawing from his early *Knowledge and Human Interests* to his later *Between Facts and Norms*, showing how in every case boundaries depend on a presupposed higher vantage point or metatheory which itself is no longer subject to hermeneutical learning. By way of conclusion the chapter aligns itself with the "horizonal" or border-crossing quality of Gadamer's hermeneutics, indicating how this approach has bearings for political praxis and the contemporary need for global boundary crossings.

As it seems to me, the notion of open borders is relevant not only for different temporalities and knowledge forms, but also for the relation between humans and the "divine." In opposition to a myopic self-enclosure, it can be shown that "secularism" for its own intelligibility requires open borders—which does not negate secularism's basic impulse directed against religious or clerical domination. In my view, the "divine"—personified in theistic language as "God"—is precisely what cannot be co-opted, manipulated, or bent into an instrument of power and exploitation; it escapes worldly abuse—without on this count being escapist or distantly aloof. While shunning dominion or imperial rule, the divine has its own peculiar potency, operating as the recessed "wonder" in ordinary things or as the "narrow gate" mentioned by Walter Benjamin; being neither domineering nor passively submissive it is liberating and transformative.[9] Under the title "Empire and Faith," the concluding chapter discusses the peculiar border-crossing quality of the divine in this world. In emphasizing this "horizonal" character, the chapter takes aim at a further set of "self-images" of our age: the images manifest in the agendas of a self-enclosed secularism and a triumphalist religious "fundamentalism." The presentation takes its cues from a biblical story narrated in John's Gospel: the interrogation of Jesus by Pontius Pilate. Asked by the Roman governor whether he was a "king," Jesus directed his response onto an entirely different plane, away from political power and nonpower, saying: "I was born for one thing, and for this I have come into the world: to bear witness to the truth" (John 18:37). As we are told, Pilate was left perplexed by this response. And indeed, Jesus' words stunningly reveal the surprising quality of "small wonder."

The appendix of this book contains a series of reviews or responses that are pertinent to the issues raised in the preceding chapters, amplifying some of their salient points or arguments. The first review pays tribute to Rabbi Jonathan Sacks, the author of an eloquent plea in favor of "the dignity of difference." As Rabbi Sacks points out in his book of that title, it is quite possible to be fervently devoted (in an orthodox way) to a particular religion while simultaneously being respectful of other religious faiths. In his words, God (as transcendence) may be the "God of all humanity," but "no single faith is or should be the faith of all humanity." Based on this insight, his book urges a new covenantal engagement: a global "covenant of hope" involving a "partnership without dominance or submission."[10] The second review deals with the relation between "religion and rationality" focusing on the manner this relation has been construed by members of the so-called Frankfurt School of critical theory. Contrary to assumptions of a smooth continuity of the School's perspective, the review draws attention to various gaps or gulfs separating the School's early founders (especially Adorno and Horkheimer) from later reformulations of critical theory in terms of "communicative rationality." The main gaps noted have to do with two changes: on the political plane, a move from radical social critique to a position closer to mainstream liberalism; and on the intellectual plane, a move from the subdued "Jewish messianism" of the founders to a secular-rational agnosticism (tempered, however, in recent years by more conciliatory gestures). The final review takes the form of a response to Charles Taylor, specifically to an essay he wrote on "moralism" and its dangers. Agreeing largely with Taylor, the response notes that a focus on moral imperatives alone egregiously neglects the affective dimension of human life, and especially the extent to which norms require for their observance an underlying engagement or "fidelity."

The pervasive tone of the entire book is what one may call a "hopeful realism," that is, a stance that is fully aware of the enormous obstacles standing in the way of a "humane global governance" but also unwilling to yield pliantly to these obstacles. Several chapters point out the enormity of existing dangers and "discontents": the unparalleled, frequently unaccountable accumulation of political, economic, and military power, reinforced by a hankering for unilateral aggression and a widespread culture of violence. But several chapters also tap into intense longings for justice and peace, longings widely disseminated among people around the globe and testifying to the presence of an enduring promise—a "small wonder"—in the midst of looming calamities. The question is whether we are willing to keep our side of the bargain by maintaining our loyalty to the promise. To believers it is clear that we have not been promised a life without hardship or grief; but they also refuse to consider grief as the end of the story. Basically, believers realize that as recipients (not givers) of the promise, we cannot unilaterally bring about its fulfillment—which does not relieve us of the task of preparing the way. In this domain I find myself in complete agreement with a contemporary philosopher of religion, Richard Kearney, who—in a remarkable book titled *The God Who May Be*—writes that if God's promise can indeed save us, "it is only to the extent that we choose to respond to it by acting to bring the coming Kingdom closer, making it more possible, as it were, by each of our actions, while acknowledging that its ultimate realization is impossible to us alone." As he adds thoughtfully and a bit provocatively, the fulfillment of the promise is not impossible to God—if we do our part and "help God to become God." How can this happen? "By opening ourselves to the 'loving possible,' by acting each moment to make the impossible that bit more possible."[11]

NOTES

1. The phrase is adapted from the title of one of Alasdair MacIntyre's early books: *Against the Self-Images of the Age: Essays on Ideology and Philosophy* (New York: Schocken Books, 1971).

2. Several books in Plato's *Republic* are devoted to the moral and intellectual education of political leaders; the same emphasis can be found in Aristotle's *Nicomachean Ethics* and *Politics*. In East Asia, Confucian scholars endowed with "great learning" were supposed to act as watchdogs of rulers reminding them of the limits of rulership. It is a sad commentary on our times that political leaders today, even so-called world leaders, are ignorant and sometimes even dismissive of classical learning (or any learning whatever). For the legacy of Confucian learning see, e.g., William Theodore de Bary, *Neo-Confucian Orthodoxy and the Learning of the Mind-and-Heart* (New York: Columbia University Press, 1981).

3. Martin Heidegger, "Letter on Humanism," in *Martin Heidegger: Basic Writings*, ed. David F. Krell (New York: Harper & Row, 1977), pp. 233-234 (translation slightly altered).

4. Walter Benjamin, "Theses on the Philosophy of History," in *Walter Benjamin: Illuminations*, ed. Hannah Arendt (New York: Harcourt, Brace & World, 1968), p. 266. See also "Letter on Humanism," in *Martin Heidegger: Basic Writings*, p. 242 (translation slightly altered).

5. The chapter insofar steers a middle course between the kind of "cosmopolitan democracy" advocated by David Held and others and the more agonistic cosmopolitics envisaged by Danilo Zolo. See, e.g., Daniele Archibugi and David Held, eds., *Cosmopolitan Democracy: An Agenda for a New World Order* (Cambridge, UK: Polity Press, 1995); Danilo Zolo, *Cosmopolis: Prospects for a World Government*, trans. David McKie (Cambridge, UK: Polity Press, 1997).

6. Arundhati Roy, *The Cost of Living* (New York: Modern Library, 1999), p. 12.

7. See Ulrich Beck, "Toward a New Critical Theory with a Cosmopolitan Intent," *Constellations* 10 (2003): pp. 453-468.

8. Maurice Merleau-Ponty, "Dialogue and the Perception of the Other," in *The Prose of the World*, ed. Claude Lefort, trans. John O'Neill (Evanston, IL: Northwestern University Press, 1973), p. 134.

9. Compare on this issue also John D. Caputo's inspiring words: "Religion on my telling is a pact or 'covenant' with the impossible. To have a religious sense of life is to long with a restless heart for a reality beyond reality, to tremble with the possibility of the impossible. If the religious sense of life is sometimes thought in terms of eternity (under the influence of Plato), my advice is to rethink it in terms of time, as a temporal way to be" (in a transformative mode). See his *On Religion* (London and New York: Routledge, 2001), p. 15.

10. Jonathan Sacks, *The Dignity of Difference: How to Avoid the Clash of Civilizations* (London and New York: Continuum, 2002), pp. 55, 208.

11. Richard Kearney, *The God Who May Be: A Hermeneutics of Religion* (Bloomington, IN: Indiana University Press, 2001), pp. 110-111. Steering a course between traditional (ontological) theology and a radical "postmodern" theology of negation, Kearney suggests (p. 4) that "the God of Exodus and Transfiguration, the God of Eros and Possibility, is a God who may be." This, he adds, is "why I argue that it is wiser to interpret divinity as a possibility-to-be than as either pure being in the manner of onto-theology, or as pure nonbeing in the manner of negative theology." He calls this approach "onto-eschatology" (p. 8).

Chapter One

Small Wonder:
Finitude and Its Horizons

(For Hwa Yol Jung)

History delights in strange twists and turns: the unexpected is usually the only thing to be expected. Nothing demonstrates this irony better than the contemporary process of globalization. What this process signals, above all, is a steady enlargement of horizons, a movement from smallness to greater and greater bigness—a movement which has its own history. Ever since the onset of Western modernity, "progress" has denoted spatial expansion: from the village to the city and the nation, and from there to regional hemispheres and the entire globe. Today, even globalization reaches beyond itself: to the still greater bigness of galactic or interplanetary space. Despite its imposing grandeur, spatial expansion exacts a price: the growing sense of the hollowness and destructiveness of all big things—a sense well captured by Walter Benjamin in the image of "Angelus Novus" (as the purveyor of accumulating debris).[1] Curiously—and testifying to historical irony—the modern drive toward global and even extraterrestrial largeness is countermanded by a nearly opposite move: the turn toward the earth and its preservation; differently and more pointedly phrased: the return from unlimited spectatorial horizons to the bounded limits of concrete earthly life, from the lure of speculative infinity to the challenges and rewards of finitude, to the small wonders of finite existence and experience.

Just like modern "progress," the countermove toward finitude—toward the intricate ways and byways of ordinary life—has its own history, which can be traced along several axes. Religiously, the clerical and monastic control of church affairs during the High Middle Ages was progressively weakened during subsequent centuries by the rise of the less hierarchical "*devotio moderna*," a development which was sharpened by the later Reformers' emphasis on "general" priesthood and on the religious merits of "ordinary" (as compared with monastic) life.[2] Politically, the movement from clerical privilege to popular piety was paralleled by a sequence of well-known transformations and substitutions: first the replacement of papal and imperial rule by national monarchies or autocracies, and later the replacement of autocracies by constitutional republics and democracies (a sequence which, like the religious movement, is far from having reached its full potential). Perhaps the most instructive and portentous illustration of the countermove to finitude can be found in the domain of philosophy, including political philosophy. Here major signposts of change are the rejection of grand metaphysical systems (by Nietzsche and Kierkegaard), and then the valorization of the ordinary "lifeworld" (by Husserl and his successors). In the words of political theorist Hwa Yol Jung, the task of exploring this life-world had been "neglected in Western philosophy since the time of Plato who considered it a [mere] 'cave world' of impermanent shadows and images"—until it was rescued from oblivion by recent (twentieth-century) philosophy.[3] The following presentation explores the turn to finitude by focusing first on some of its manifestations in recent philosophical literature. Next, the question is raised whether finitude is recalcitrant to philosophical (and religious) modes of "transcendence" or else harbors within itself its own "horizons of finitude." By way of conclusion, the discussion turns to the implications of the countermove for political and cross-cultural studies in our globalizing age.

"TO THE THINGS THEMSELVES"

In large measure, the history of Western philosophy can be seen as a story of humanization, that is, as a series of attempts to transform philosophers from purveyors of eternal vistas into participants in the joys and agonies of finite existence. Such participation was still evident in the case of Socrates and some of the pre-Socratic thinkers; but it was progressively eclipsed by the rise of classical metaphysics. Basically, what is meant by "metaphysics" in this context is the formulation of a complete overview or inventory of all modes of being as seen "*sub specie aeternitatis*" (from an eternal or infinite perspective). The obvious question was: who could claim to occupy an infinite standpoint permitting such a complete overview? What is sometimes called the "naiveté" of classical philosophy is the assumption of an infinite vista without the explicit elaboration of a privileged consciousness or subjectivity (what in modern times is termed the "*cogito*"). Even Aristotle—whose ethical and political thought is eminently praxis-oriented—succumbed at points to the lure of metaphysics by stipulating a complete list or catalog of all possible substances and modes of thought. In Roman times, the Stoics continued classical metaphysics through the invocation of a timeless and universal "reason" (whose universalism conveniently coincided with the scope of the expanding empire). Classical metaphysics persisted into the Christian Middle Ages in the form of scholastic philosophy, a system of thought which assigned to God the role of privileged knower (*sub specie aeternitatis*) but granted to human thinkers a sizable share in divine knowledge.

The first rumblings of change came in the late Middle Ages with the onset of "nominalism," which, challenging the "reality" of universal vistas, allowed them to persist only as words or phrases. The challenge was deepened by the rise of modern skepticism and human-centered rationalism, especially by Descartes' program of radical doubt. The result of this program was twofold. First of all, it removed or called into question those aspects of classical metaphysics that pretended to a naïve grasp of cosmic truth (or reality). Secondly, and more importantly, it pinpointed for the first time explicitly the standpoint required for genuine knowledge: the standpoint of purified consciousness or subjectivity (termed "*cogito*" or "thinking substance"). What, despite his protestations, linked Descartes' framework with earlier metaphysics was the premise of a privileged or extramundane perspective—a premise evident in the removal of the *cogito* from everything alien to it, that is, from the space-time coordinates of the "external" world. Despite significant modifications and refinements, this removal (of consciousness from the world) carried over into the most massive assault on traditional metaphysics launched in modern times: the critical philosophy of Immanuel Kant. With his separation of *apriori* and *aposteriori* forms of knowledge, Kant's approach exempted immutable categories of reason from mundane learning experiences, just as his distinction between "noumenal" and "phenomenal" realms elevated categorical moral imperatives above the contingencies of moral life. In many ways, Kant's linchpin of "transcendental consciousness" thus remained heir to philosophizing "*sub specie aeternitatis*"—with eternity now being assigned to human reason. Elements of this Kantian approach can still be found in the founder of modern "phenomenology," Edmund Husserl—whose later work, however, initiated a decisive break with the past through the discovery of the "life-world," the world of finite experience undergirding reason or consciousness itself.

In the meantime (even prior to this discovery), the edifice of traditional metaphysics had been severely shaken by two thinkers whose writings resembled major earthquakes: Friedrich Nietzsche and Søren Kierkegaard. Both thinkers, in their different ways, tried to rescue concrete life experience from the "accumulating debris" of metaphysical systems. In the case of Kierkegaard, the main target of critique was Hegel's encyclopedic system that aimed to encompass all possible facets of life in a tight logical or conceptual structure. To the Danish thinker, such a structure appeared like a vast mausoleum; it allowed the "scientific logicism" to bury all real-life contingencies under the cloak of conceptual formulas.[4] Nietzsche's line of attack was even more sweeping, extending from classical (Platonic) metaphysics via scholasticism to Hegel's idealism. In his view, the gist of traditional metaphysics resided in the "doubling" of the world, the assumption that there is a permanent, unchanging, and truly "real" world behind the flux of ordinary life. Without this assumption, or rather "dream," he noted, "one would have found no occasion for a doubling of the world." In opposition to this dream, Nietzsche urged the cultivation and affirmation of finite life, the willingness to "remain faithful to the earth" and its subtle and inexhaustible "meaning." What he termed "tranvaluation of values" was based on the need to rescue life-sustaining sense underneath the metaphysical debris of "eternal values"—that, over time, have been appropriated and instrumentalized by ideologues and managerial elites. Here is a passage from *Twilight of the Idols* where Nietzsche denounces traditional philosophers for

> their lack of historical sense, their hatred of the very idea of becoming, their Egypticism. They think that they show their respect for a topic when they dehistoricize it, *sub specie aeterni*—when they turn it into a mummy. All that [these] philosophers have handled for thousands of years have been concept-mummies; nothing real escaped their grasp alive. . . . Whatever has being does not become; whatever becomes does not have being.[5]

By comparison with Nietzsche's dramatic gesture, Husserl's philosophy appears more reticent and academic; however, precisely because of the slow and painstaking character of his arguments, his work was able to initiate a broad reorientation in the course of modern Western philosophy. With his emphasis on the "intentionality" of consciousness, Husserl dislodged a major pillar of the Cartesian legacy: the so-called subject-object dichotomy, that is, the segregation of thinking subject (*cogito*) from the rest of the world. His chief and lasting contribution, however, resides in his embrace of "phenomenology": his willingness to take mundane phenomena seriously (captured in his motto "to the things themselves"), a move that ultimately led to his discovery of the "life-world." In the words of Hwa Yol Jung: "Husserl's famous urging to go back 'to the things themselves' means a return to the primordial and original world of everyday existence that is prior to the derivative and secondary expression of theorizing activity in philosophy and science." This primordial domain is the life-world seen as the "ultimate horizon" of natural, cultural, and social phenomena. As Husserl himself wrote in his famous *Crisis of European Sciences*: The life-world is "the constant ground of validity, an ever available source of what is taken for granted, to which we, whether as practical men or as scientists, lay claim as a matter of course."[6] Precisely because of its precognitive or prereflective character, the life-world and its mundane phenomena are available for ever-renewed interpretive studies—without being able to be exhaustively mapped by a domineering conceptual rationality. In this respect, Jung is able to draw a parallel between phenomenology and the "radical empiricism" of William James. Just as in the Jamesian approach, he notes, phenomenology "recognizes the dependence of reflection on directly lived experience, that is to say, it accepts the idea that reflection is founded upon lived experience." While remaining recalcitrant to complete cognitive (and metaphysical) grasp, immediate experience "provides the material for later conceptual activity."[7]

Husserl's initiatives were continued and further radicalized by his student and associate Martin Heidegger whose work can be regarded as a preeminent example of a philosophy of finitude. Going beyond Husserl, Heidegger undermined the pivot of intentional consciousness—the remnant of the *cogitio*—by inserting it squarely in the context of a worldliness in which it has to find its bearings. In his famous formulation, human existence (*Dasein*) is described as "being-in-the-world"—where "world" is not a limiting container but an ever-present ambience or horizon of lived experience.[8] For Heidegger, the availability of horizons is not in conflict with, but rather a corollary and consequence of the finitude of existence. In *Being and Time*, this finitude is prominently discussed under the rubric of human "being-toward-death"—a phrase that indicates that human striving in this world is always surrounded by a penumbra of incompleteness, negativity, or loss. Seen from this angle, human life remains a journey whose sense or meaning can never be fully grasped or conceptually exhausted (*sub specie aeternitatis*). Opposing itself to Western metaphysics, Heidegger's thought undercuts the traditional "doubling of the world" chastised by Nietzsche—the juxtaposition of timeless "being" and worldly flux—by temporalizing "being" itself and portraying its worldly manifestation as a conceptually uncharted and unmanageable disclosure (or *parousia*). As he writes at one point, the "being" of the world is not guaranteed by any metaphysical formula; rather, its meaning inserts itself laterally or furtively into mundane experience as a counterpoint or "absent presence." To this extent, its advent remains "essentially finite."[9]

Heidegger's departure from metaphysics—especially from modern Cartesianism—is well articulated by Lawrence Hatab in his book *Ethics and Finitude*. Inaugurated by René Descartes, he writes, modern Western philosophy was "governed by the subject-object binary unfolding out of scientific reason," where "world" was construed "as a set of objective conditions divorced from human involvement and meaning, a divorce accomplished by the disengaged subjectivity of rational reflection." Such disengagement permitted a "deliverance from the contingency, flux, and limits of lived experience," and thus prevented a serious confrontation with finitude. By contrast to this tradition, Heidegger's work insists on the primacy of "engaged being-in-the-world" vis-à-vis abstract reflection and conceptual analysis. In line with this emphasis, his work center stages the "finitude of being," where "finitude" does not simply refer to spatial, temporal, or cognitive limits but has an ontological status. In Hatab's words, finitude for Heidegger includes an "indigenous negativity in being," in the sense that "an absence or otherness is always part of a thing's being"—with the result that "being cannot be associated with full or constant presence" (a presence that could be conceptually mastered or domesticated). For human beings, he adds, finitude includes "a sense of absence in the midst of presence," that is, "an awareness of the pervasive possibility of loss and privation"; it also entails a kind of self-decentering or self-dispersal as opposed to "the intimations of sovereignty and mastery" contained in modern subjectivity.[10] The crucial change involved in Heidegger's thought is well expressed also by another American philosopher who writes:

> The recovery of the finite, the philosophic recognition of its ubiquity, is not simply a matter of altering our philosophic "positions" and renegotiating the possibilities of theoretical understanding; it is rather a matter of fundamentally altering the prejudices and temperament that have long guided philosophy. Most of all, it is every form of "final solution" that needs to be abandoned.[11]

In recent Western philosophy, the turn to finitude—and away from final (metaphysical) solutions—has not been the monopoly of Heidegger alone. Among French phenomenologists, a similar path was pursued by Maurice Merleau-Ponty who, like Heidegger, bent the Husserlian call "to the things themselves" in the direction of a more intimate involvement with worldliness. From his earliest writings, Merleau-Ponty's work was opposed both to a reductive empiricism (or positivism) and a detached intellectualism: while the former reduces the human journey to fact-gathering, the latter conjures up the prospect of an ultimate overview (amenable to mastery and control). In the history of Western metaphysics, the yearning for such finality has been the chief temptation. In one of his writings, Merleau-Ponty sharply castigates what he calls the "myth about philosophy," which presents it as "an authoritarian affirmation of the mind's absolute autonomy." Shunning the need for reflective learning, authoritarian philosophizing congeals thought into a "body of doctrines" predicated on an "absolutely unfettered spirit in full possession of itself and its ideas." As an antidote to this metaphysical self-possession, phenomenology—in Merleau-Ponty's account—is a philosophy "for which the world is always 'already there' before reflection begins—as an inalienable presence"; as a consequence, all the efforts of phenomenological inquiry are directed toward "reachieving a direct and primitive contact with the world, and endowing that contact with a philosophical status." Seen from this angle, Husserl's motto "to the things themselves" signifies a renewed engagement: a "return to that world which precedes knowledge, of which knowledge always *speaks*, and in relation to which every scientific schematization is an abstract and derivative sign-language"—just as professional geography is in relation to "the countryside in which we have learned beforehand what a forest, a prairie or a river is."[12]

Parallel initiatives can be found outside the camp of phenomenology, especially in the confines of the early Frankfurt School. In their famous study, *Dialectic of Enlightenment*, Theodor Adorno and Max Horkheimer strongly complained about the growing complicity of modern rationalism—restyled as "enlightenment"—with the ascent of technological mastery and top-down final solutions. In the authors' view, this development was not fortuitous or accidental. Given the exodus of modern reason (*cogito*) from all surrounding contexts, the world and its phenomena were bound to be transformed into mere targets of managerial and technical control. The same development boomeranged on human life to the extent that human agents were progressively reduced to "subjects" (in the sense of privatized individuals and passive consumers). For Horkheimer and Adorno, what was most disturbing was the close linkage between modern epistemology (and metaphysics) and growing modes of societal domestication and surveillance. As they pointed out, modern epistemology is wedded to discursive logic and a conceptual universalism to which all particular phenomena are rigidly subordinated or subsumed; in this manner, the diversity and elusiveness of concrete experience are sacrificed to general rules. In their words: "The universality of concepts as developed by modern logic—their supremacy in the conceptual sphere— is erected on the basis of actual supremacy or domination." Hence, the rational replacement of "magical-mythical" legacies, promised by "enlightenment," ushers forth a "hierarchical social constitution determined by freemen and implemented through chains of command." In terms of *Dialectic of Enlightenment*, the chief offshoot of this development is a certain "world alienation" or "loss of world" (*Weltverlust*): namely, the loss of the qualitative richness of phenomena as well as of the resources of imagination and sensibility undergirding reason itself. The remedy for this impoverishment had to be found in a reconnection of reason and world, that is, in reason's turn to the domain of "otherness" (or nonidentity) by means of a "remembrance of alienated nature."[13]

The trajectory initiated in *Dialectic of Enlightenment* was fleshed out and brought to full fruition in the authors' later works, particularly in Adorno's crowning opus titled *Negative Dialectics*. The title of the study signaled a challenge to all kinds of metaphysical finality, but especially to Hegel's dialectical system anchored in the potency of absolute reason (or subjectivity). The term "negative" in this context was not a synonym for pessimism or nihilism, but rather pointed to reason's intrinsic finitude: to the entwinement of reason and nonreason, presence and absence. Basically, "negative dialectics" heralded a move away from rationalist metaphysics—and its corollary of technical mastery—in the direction of a renewed openness to the world and the "otherness" of phenomena. In Adorno's words: "To change the direction of conceptuality and turn it toward nonidentity (otherness), this is the emblem or point of negative dialectics." Speaking phenomenologically, the turn to "nonidentity" involved an effort to "save the appearances," that is, a determined attentiveness to the richness and diversity of phenomena not yet streamlined or domesticated by rationalist constructs. Attention to phenomena required not only a cognitive (or epistemic) change but a more profound human transformation: one enabling human beings to emancipate themselves from self-enclosure and self-possession in favor of a new empathy or sympathy for the world. Basically, liberation of this kind, he noted, could unleash a genuine "love for things" (and all beings), a disposition which would not imply a desire for possession or control but rather a generous acceptance and recognition of difference.[14]

FINITUDE AND TRANSCENDENCE

As shown in the preceding account, the history of Western philosophy can, with some plausibility, be read as a story of unfolding modesty, of the growing willingness of philosophers to share the lot of finite existence. Yet, unsurprisingly, this story is also fraught with subtle complexities, that is, with the unexpected twists and turns noted at the beginning. A major complication derives from the fact that the story is not unilinear and cannot be told as the simple move from metaphysics to anti-metaphysics, from absolute knowledge to contingency (which would merely rearrange priorities). Surely, more is involved than a mere rejection of the past—but the nature of this "more" is baffling and contested. In the eyes of many well-intentioned observers, the turn to finitude is beset with grave dangers and may even herald the doom of Western civilization in its traditional form. Religiously motivated intellectuals are likely to be troubled by questions like these: With the stress on human finitude what is happening to infinity? With the accent on "immanent" life what is the status of "transcendence" as vouchsafed by revelation? More philosophically inclined observers are disturbed by a further set of questions:

Does the emphasis on finite temporality not erode the "timeless" status of rational norms and principles? And what is the impact of recent philosophical developments on "truth"?

Clearly, questions of this kind cannot quickly be brushed aside. In some quarters, such questions have triggered an openly restorative mood: a desire or longing to return to traditional metaphysics, and especially to some of the great system-builders of the past (from Plato and the scholastics to Descartes, Kant, and Hegel). Of late such longing has surfaced even in the confines of phenomenology—despite the latter's nonmetaphysical bent. In a book titled *Phenomenology and the "Theological Turn,"* Dominique Janicaud has discussed the renewed "veering" toward transcendence and infinity inside a philosophical perspective ostensibly wedded to ordinary experience. As he asks pointedly: is this veering still compatible with phenomenology, or does it not rather constitute a "rupture within immanent phenomenality"? A primary example of this turning, for Janicaud, is the work of Emmanuel Levinas, one of whose major writings was provocatively titled *Totality and Infinity.* In that context, "totality" was the name for the sum of all mundane or "immanent" phenomena, whereas "infinity" signaled the irruption into the world of a radical transcendence or "exteriority"—an irruption that ultimately carried the earmarks of divine revelation. Critiquing the Levinasian project, Janicaud traces the transcendental urge to a "nonphenomenological, metaphysical desire" which, coming from "a land not of our birth," is predicated on a "metaphysico-theological montage." More sharply phrased, he views this urge as "a veritable *captatio benevolentiae* of the phenomenological method" whereby phenomenology is "taken hostage by a theology that does not want to say its name." In the end, he juxtaposes Levinasian transcendence to Merleau-Ponty's more sober outlook, leading up to a basic alternative: "Between the unconditional affirmation of transcendence and the patient interrogation of the visible, the incompatibility cries out; we must choose."[15]

Commenting on recent developments in Continental thought, Italian philosopher Giorgio Agamben detects two divergent and even opposite tendencies: one pointing toward radical immanence and the other toward radical transcendence. The first tendency—which can trace its roots ultimately to Spinoza—finds expression in recent times chiefly in the works of Gilles Deleuze and Michel Foucault; the second trajectory—indebted distantly to Husserl, Kant, and Descartes—is prominently represented by Levinas and Jacques Derrida. Curiously, in this genealogical scheme, Heidegger's thought appears as the nodal point through which both trajectories move and beyond which they diverge. In Agamben's account, primary attention is given (and deserves to be given) to Deleuze as the most resolute defender of a "pure" and even "absolute" immanence. As Deleuze himself wrote at one point: "One can say of pure immanence that it is a LIFE, and nothing else. It is not immanence to life; rather, immanence that is in nothing is in itself a life. A life is the immanence of immanence, absolute immanence." Insisting on this vantage point, Deleuze sharply criticized the transcendental "veerings" of Husserl and Levinas in whose writings, he says, "immanence itself is made to disgorge the transcendent everywhere." As Agamben comments: just as in the case of Spinoza, "the principle of immanence here is nothing other than a generalization of the ontology of univocity, which excludes any transcendence of Being." In the same context, Agamben refers to Deleuze's use of the term "beatitude" to designate the essential character of life and the intrinsic movement of absolute immanence. If "life" is taken in the broadest possible sense, he concludes (somewhat obscurely), then "blessed life lies on the same terrain as the biological body of the West."[16]

Although undeniable and striking, the divergence of trajectories probably should not be overstated or carried too far. A main reason for this is that, in the wake of phenomenology, the two trends are too much embroiled and implicated with each other. Deleuze's use of "beatitude"—a term clearly deriving from biblical and metaphysical sources—illustrates this embroilment. Moreover, in a contemporary context, Deleuze himself finds it nearly impossible to segregate the two perspectives—as is evident in Agamben's comment: "Insofar as immanence is the 'movement of the infinite' beyond which there is nothing, immanence has neither a fixed point nor a horizon that can orient thought; the 'movement has engulfed everything' and the only possible point of orientation is the vertigo in which outside and inside, immanence and transcendence, are absolutely indistinguishable."[17] Clearly, once outside and inside are indistinguishable, the notion of an "absolute immanence" becomes puzzling or enigmatic. On the other hand, the Levinasian use of "infinity" and "transcendence" is not nearly as clear-cut and univocal as the neat distinction between (mundane) "totality and infinity" would suggest. As Levinas himself writes in his cited text, the relation between the "finite" and the "infinite" is neither one of radical antithesis nor of mutual coincidence. Basically, it is not a matter of the finite being integrated into or simply absorbed by a larger whole termed infinity. Rather, in turning to transcendence or "exteriority," one leaves behind the pretense of a panoramic overview or synthetic totality and begins to understand finitude on its own terms (without holistic nostalgia), just as infinity appears no longer as completion but as the simple "desire for infinity." In the end, Levinas asserts, infinite exteriority is neither a simple completion nor a negation of immanence, but a wonder or "marvel."[18]

Given the mutual entanglement of outside and inside, transcendence and immanence, traditional terminology is strained or placed under siege. In many ways (so it seems to me), use of this terminology retains only a pragmatic or strategic significance. Both the trajectories of immanence and transcendence are fraught with grave perils, which can be ignored only at great risk. Insistence on pure immanence too readily shades over into a reductive empiricism or "positivism"—perspectives which in turn can give rise politically to "this-worldly" mastery and totalitarian domination. This is clearly a motivating factor in Levinas's writing that speaks of the danger of a totalizing synthesis and a reified or objectified mundane existence. On the other side of the coin, there is also a danger—perhaps an even greater one—in the elevation of transcendence into an absolute idea or universal conceptual scheme to which all particularities would be subordinated (if not sacrificed). As experience teaches, absolute schemes of this kind are too readily appropriated and manipulated by ruling elites and transformed into quasi-missionary ideologies. Once this happens, transcendence turns into those "higher values" criticized by Nietzsche or that metaphysical debris so eloquently denounced by Benjamin. Levinas himself wants to have no truck with this debauched form of transcendentalism. Properly conceived, he writes, transcendence refuses any totalizing ambition and hence does not lend itself to a perspective that "would encompass it from the outside" and be amenable to dogmatic manipulation. Every claim to have grasped or "comprehended" transcendence involves its betrayal. In fact, the inability to be fully grasped is the very hallmark or definition of transcendence, which uses "no theological banisters."[19]

Given the sketched dangers, it seems advisable to proceed cautiously in this domain. Instead of treating them as absolutes it appears preferable to use immanence and transcendence in a critical vein or as sources of resistance: that is, to invoke transcendence as an antidote to totalizing reification and to invoke immanence as a counterpoint to transcendental conceit. Seen in this light, transcendence (or the transcendent) is neither a positive doctrine nor a mere negativity (or emptiness); rather, it is the negative *of* the positive (or slumbering in the positive), the absence *of* the presence. In Merleau-Ponty's account, transcendence turns into the outside *of* the inside, the invisible *of* the visible. As he writes in his late "Working Notes": "The invisible is not another visible . . . It is *Verborgenheit* [concealment, latency] by principle, that is, the invisible *of* the visible, *Offenheit* of the Umwelt and not *Unendlichkeit* [positive infinity]."[20] Formulations of this kind no doubt are complicated and unsettling—but not in a disabling way. Commenting on the interlacing of immanence and transcendence Deleuze speaks (somewhat hyperbolically) of "vertigo." As indicated before, Levinas portrays the same interlacing as a kind of marvel or wonder. Surely, we are here not in the presence of a big spectacle or a triumphalist epiphany, but of something much more modest and reticent—a small wonder, a marvel harbored in small everyday things. It is this kind of marvel that Benjamin had in mind when he spoke of nearly imperceptible "chips of Messianic time" and of "the narrow gate through which the Messiah might enter."[21] In his own way, Adorno addresses this theme when he states that today "no recollection of transcendence is possible except through finitude; eternity no longer appears as plenitude but only via perishable things. . . . [From this angle] the smallest inner-worldly traces gain relevance for the absolute."[22]

Despite his explicit turn to worldliness (being-in-the-world), Heidegger's thought likewise cannot be stabilized in a factual immanence. His writings repeatedly make reference to transcendence—as when, in *Being and Time*, he portrays "being" as "transcendence as such."[23] To be sure, what is involved here is not a positive plenitude nor an absolute epiphany—for "being," in his writings, always remains sheltered in partial concealment (thereby preventing any manipulative grasp). In his "Letter on Humanism," he clarifies his "worldly" approach by differentiating it sharply both from a self-contained immanence and an aloof otherworldliness. As he writes: the notion of "being-in-the-world" does not assert "that humans are merely 'this-worldly' creatures in a Christian sense, that is, turned away from God and cut loose from 'transcendence.'" By the same token, the phrase "does not refer to a merely 'earthly' as opposed to a 'heavenly' realm, nor to a 'secular' in contrast to a 'spiritual' domain." Instead of pinpointing a distinct sphere, the phrase rather captures the intrinsic "openness of being" into which human existence (*Dasein*) is inserted or propelled. In the same context, Heidegger offers a rewording of the term "existence" by emphasizing its transgressive or "ecstatic" character, its ability to move into uncharted terrain. Seen from this angle, "world" appears as a kind of clearing into which "*Dasein* stands out in the midst of its finitude"; it designates precisely the opening or "beyond" harbored in existence—a kind of horizon of finitude.[24] This combined accent on finitude and transgression also casts light on the enormously subdued or recessed role of religion in Heidegger's work. His "Beiträge zur Philosophie" alludes briefly to a possible advent or "passing-by" of a "last God"—but in language that is far removed from any religious triumphalism. Drawing on this and similar passages, one commentator speaks of Heidegger's "*attentismo*," his patient "waiting for God" (*Erharren vor Gott*)—a posture involving neither dogmatic exuberance nor despair. In the philosopher's own words, religious reticence—bracketing grand vistas—may today be the only way, admittedly a "difficult way," of honoring the divine.[25]

ORDINARY LIFE AND POLITICS

With the advent of phenomenology (and its allies), philosophy and religion are no longer remote enclaves, controlled by privileged elites, but have come to inhabit a world shared by ordinary laypeople. This world is inevitably a social and political world—an arena where philosophical and religious teachings are ultimately put to the test. Unsurprisingly, the philosophers' turn to finitude and the life-world has been embraced and seconded by a number of political thinkers, especially thinkers concerned with the prospect of ordinary democratic life. A good example of this embrace is Hwa Yol Jung whose work was briefly noted before. From the time of his early writings, Jung has followed the phenomenological path—attentive to its social and political implications. As he wrote in his preface to *Rethinking Political Theory*: Faithful to the "originary" (or preconceptual) evidence of human life, "phenomenology attempts to *show* the experiential basis of all conceptualization, both philosophical and scientific." As envisaged by Husserl and continued by Heidegger, Merleau-Ponty, and others, phenomenology inaugurates a mode of "philosophizing with a human face." Although subtle and self-reflective, this mode of philosophizing inevitably remains wedded to a social and political context as the fertile soil of its inquiries. Shunning intellectual and social alibis, he adds, the phenomenologist is one who is "willing to take on the challenge and responsibility of strengthening the moral solidarity of humanity, that is, to transcend [narrow] disciplinary boundaries," to challenge invidious parochialisms, and to "tear down continental divides of culture in the age of academic specialization and compartmentalization."[26]

Jung's embrace of phenomenology did not occur in a vacuum, but was meant as a countermove to dominant intellectual frameworks or paradigms. Most prominent among these frameworks were positivism (or empirical scientism) and "essentialism" (or the return to traditional metaphysics). While positivism eschews the question of meaning and moral standards, essentialism locates these standards beyond experience, in a world beyond "this" world. As Jung describes his own intellectual trajectory: "When I was first introduced to phenomenology" [via Heidegger and Merleau-Ponty], "I quickly came to the realization that it is *the* alternative, though far less traveled and virtually unknown in political theorizing, to political behaviorism [positivism] and to essentialism . . . , which then happened to be the two major competing paradigms in the study of politics." Wedded to the program of "unified science," behavioral positivism ignored the distinctiveness of social and political inquiry, while also being "stricken with ethical amnesia." On the other hand, elevating itself radically beyond lived experience, essentialism sidestepped "the human being's historicity or time-boundedness" and was incapable of "understanding history as transformation." Although sharing the essentialist's opposition to scientism, Jung diverges from the former on a number of crucial points: including the privileging of theoretical contemplation over practice, of eternal sameness over change (and difference), and also of "vision" (rooted in the solitary *cogito*) over "hearing" in a lived community. Among the negative effects of essentialist thought, he notes, is the disregard of change and the rejection of human practice as "something 'irrational'"—a rejection deriving from the primary concern "with what humans think rather than with what they do." A corollary of this disregard is the focus on universal sameness and a kind of "ontological determinism" which discounts the future as "an ecstatic dimension of existence." The most important consequence of metaphysics, especially modern Cartesian metaphysics, however, is the stress on vision, on the *cogito* as the privileged overseer of the world, in contrast to the communicative exchange among partners in a shared world.[27]

In a stunning passage in *Rethinking Political Theory*, Jung links modern metaphysics with the steadily expanding systems of supervision or surveillance in modern Western society. Cartesian metaphysics based on the *cogito*, he writes, "is identifiable with, and epitomizes, the aristocracy of vision or sight as unambiguous." Unlike other modes of human sensibility, vision tends to be solitary and distancing; whereas sounds are prone to "socialize, unify, and synthesize," the effect of sight (taken by itself) is to "isolate, divide, and analyze." Taking a leaf from Heidegger's teachings, Jung at this point establishes a parallel or isomorphism between the subjectivity of the *ego cogito* ("I think") and the "eye-viewpoint" of visual metaphysics, both bent on providing a theoretical overview. From Heidegger, a line can be drawn to the writings of Michel Foucault, especially his observation on total surveillance epitomized by the "Panopticon" or central "Inspection House." As Jung comments sharply, this modern surveillance mechanism is preeminently a "Cartesian plot":

> The Panopticon is literally the prison-house of visualism. Its prisoners, who live in perpetual solitude in the "islands" of cells partitioned by impregnable walls, may be likened to the solitary confinement of the *cogito* or epistemological subject as bodiless substance. Moreover, the Panopticon epitomizes the inextricable link between visualism and the ironclad network of what Michel Foucault calls "disciplinary technologies."[28]

Similar lines of argument, with a clear political edge, can also be found in other thinkers highlighted before. Adorno's *Negative Dialectics* is astutely critical of Cartesian metaphysics, on both philosophical and political grounds. As he notes, modern metaphysics provided the basis both for a subject-centered epistemology and a state- or elite-centered politics. His study is meant to provide an antidote. "Ever since he came to trust his own intellectual impulses," the preface states, "the author has considered it his task to dismantle the fallacy of self-centered subjectivity" because of its disturbing implications. The most troubling aspect of this outlook has been its complicity with mastery and comprehensive (or totalizing) control. "The dominant trend of modern epistemology," we read, "has been to reduce more and more of the natural world to the *cogito*'s grasp," a trend which in due course was bound to boomerang against ordinary life experience. For, "the more autocratically the ego rises above the world, the more fully it falls prey to reification," that is, to the temptation of comprehensive organization, management, and surveillance. In its implicit trajectory, the temptation finally leads to the prospect of a "totally administered society" in which modernity's promise of human emancipation is cancelled. The danger was formulated even more dramatically by Adorno's associate and friend, Horkheimer. "The history of man's efforts to subjugate nature," the latter wrote," is also the history of man's subjugation by man. The development of the concept of the ego reflects this twofold history." By assuming the stance of privileged overseer, the modern "I/eye" becomes habituated to the functions of "domination, command, and organization." As illustrated by recent totalitarian regimes, the symbol and characteristic gesture of the *cogito* (as the embodiment of power/knowledge) is the "outstretched arm of the ruler, directing his men to march or dooming the culprit to execution."[29]

The political implications of rationalist metaphysics are also a prominent concern in the work of Merleau-Ponty—who, at the same time, offers valuable guideposts for a political reorientation. As previously indicated, Merleau-Ponty was strongly opposed to "authoritarian philosophizing," to a kind of narcissistic metaphysics claiming to emanate from an "absolutely unfettered spirit in full possession of itself and its ideas." In another context, he castigated the danger of a haughty celebration of abstract doctrines, of a philosophizing "placed in books" that in effect has "ceased to challenge or touch" human minds and hearts. As a counterpoint, he appealed to the example of Socrates, a thinker who "never wrote and never taught," a gadfly who roamed the market place, "who talked with anyone he met on the street, and who had certain difficulties with public opinion and with the ruling powers."[30] The return to the market place equals a return to the life-world, the world of ordinary social life—which is preeminently the place of democratic politics. On this point, too, Merleau-Ponty's work offers important insights (which deserve to be remembered in a time saturated with haughty principles and factual surveillance). "Whatever one's philosophical or even theological position," he states in one of his early writings, "a society is not the temple of value-idols that figure on the front of its monuments or in its constitutional scrolls." In contrast to the abstract slogans disseminated by ruling elites and the media, the test of a society resides in "the value it places upon concrete human relations." Hence, to understand and properly judge a society, he adds, "one has to penetrate its basic structure to the human bond upon which it is built"—which undoubtedly "depends on legal relations, but also on forms of labor, ways of loving, living, and dying."[31]

Taking his bearings from phenomenology and its embroilment in the market place, Jung strongly seconds the French thinker's observations. "A definition of democracy," he states at one point, begins or should begin "from our felt or tacit meaning of it." Although this felt sense may not be "logically prior" to a conceptual definition, it happens *"experientially prior"* to the formulation of abstract rules and principles. With this accent, Jung places himself squarely on the side of ordinary human life, on the side of finitude and its horizons—as against the pretensions of grand political doctrines and top-down ideologies. With the same accent or gesture, he also reveals his loyalty to his own cultural background—the legacy of Asian thought—with its traditional emphasis on verbal reticence and ordinary, nearly inconspicuous actions in concrete contexts. The closing pages of *Rethinking Political Theory* refer to the teachings of Lao Tzu who, in opposing metaphysical grandiloquence, "warned against the danger of insincere and excessive verbalization," against the political proclivity for "image-making, half-truth, and deceptions." In another context, while discussing Roland Barthes' semiology, Jung refers to the famous Japanese *haiku*: "The old pond / A frog jumps in: / Oh, the sound of water"—to illustrate both the virtue of verbal parsimony and the "small wonder" inhabiting or being sheltered in everyday life. In a surprising and nearly miraculous way, this kind of finite smallness is able to resist and disarm mighty political rulers and their presumptuous projects. Jung here would surely recall the lines from Lao Tzu's *Tao Te Ching* (which are like a balm for a wounded world):

> Those who would take over the earth
> And shape it to their will
> Never, I notice, succeed.
> The earth is like a vessel so sacred
> That at the mere approach of the profane
> It is marred
> And when they reach out their fingers it is gone.[32]

NOTES

1. See Benjamin, "Theses on the Philosophy of History," in Benjamin, *Illuminations*, pp. 259-260.

2. The importance of "ordinary life" in the development of Western modernity has been prominently outlined by Charles Taylor in *Sources of the Self: The Making of Modern Identity* (Cambridge, MA: Harvard University Press, 1989), pp. 211-247.

3. Hwa Yol Jung, *Rethinking Political Theory: Essays in Phenomenology and the Study of Politics* (Athens, OH: Ohio University Press, 1993), p. 5. For a discussion of the notion of the "life-world" and its different formulations see Stephen K. White, ed., *Life-World and Politics: Between Modernity and Postmodernity* (Notre Dame, IN: University of Notre Dame Press, 1989).

4. See Søren Kierkegaard, *Concluding Unscientific Postscript*, trans. David F. Swenson (Princeton, NJ: Princeton University Press, 1944), pp. 109, 270-273.

5. Friedrich Nietzsche, "Twilight of the Idols," in *The Portable Nietzsche*, ed. and trans. Walter Kaufmann (New York: Viking Press, 1968), p. 479; see also "Human, All-Too-Human," p. 52; and "Thus Spoke Zarathustra: First Poet," p. 188.

6. Edmund Husserl, *The Crisis of European Sciences and Transcendental Phenomenology*, trans. David Carr (Evanston, IL: Northwestern University Press, 1970), p. 122. See also Jung, *Rethinking Political Theory*, p. 6. Husserl's turn to mundane phenomena can be (and has been) compared with the development of modern painting: specifically the move from the studio to open-air painting accomplished by impressionism. While, in the Middle Ages, transcendence was captured in sacred figures silhouetted against a golden (eternal) background, and while the onset of modernity discovered the role of perspective as seen from a privileged observer (*cogito*), impressionist and Postimpressionist art has turned to ordinary life (for example, Vincent Van Gogh's *Peasant Shoes*). Moving beyond the standpoint of the privileged observer, cubism has scrambled and multiplied perspectives (anticipating the philosophical celebration of difference and multiplicity).

7. Jung, *Rethinking Political Theory*, p. 7. See also William James, *The Principles of Psychology*, 2 vols. (New York: Dover, 1950).

8. In Jung's words: *Dasein* is defined as "being-in-the-world," the hyphenated phrase aiming "to pinpoint human specificity in an inseparable relatedness of human beings and the world. . . . For Heidegger, the world is the inseparable correlate of humankind's being and is divided into three distinguishable regions: (1) 'being-with' others (*Mitsein*) or the social world (*Mitwelt*); (2) the world of natural things; and (3) the world of human-made objects or artifacts, whose purpose is determined by their serviceability, usability, and manipulability." See *Rethinking Political Theory*, pp. 139-140.

9. Martin Heidegger, "What is Metaphysics?" in *Martin Heidegger: Basic Writings*, p. 108. See also Heidegger, *Being and Time*, trans. Joan Stambaugh (Albany, NY: State University of New York Press, 1996), pp. 219-246.

10. Lawrence J. Hatab, *Ethics and Finitude: Heideggerian Contributions to Moral Philosophy* (Lanham, MD: Rowman & Littlefield, 2000), pp. 2-3.

11. Dennis J. Schmidt, *The Ubiquity of the Finite: Hegel, Heidegger, and the Entitlements of Philosophy* (Cambridge, MA: MIT Press, 1988), p. 227.

12. See Maurice Merleau-Ponty, "What is Phenomenology?" and "The Philosopher and Sociology," in *The Essential Writings of Merleau-Ponty*, ed. Alden L. Fisher (New York: Harcourt, Brace & World, 1969), pp. 27, 29, 65. At another point, Merleau-Ponty insisted on the open-ended finitude of human existence, as contrasted with metaphysical "two-world" theories. In opposition to those metaphysicians (and absolute rationalists) who "wish for man, like things, to be nothing

but a nature heading toward its perfection"—he wrote—a human being should be seen as "a creature who never achieves completion . . . a rift, as it were, in the peaceful fabric of the world." See "The Battle over Existentialism," in *Sense and Non-Sense*, trans. Hubert L. and Patricia A. Dreyfus (Evanston, IL: Northwestern University Press, 1964), pp. 75-76.

13. Max Horkheimer and Theodor W. Adorno, *Dialectic of Enlightenment*, trans. John Cumming (New York: Seabury Press, 1972), pp. 9, 14, 26, 36.

14. Theodor W. Adorno, *Negative Dialectics*, trans. E. B. Ashton (New York: Seabury Press, 1973), pp. 6, 12, 27-28, 277-278.

15. See Dominique Janicaud et al., *Phenomenology and the "Theological" Turn": The French Debate* (New York: Fordam University Press, 2000), p. 17, 26-27, 43. Janicaud's own contribution to the volume is called "The Theological Turn of French Phenomenology" (first published in France in 1991). In addition to Levinas, Janicaud also critiques the writings of Jean-Luc Marion, Michel Henry, and Jean-Louis Chrétien.

16. Giorgio Agamben, "Absolute Immanence," in *Potentiality: Collected Essays in Philosophy*, ed. and trans. Daniel Heller-Roazen (Stanford, CA: Stanford University Press, 1999), pp. 226-228, 238-239. See also Gilles Deleuze, "Immanence: Une vie . . . ," *Philosophie* 47 (1995): p. 4; and Deleuze and Félix Guattari, *What is Philosophy?* trans. Hugh Tomlinson and Graham Burchell (New York: Columbia University Press, 1994), pp. 46-47.

17. Agamben, "Absolute Immanence," in *Potentiality*, p. 228.

18. Emmanuel Levinas, "The Finite and the Infinite," in *Totality and Infinity: An Essay on Exteriority*, trans. Alphonso Lingis (Pittsburgh, PA: Duquesne University Press, 1969), p. 292.

19. Levinas, "The Finite and the Infinite," p. 293 (translation slightly changed).

20. Maurice Merleau-Ponty, *The Visible and the Invisible, Followed by Working Notes*, ed. Claude Lefort, trans. Alphonso Lingis (Evanston, IL: Northwestern University Press, 1968), p. 251. As he adds (p. 251): "For me the infinity of Being that one can speak of is *operative*, transgressive finitude: the openness of the *Umwelt*. I am against finitude in the empirical sense, a factual existence that *has limits*, and this is why I am for metaphysics. But its point lies no more in infinity than in factual finitude." Compare also his statement (p. 250): "The progress of inquiry toward the *center* is not the movement from the conditioned unto the condition, from the founded to the *Grund*: the so-called *Grund* is *Abgrund*. But the abyss one thus discovers is not such *by lack of ground*; it is upsurge of a *Hoheit* which supports from above, that is, of a negativity that *comes to the world*."

21. Benjamin, "Theses on the Philosophy of History," in *Illuminations*, pp. 265–266.

22. Adorno, *Negative Dialectics*, pp. 360, 408. Opposing transcendentalist conceit, Adorno at another point (p. 207) invokes the Jewish-theological "ban on images" which does not permit utopia or the redeemed condition to be positively pictured or represented.

23. Heidegger, *Being and Time*, pp. 33-34. On the role of transcendence in Heidegger's philosophy see, e.g., Jean Greisch, "The 'Play of Transcendence' and the Question of Ethics," in *Heidegger and Practical Philosophy,* ed. François Raffoul and David Pettigrew (Albany, NY: State University of New York Press, 2002), pp. 99-116; also Sonia Sikka, *Forms of Transcendence: Heidegger and Medieval Mystical Theology* (Albany, NY: State University of New York Press, 1997).

24. Heidegger, "Letter on Humanism," in *Martin Heidegger: Basic Writings*, pp. 228-229. Compare also Heidegger's *Einleitung in die Philosophie* (*Gesamtausgabe*, vol. 27; Frankfurt-Main: Klostermann, 1996), where he states (p. 307) that, in its ecstatic quality, *Dasein* does not step over the world but rather thereby first "comes to the world: transcendence means being-in-the-world. . . . That, upon which the basically transgressive *Dasein* transcends, we name 'world.' In stepping-over, however, *Dasein* does not step out of itself . . . but precisely first becomes it."

25. See Manfred Riedel, "Frömmigkeit des Denkens," in *"Herkunft aber bleibt stets Zukunft": Martin Heidegger und die Gottesfrage*, ed. Paola-Ludovica Coriando (Frankfurt-Main: Klosterman, 1998), p. 39; Heidegger, *Beiträge zur Philosophie: Vom Ereignis* (*Gesamtausgabe*, vol. 65; Frankfurt-Main: Klostermann, 1989), p. 406; and "Philosophische Interpretationen zu Aristoteles" (1922), in *Dilthey Jahrbuch*, vol. 6 (1989), p. 197. Compare also Heidegger, *The Phenomenology of Religious Life*, trans. Matthias Fritsch and Jennifer Anna Gosetti-Ferencei (Bloomington, IN: Indiana University Press, 2004); Gianni Vattimo, "Heidegger and Christian Existence," in *After Christianity*, trans. Luca d'Isanto (New York: Columbia University Press, 2002), pp. 123-137; and Richard Kearney and J. O'Leary, eds., *Heidegger et la question de Dieu* (Paris: Grasset, 1980).

26. Jung, *Rethinking Political Theory*, pp. xiii, xviii. Following in the footsteps of Gabriel Marcel and Merleau-Ponty, Jung also stresses the "embodied" character of ordinary life (p. xv): "The most distinctive discovery of phenomenology is, I submit, the notion that the body—the shadowy *other* of the mind or the soul—is not just an object among other objects in the world, but a sentient subject (*Leib, corps vécu*). . . . Only because humans are fully embodied are they naturally rooted in the world both social and natural." As a corollary, phenomenology lends strong support to feminism and feminist theory, given that "the valorization of the feminine intends to subvert the canonical institution of philosophy as the *specular theory* of knowing and doing, as the ethics of *specular man*" (p. xvii).

27. Jung, *Rethinking Political Theory*, pp. xiv, 129. Jung singles out the work of Leo Strauss as a prime example of an essentialist political philosophy. Given his stress on "esoteric" knowledge, he observes (p. 129), "the traditional essentialism of Strauss has 'a kernel of subjectivism' at its very root. Strauss himself admits that philosophizing is the ascendance from what he calls 'public dogma' to 'private knowledge.' Truth, however, is not a 'private knowledge' accessible to a divinely inspired elite but, as Karl Jaspers says, is communicability."

28. Jung, *Rethinking Political Theory*, p. 79. The references in the text are chiefly to Heidegger, *The Question Concerning Technology and Other Essays*, trans. William Lovitt (New York: Harper & Row, 1977), especially "The Age of the World Picture," pp. 115-154; and Michel Foucault, *Discipline and Punish*, trans. Alan Sheridan (New York: Pantheon Books, 1977), pp. 195-228. Compare also Charles B. Guignon, *Heidegger and the Problem of Knowledge* (Indianapolis, IN: Hacket, 1983), and Guy Debord, *Society of the Spectacle* (Detroit, MI: Black & Red, 1983).

29. See Max Horkheimer, *Eclipse of Reason* (1947; repr., New York: Seabury Press, 1974), pp. 93-94; Adorno, *Negative Dialectics*, pp. 176-177. For a similar critique of metaphysical subjectivity compare Stephen K. White's observation: "The dominant, modern philosophical perspective has privileged a portrait of the self as essentially

'disengaged' from its world. This self wants to gain epistemological purchase on, and practical control of, its world. It aims to master the terms of engagement." See *Sustaining Affirmation: The Strength of Weak Ontology in Political Theory* (Princeton, NJ: Princeton University Press, 2000), p. 42.

30. Merleau-Ponty, *In Praise of Philosophy*, trans. John Wild and James M. Edie (Evanston, IL: Northwestern University Press, 1963), pp. 33-34.

31. Merleau-Ponty, *Humanism and Terror*, trans. John O'Neill (Boston: Beacon Press, 1969), p. xiv. Giving a concrete example, the text adds (pp. xiv, xxiv): "It is not just a question of knowing what the liberals have in mind but what in reality is done by the liberal state within and beyond its frontiers. . . . An aggressive liberalism exists which is a dogma and already an ideology of war. It can be recognized by its love of the empyrean of principles. . . . Its nature is violent, nor does it hesitate to impose itself through violence."

32. See *The Way of Life, According to Lao Tzu*, trans. Witter Bynner (New York: Perigee Books, 1972), p. 58; also Jung, *Rethinking Political Theory*, pp. 9, 209, and *The Question of Rationality and the Basic Grammar of Intercultural Texts* (Niigata: International University of Japan, 1989), p. 94.

Chapter Two

The Underside of Modernity: Adorno, Heidegger, and Dussel

Theories or ideas, no matter how lofty, are not immune from historical circumstance: the latter often disclose what otherwise is left unsaid. Far from being an assortment of random data, history from this angle remains a great taskmaster—by teaching us about the complex ambivalences and unintended consequences of rational designs. The ideas of "modernity" and "enlightenment" are a prominent case in point. No one can doubt the loftiness and even intrinsic nobility of these labels. Basically, modernity (as understood in the West) was meant to inaugurate a new age of human freedom and self-determination, as contrasted with previous eras marked by political, clerical, and intellectual tutelage. In turn, enlightenment—in Kant's memorable phrase—was meant to awaken humankind from the "slumber of self-induced immaturity" and ignorance, thereby paving the way for the undiluted reign of scientific knowledge and moral self-legislation. As history teaches, these and related ideas did indeed generate some of the desired results—but often in unforeseen ways and straddled with dubious or less noble implications. Like a deep shadow, these implications accompanied from the beginning the modern spreading of "light." At the very onset of the new age, Francis Bacon proclaimed the equation of knowledge with power—thereby vindicating the prospect of human mastery over nature (as well as over less knowledgeable people). In the domain of politics and ethics, the modern maxim of freedom exacerbated a formula that Aristotle already had used against non-Greeks: "meet it is that barbarous peoples should be governed by the Greeks."[1]

The merits and demerits of modernity have been widely discussed in recent decades from a variety of angles (antimodern, modernist, postmodern)—but often in a purely academic vein. Here again, historical circumstance demands its due. It was during the past (twentieth) century that some of the most disturbing and hideous connotations of the modern project of unlimited mastery

33

came out into the open, and it was in response to these implications—manifest in fascism and Stalinist communism—that some of the most penetrating analyses of this project were formulated. In view of the hundredth anniversary of Theodor Adorno's birth (1903), it is fitting that close attention should be given again to his critical work—particularly to the magisterial *Dialectic of Enlightenment* (written in collaboration with Max Horkheimer) and the magnum opus of his later years, *Negative Dialectics*. Roughly in the same historical context, another leading German thinker—Martin Heidegger—launched an equally devastating attack on the totalizing machinations of modern technology and modern politics (in writings which only recently have become available). The following pages start out by reviewing the arguments of these two thinkers, with an emphasis on both their similarities and their differences. With the demise of fascism and Stalinist communism, these arguments seem to have lost their contextual force; this, however, is far from being the case. Under the aegis of globalization, the totalizing ambitions of Western modernity are revealed today on a planetary scale: in the opposition between the hegemonic "North" and the dominated "South." Speaking no longer from the European "center" of modernity but from the non-Western periphery—and drawing freely on the insights of Adorno and Heidegger—the Latin American Enrique Dussel has formulated a new critique of the modern project, a critique which—without denying its liberating potential—takes aim at the prospect of global mastery as the "underside of modernity."

ADORNO AND MODERNITY'S "DIALECTIC"

Adorno's life reflects the entire drama of his period. A cofounder of the Frankfurt Institute for Social Research during the Weimar years, he—like many of his colleagues—was forced into exile by the rise of fascism in Germany. Under the impact of fascist policies, and especially the unfolding specter of the Jewish Holocaust, Adorno came to realize the darkly sinister undertone of Western modernity—an awareness prompting him to temper the confident progressivism of his earlier years (inspired by Left-Hegelian ideas). To be sure, past history had always been punctuated by grim episodes of persecution and oppression; however, what rendered contemporary politics distinctive was the totalizing or "totalitarian" reach of political control—a reach indebted in no small measure to the triumphant sway of modern rationality wedded to the Baconian motto of knowledge/power. Some of the dangers lurking in this motto were clearly exposed by Max Horkheimer, Adorno's friend, in a study written during the war years and entitled *Eclipse of Reason*. Without simply abandoning modernity or the promises of enlightenment,

Horkheimer's text severely castigated the ongoing shrinkage of critical reason and self-reflection into a mere instrument of calculation and managerial control. To a large extent, this shrinkage in his view could be traced to the Baconian (and Cartesian) split between subject and object, between rational knowledge and external matter or nature. The end result of this division, he noted, was on the one hand an "abstract ego emptied of all substance" except its will for self-preservation, and on the other, "an empty nature degraded to mere material, mere stuff to be dominated, without any other purpose than that of this very domination."[2]

Themes of this kind were further explored and deepened by Horkheimer and Adorno during the same wartime period—an exploration which culminated in their epochal work, *Dialectic of Enlightenment.* Here, as in Horkheimer's text, the animus was not directed against reason and enlightenment as such—provided these labels preserved the connotation of critical understanding and self-reflection. As it happened, however, the unfolding scenario of modernity led to a steady curtailment of the latter in favor of a progressive congealment or "reification" of both rational knowledge and the empirical target of knowledge (the two poles of the subject-object split). According to the authors, the advancement of modern scientific knowledge basically heralded an exit or exodus—a largely welcome exodus—from primitive myth or an unreflective and oppressive "naturalism" (utterly opaque to human understanding); yet, precisely by virtue of this exodus and the resulting subjugation of nature, modern reason is in danger of being "remythologized" by turning into an instrument of unreflective power. Although the program of rational inquiry always entails in some way "the disenchantment of the world, the dissolution of myths, and the substitution of knowledge for fancy," the process begins to boomerang when reason loses its critical edge by blending into "positivist" formulas. At this point, enlightenment reveals its own dark undercurrent, and social progress, its complicity with regress. Here is a passage that eloquently expresses the authors' concerns:

> We are wholly convinced—and therein lies our *petitio principii*—that social freedom is inseparable from enlightened thought. Nevertheless, we believe just as clearly to have recognized that this very way of thinking—no less than the actual historical forms (the social institutions) with which it is interwoven—already contains the seed of the reversal universally apparent today. If enlightenment does not allow reflection on this regressive element, it seals its own fate.[3]

In terms of the text, the regressive counterpoint of enlightenment—its dialectical underside—derives from the streamlining of rational thought into a calculating, instrumental form of rationality, a process which underscores the growing division between human beings and nature, between cognitive

power and its external targets. Ever since the time of Bacon, Horkheimer and
Adorno assert, cognitive rationality has shown a "patriarchal" face: by conquering superstition, human reason is meant to "hold sway over the disenchanted nature." In the course of modernity or modernization, this patriarchal
legacy has led to a steady widening of the rift between *res cogitans* (thinking
subject) and *res extensa* (extended matter)—which coincides with the gulf between inside and outside, between logical form and substantive content. On
the internal or "subjective" side, the *cogito* in modernity tends to be stylized
into a sovereign selfhood, a self-contained "identity" that ejects from itself all
forms of otherness as modes of alienation and reification; in large measure,
modern freedom or "emancipation" has this connotation of self-recovery or
self-possession. It is only through this retreat into inwardness, the text states,
that individuals gain "self-identity," a selfhood that cannot be "dissipated
through identification with others" but that "takes possession of itself once
and for all behind an impenetrable mask." The upshot of this development is
the radical subordination of matter to mind, of nature—both internal and external nature—to the dictates of a rationally emancipated humankind. As the
authors add intriguingly, in a foray into political theology: "Systematizing
reason and the creator-God resemble each other as rulers of nature. Man's
likeness to God consists in the sovereignty over the world, in the countenance
of mastery, and in the ability to command."[4]

In the modern era, the streamlining effect of cognitive rationality was first
evident in the sequence of grand philosophical "systems"—all intent on
grasping the universe as a whole. Later, the same tendency surfaced in social-
scientific systems, especially in functional-sociological models pretending to
capture the totality of social life. In the authors' words: "From the start, enlightenment recognizes as real occurrence only what can be apprehended in
rational unity; its ideal is the 'system' from which all and everything follows." The primary means for accomplishing this unity—a means extolled especially by positivism and the "unified science" movement—is number, that
is, the reduction of all qualitative differences to quantitative measurement.
"Number," we read, "became the canon of enlightenment: the same equations
govern bourgeois [abstract] justice and economic commodity exchange." In
expelling or cleansing itself of qualitative differences, cognitive rationality
inevitably prepared the ground for the "systematization" or homogenization
of social life and thus for the establishment of increasingly effective social
controls and disciplines. At the same time, the priority of number or formal
calculus promoted a distinctive kind of social and intellectual hierarchy (or
patriarchy). By defining knowledge or "truth" as the primacy of universal
form over particular content, of rational system over nonrational experience,
modern rationality exacted a price: namely, the alienation of reason from the

target of knowledge or, more precisely, the isolation of reason from possible learning experiences induced by its targets. Among these learning experiences are the lessons provided by human sensuality and affectivity (that is, the realm of "inner" nature). From the vantage of modern rationality, Horkheimer and Adorno state, sensuality and instinct are "as mythical as religious superstitions" (and hence subject to the same exorcism), while the idea of serving a God not constructed by the rational self is considered "as irrational as drunkenness."[5]

As in Horkheimer's text, exposing the "dialectic of enlightenment" was not meant as a plea for primitivism or nostalgic regression. Some help in avoiding the twin dangers of regression and rational triumphalism could be found in Hegelian dialectics, and particularly in his notion of "determinate negation." With that notion, Horkheimer and Adorno affirm, Hegel "revealed an element that separates [genuine] enlightenment from the positivist decay with which he lumps it together." Yet, this endorsement is qualified: by ultimately "absolutizing" the outcome of dialectics—namely, his own system of totalizing synthesis—Hegel himself "contravened the prohibition (of images) and lapsed into mythology." As a result, the authors recommend a more subdued, post-Hegelian dialectics—but one clearly geared toward the healing or reconciliation of modern divisions. To be sure, hope cannot be pinned on magical formulas or instant solutions. Only through critical reflection—one mindful of its tendential complicity with power—is reason able to break the spell of (ancient or modern) mythology and reification. Only in this manner is reason capable of regaining its liberating élan: an élan whereby enlightenment transcends domineering rationality by regaining access to a nature "which becomes perceptible in its otherness or alienation." Thus, a healing of modern divisions is at least initiated (if not completed) through radical self-reflection pushing beyond instrumentalism—more boldly phrased: through a "recollection of nature in the rational subject," a remembrance which holds the key to the "truth of all culture." As the authors conclude, enlightenment fulfills and "sublates" itself when the means-ends nexus is suspended—at the point where the "nearest practical ends" reveal themselves as the "most distant goal" and where repressed nature is remembered as the "land of origin" as well as the portent of an "unmanageable" hope.[6]

Qualified endorsement of Hegelian dialectics is the hallmark also of Adorno's later writings, particularly his sprawling *Negative Dialectics*. "Qualified" here means acceptance of healing mediations *minus* resort to the "absolute" or to any kind of comprehensive or totalizing synthesis. It is this *minus* feature that renders genuine dialectics "negative": namely, by confining itself to the determinate negation of existing ills and divisions while radically refusing to portray and conceptually define a fully reconciled utopia. One of

Adorno's main complaints here is directed at Hegel's relentless rationalism or "conceptualism": his effort to bring all experience under the domineering sway of concepts (culminating in the "absolute" concept or idea). Although recognizing experiential "otherness," he remonstrates, Hegel's system tended to "prethink" and conceptually prearrange every concrete particularity, with the result that the diversity of phenomena was streamlined into a grand, holistic synthesis governed by reason. Proceeding in this manner, Hegelian dialectics ultimately reduced concrete phenomena to mere "exemplars of concepts" while confining reason to the rehearsal of its own categories. In Adorno's view, the only way to rupture this self-enclosure is through thought's attentiveness to nonthought or reason's turn toward the (conceptually) "nonidentical"— which precludes any premature synthesis. Only in this manner is reason able to regain (in Hegel's own terms) its "freedom toward the object," a freedom lost under the spell of the subject's "meaning-constituting" or meaning-imposing autonomy. Basically, philosophy's genuine concern in our times, he adds, is with those matters in which Hegel (following a long philosophical or metaphysical tradition) expressed little or no interest: namely, "nonconceptuality, singularity, and particularity"—things which ever since Plato have been dismissed as "transitory and insignificant," as a *qualité negligeable*."[7]

According to Adorno's text, the corrective to Hegel's conceptual system is the rigorous insistence on nontotality, that is, on the inescapable "nonidentity" between reason and its targets, between concepts and the world (or the stubborn excess of the latter over the former). "To change the direction of conceptuality, to turn it toward nonidentity," we read, "is the hinge or emblem of negative dialectics." Tied to traditional metaphysics, idealist philosophy offered only a truncated dialectics that ultimately was unable to come to grips with modern social dilemmas and divisions. Basically, in its idealist version, dialectics was tied to the "sovereign subject" as the source of rational conceptualization—an outlook which now has become "historically obsolete," given that none of the idealist formulas have stood the test of time. Under present circumstances, Adorno argues, only a negative dialectics holds out both intellectual and social promise: by being attentive to the "otherness" or underside of reason as well as to the social-political underside of modernity, the legions of marginalized and oppressed peoples at its fringes. In his stark formulation, traditional idealism by privileging the *cogito* (or subjectivity) only "spiritualized" the Darwinian struggle for survival, thus reinstating or confirming a repressive naturalism. By proclaiming itself the Baconian master and even idealist "maker" of all things, the modern epistemological *cogito* inevitably entangled itself in the nexus of power/knowledge: "In exerting mastery it becomes part of what it believes to master, succumbing like the lord" (in the Hegelian master-slave relationship).[8]

In departing from the idealist legacy, negative dialectics counters not only speculative illusions but also the nexus of domination prevailing in modernity with regard to both nature and society. In relinquishing the primacy of the *cogito* (or subjectivity), such a dialectics is able to confront the power/ knowledge nexus that, in modernity, pits against each other reason and experience, humanity and nature, privileged or dominant and oppressed populations. As Adorno writes, dialectical thinking "respects that which is to be thought—the object or target of knowledge—even where the latter exceeds or does not heed the rules of formal logic." Differently phrased: such a thinking is able "to think against itself without self-cancellation or self-erasure." Proceeding along these lines, negative dialectics extricates itself from the modified Darwinism of traditional idealist thought, by allowing things "to be" and by giving a hearing to voices otherwise excluded by modern reason. In Adorno's words, attention to the underside of reason means a willingness to "heed a potential slumbering in things" and thereby "make amends" to them for its own incursions. This "potential slumbering in things" is the domain of otherness or difference—a domain captured in Josef Eichendorff's phrase of "beautiful strangeness" (*schöne Fremde*). As he concludes:

> The hoped-for state of reconciliation would not annex the alien through an act of philosophical imperialism. Instead, its happiness would consist in allowing it to remain distant and different even in proximate surroundings, beyond the pale of both heterogeneity and sameness or identity.[9]

HEIDEGGER AND MODERN "MACHINATIONS"

The relation between Adorno and Heidegger is complex and hard to disentangle; probably for this very reason it is infrequently discussed in the literature.[10] Some of the differences between the two thinkers are relatively easy to pinpoint, having to do mainly with their respective life stories and intellectual backgrounds. As indicated, Adorno's life story was relatively turbulent, leading him from Weimar Germany into the New World (New York and California) and finally back to Frankfurt after the war. By comparison, Heidegger's personal life was relatively sheltered, being spent for the most part in and around Freiburg and the Black Forest region. In terms of intellectual background, Adorno drew his inspiration chiefly from Left Hegelianism and aspects of humanist Marxism; by contrast, Heidegger's intellectual pedigree is of *longue durée*, stretching from the pre-Socratics via Aristotle to Husserlian phenomenology and hermeneutics. The most obvious difference, of course— and the one most widely debated—has to do with their respective responses to 1933 and its aftermath. Yet, it is precisely in this regard that initial impressions and popular assessments may be thoroughly misleading and hence in need of revision. During recent years, several writings have become available which Heidegger wrote in the decade following 1933, that is, during the apogee of the Nazi regime. Far from showing a continued attachment to this regime, these writings on the contrary reveal Heidegger's steady estrangement—or what one may call his "inner emigration"—from the hegemonic powers of his time. With growing intensity, his opposition is directed at the totalizing or totalitarian features of the regime, features which in no small part derive from modernity's infatuation with "making" and domineering fabrication—what Heidegger calls *"Machenschaft."*

The texts from the Nazi period which recently became available are mainly three: *Beiträge zur Philosophie* (Contributions to Philosophy) of 1936; *Besinnung* (Meditative Thinking) of 1938-1939; and *Die Geschichte des Seyns* (The History of Being) of 1939-1940. Taken together, the texts give evidence of a profound intellectual drama that Heidegger underwent during this period—a drama that is customarily described as his *"Kehre"* or "turning" (labels which should not be taken as synonyms for a reversal or simple "turning away," but rather as signposts of a deepening and more intensive "turning toward" primary philosophical concerns). Of the three texts, the first is the most voluminous and also the most dramatically ambitious, setting forth an entire, detailed trajectory of intellectual and existential transformation and reorientation. This trajectory basically leads from the condition of modernity anchored in knowledge/power and the domineering designs of the *cogito* in the direction of a freer and more generously open mode of co-being among humans and between humans and the world (guided by "letting-be"). The text is challenging and provocative not only philosophically, but also on a more mundane, political level. Taking direct aim at National Socialism and its motto of "total mobilization," Heidegger comments that such a "total (or totalizing) worldview" must "close itself off against the probing of its own ground and the premises of its actions," and it must do so because otherwise "total ideology would put itself into question." It is in connection with this critique that the term *"Machenschaft"* surfaces prominently—and with starkly pejorative connotations. The rise of worldviews to predominance, Heidegger notes, is a result of modern metaphysics, and in that context "worldview basically means *Machenschaft*," that is, a mode of contrived "machination" where creative praxis is replaced by organized "business" (*Betrieb*) and managerial control.[11]

Elaborating on this point, the text links the term with the modern prevalence of "making (*Machen, poiesis, techne*)," a making seen not solely as a form of human conduct, but as a distinct type of ontological disclosure. In modernity, Heidegger points out, *Machenschaft* is promoted by the sway of science and technology that renders everything "makeable" (*machbar*). Under these auspices, the instrumental cause-effect nexus becomes all-dominant, though in varying guises: "Both the mechanistic and the biologistic worldviews are only consequences of the underlying *machenschaftlich* interpretation of being." Preceded by biblical accounts of creation (construed as fabrication), the modern rise of *Machenschaft* was decisively inaugurated by the Cartesian *cogito*, especially by Descartes' equation of *ens creatum* with *ens certum* (fixed, determined being). Subsequently, this approach was further solidified by the advances of mathematical physics and technology (*Technik*), a process leading to the progressive technical-calculating management of the world and its resources. Against this background, Heidegger asks "What is *Machenschaft?*" and responds: "It is the system of complete explanatory calculability whereby every being is streamlined and uniformly equated with every other being—and thereby alienated, and more than alienated, from itself" (or its own distinctive potential). As he further elaborates, calculability and anonymous sameness are curiously allied in *Machenschaft* with something seemingly very different: namely, subjective feeling or emotion (*Erlebnis*). But the contrast is only apparent because anonymity and subjectivism are only two sides of the same coin: the cognitive and the emotive sides of the ego. Both reveal the subject's incapacity for self-transformation and its "oblivion of being."[12]

Jointly with the critique of *Machenschaft*, *Beiträge* also offers intriguing reflections on the meaning of "power," "violence," and related terms. Departing from an earlier ambivalent usage, the text stipulates a series of definitions with clearly demarcated contours. Closely associated with *Machenschaft* are the two terms "power" (*Macht*) and "violence" (*Gewalt*). In Heidegger's formulation, violence (*Gewalt*) signifies the willful but impotent attempt to change things or conditions without deeper insight or ontological attunement: "Wherever change is sought by 'ontic' means alone (*Seiendes durch Seiendes*), violence is needed." Power (*Macht*) stands purely in the service of willful machination and signifies "the ability to secure the control of possibilities of violence." In sharp contrast to these terms, *Beiträge* mentions "authoritative rule" (*Herrschaft*) as a mode of ontological potency or capability deriving its authority from its liberating openness to "being." "Herrschaft," Heidegger writes, "is the need of freedom for freedom" and happens only "in the realm of freedom"; its greatness consists in the fact "that it has no need of power or violence and yet is more potent (*wirksamer*) than they." Such liberating and nonmanipulative *Herrschaft* is impossible under the reign of modern worldviews, especially totalizing worldview-ideologies, which have no room for human freedom and level everything into the uniform system of *Machenschaft*. Under the auspices of this system, human beings individually and people at large are reduced to mere resources of power, and the only issue is the preservation and enhancement of their utility. The only way for *Dasein* and people to live genuinely and freely, *Beiträge* insists, is through an act of self-transcendence or self-transformation (ek-stasis) that is simultaneously an act of self-finding, highlighted by the term "*Ereignis.*" For *Ereignis* means basically the chiasm or entwinement between humans and the openness of "being" (or the divine), a differentiated and needful encounter which opens up the prospect of the arrival of "the godhead of the other God" (*die Gottheit des anderen Gottes*).[13]

The critique of totalizing and domineering *Machenschaft* was further sharpened in the book titled *Besinnung*. As in the case of *Beiträge*, the text can be read both on a recessed, philosophical and a more mundane, political level—although the two levels are closely interlaced. Philosophically, *Besinnung* urges a more reflective rethinking of human being-in-the-world, a rethinking opening human hearts and minds again to the "call of being" (which guides them into a more careful and caring mode of living). As before, Heidegger dwells on the meaning of *Machenschaft* and its relation to *Macht* and *Gewalt*. "*Machenschaft,*" he reiterates, "means the all-pervasive and totalizing 'makeability' of everything" and the general routine acceptance of this process in such a way that "the unconditional calculability of everything is assured." In pursuing its leveling and domineering path, *Machenschaft* employs violence (*Gewalt*) and the latter is stabilized through the "secure possession of power (*Macht*)" aiming at universal or total subjugation. In modernity, the text continues, the aims of *Machenschaft* are promoted and abetted by technology (*Technik*) that reduces human beings to mere empirical resources whose value is assessed purely in terms of utility or productivity. It is in this context that Heidegger launches an attack on the *Führer* himself who, in an address to the *Reichstag* in 1939, had made this statement: "There is no stance or attitude (*Haltung*) which would not receive its ultimate justification from its utility for the totality (of the nation)." Reacting angrily to this statement, Heidegger raises a number of acerbic questions, such as the following: What is the "totality" that is postulated here? What is the "utility" of an attitude or outlook, and by what standard is it to be judged? Does the entire statement not signify "the denial of the basic questionability (*Fraglichkeit*) of human *Dasein* with regard to its hidden relation to being" (and its care)?[14]

Moving beyond the critique of *Machenschaft*, *Besinnung* offers glimpses of a radically "other" possibility: namely, the reflective recovery of the question of and care for being, a care completely immune to managerial manipulation. As before, Heidegger distinguishes between power and violence, on the one hand, and genuine "authority" (*Herrschaft*), on the other. "Apart from exuding intrinsic dignity or worth," he writes, "*Herrschaft* means the free potency or capacity for an original respect for being" (rather than merely empirical things). To characterize this dignity, *Besinnung* introduces a new vocabulary by presenting being (*Seyn*) as a basically "power-free domain (*das Machtlose*) beyond power and nonpower or impotence (*jenseits von Macht und Unmacht*)." As Heidegger emphasizes, "power-free" does not mean powerless or impotent, because the latter remains fixated on power, now experienced as a lack. From an everyday "realist" angle, being's realm may appear powerless or impotent; but this is only a semblance or illusion resulting from its reticent unobtrusiveness. Due to its reticence, being's realm can never be dragged into human machinations, into the struggles between the powerful and the powerless (as long as the latter merely seek power); but precisely in this manner it reveals its *Herrschaft*, a reign that "cannot be matched by any power or superpower because they necessarily ignore the nature of the *basically* power-free possibility." To be sure, access to this reign is difficult and radically obstructed by the *Machenschaft* of our age. Yet, an important pathway through and beyond these obstructions is offered by meditative thinking (*Besinnung*) that opens a glimpse into the "time-space-play" (*Zeit-Spiel-Raum*) of being as *Ereignis*, that is, into the interplay and differential entwinement of being and beings, of humans, nature, and the divine.[15]

Themes and insights of this kind are carried forward in *Die Geschichte des Seyns*, a series of texts dating from the onset of World War II. Politically, the texts are still more nonconformist and rebellious than preceding writings—an aspect largely attributable to their grim context. Central to the volume is again the critique of *Machenschaft* defined as a mode of being that "pushes everything into the mold of 'makeability.'" As before, *Machenschaft* is intimately linked with the glorification of power (*Macht*), and the latter is anchored ultimately in "will" to power and in "unconditional subjectivity" (a chief trait of modern metaphysics). To effectuate its rule, power relies on violence (*Gewalt*) as its chief instrument. When violence or brutality becomes predominant, matters are starkly simplified: everything is geared toward the "unconditional annihilation (*Vernichtung*) of opposing forces by unconditional means." The unleashing of brutal violence carries in its train the "devastation" (*Verwüstung*) of everything with the result that a "desert" (*Wüste*) spreads where nothing can grow any longer—especially not thoughtfulness and care for being. A particularly vivid and harrowing sign of this devastation is the hankering for warfare—a warfare that, due to the totalizing ambitions of *Machenschaft*, now turns into "total war" (*totaler Krieg*). Given the steadily widening range of modern technology and weaponry, Heidegger adds somberly, the relentless struggle for power and more power necessarily leads to "unbounded or limitless wars (*grenzenlose Kriege*) furthering the empowerment of power." Unsurprisingly, such wars ultimately take the form of "world wars" in the service of a globally unleashed *Machenschaft*.[16]

As an antidote or counterpoise to these trends, the texts refer again to the possibility of "authoritative rule" (*Herrschaft*). However, in view of its lingering proximity to power, the term now appears sufficiently suspect to Heidegger that he is willing to drop it (in favor of an unmitigated "power-free" realm). The sharpened denunciation or distantiation from *Macht* is paralleled by an intensification of political polemics. *Die Geschichte des Seyns* openly ridicules fascist leaders for their self-glorification as "mighty rulers" (*Machthaber*) whose great achievement resides in their "seizure of power" (*Machtergreifung*). Leaders, Heidegger states, are never "possessors of power" (*Machthaber*) but rather puppets in the grip of *Macht* and *Machenschaft*; they cannot "seize" or "possess" power because they are "possessed by it" (in the manner of an obsession). The texts also critique National Socialism directly by debunking its chosen terminology. Drawing on his argument that modernity is marked by "unconditional subjectivity," Heidegger comments that "the consequence of this subjectivity is the 'nationalism' of nations and the 'socialism' of the people (*Volk*)." Proceeding even more boldly, the texts raise the issue of political and moral responsibility. Despite the fact that power cannot be "possessed" but operates obsessively, the book does not hesitate to link power and violence with "criminality" (*Verbrechen*). Given the unleashing of *Machenschaft* and unconditional global warfare, Heidegger asserts, our age also produces "the great criminals" (*die grossen Verbrecher*)—criminals whose misdeeds far exceed ordinary human guilt and who, in fact, can be described as "global master criminals" (*planetarische Hauptverbrecher*). As he adds: "There is no punishment which would be sufficiently great to punish these criminals."[17]

DUSSEL AND TRANSMODERNITY

Roughly half a century has passed since the time of Adorno's and Heidegger's major writings. In the meantime, the world has dramatically changed. With the destruction of the Nazi regime, fascism—at least in its overt totalitarian guise—has passed from the scene. With the demise of the Soviet Union, Soviet-style totalitarianism likewise has disappeared. However, appearances are deceiving. In new guises and under new labels *Macht* and *Machenschaft* continue to haunt the world. Under the aegis of globalization, totalizing ambitions are no longer limited to intra-societal domination but have acquired global or planetary dimensions. As a result, social and political divisions are no longer confined to domestic class conflicts but assume the character of a global divide: that between developed and developing societies, between North and South, between center and periphery. Given the enormous accumulation of technological, military, and economic power in the "developed" hemisphere, the divide readily translates into the hegemonic domination of the North over the South or—in Samuel Huntington's phrase—of the "West" over the "Rest." In this situation, the dialectic of enlightenment and modernity is bound to be most intensely experienced by its victims or "subaltern" targets: ordinary people and intellectuals living at the borders or margins of development. One of the most eloquent and trenchant contemporary intellectuals hailing from the South is the Argentinian-Mexican Enrique Dussel whose name is closely linked with the (so-called) "philosophy of liberation." For present purposes, the discussion will be limited to two of his major texts: *The Invention of the Americas* (of 1992) and *The Underside of Modernity* (of 1996).

In terms of intellectual background, Dussel's work has been strongly influenced by a number of European writers: ranging from Marx, Gramsci, and Adorno to Heidegger, Ricoeur, and Levinas. From Marx he derived insight into the dynamics of economic class conflicts and their progressive globalization under neoliberal capitalist auspices—although he carefully steered clear of any type of determinism (an aspect linking him with Gramsci). From Adorno he learned about the "mythical" feature of Western modernity, and also about the need to avoid the totalizing ambitions of Hegel's conceptual dialectics. Connections with Heidegger's writings are particularly pronounced. With the latter he shares, among other things, the emphasis on concretely situated human existence, on finite *Dasein* as "being-in-the-world"—where "world" is not external to, but co-constitutive of human being (in contrast to the Cartesian legacy). Like Ricoeur and Gadamer, Dussel is committed to hermeneutics or hermeneutical interpretation, deriving from the conviction that seeing is always a "seeing as" and action, an imagining or "shaping as" inspired by sedimented memories and prejudgments. In pursuing his intellectual path, Dussel in recent years was also deeply drawn to the teachings of Emmanuel Levinas—although the latter never fully eclipsed his earlier philosophical moorings. What attracted him in Levinas's work was especially the debunking of egocentrism, that is, the insistence on nontotality in the sense of an openness to the ethical demands of the "Other," especially the marginalized and disadvantaged—a debunking which clearly resonates with Adorno's stress on nonidentity and Heidegger's accent on self-transcendence. What emerged from this confluence of intellectual mentors is a "philosophy of liberation" particularly attentive to "third world" needs or (in a different formulation) an "ethical hermeneutics" taking its departure from the vantage of the oppressed (paralleling the "preferential option for the poor" favored by liberation theology).[18]

The full title of the first study mentioned above is *The Invention of the Americas: Eclipse of the "Other" and the Myth of Modernity*. The title immediately announces the book's central target: the rise of "Eurocentrism" manifest in the West's totalizing hegemonic ambitions. For Dussel, the "birth-date of modernity" was 1492, that is, the discovery and ensuing conquest of the Americas. While foreshadowed by some tendencies of the later Middle Ages, he writes, modernity "came to birth in Europe's confrontation with the Other: by controlling, conquering, and violating the Other, Europe defined it-self as discoverer, conquistador, and colonizer of an alterity that was likewise constitutive of modernity." Using language borrowed in part from Horkheimer and Adorno, he adds: "Modernity dawned in 1492 and with it the myth of a special kind of sacrificial violence which eventually eclipsed what-ever was nonEuropean." Although insisting on the tensional relation between Europe and its "Other"—or between the "West" and the "Rest"—Dussel does not erect the conflict into an unbridgeable or incommensurable gulf. The re-lation for him remains dialectical—but not in the sense of Hegel's dialectic where the "Other" is ultimately absorbed in a higher synthesis. One of Dus-sel's distinctive contributions is the notion of an "analectical" mode of rea-soning and interacting, a mode that preserves the linkage between dialectics and (a certain kind of) dialogue. As he writes at one point: analectics desig-nates a method "which begins from the Other as free, as one beyond the sys-tem of totality; which begins, then, from the Other's word, from the revela-tion of the Other, and which, trusting in the Other's word, labors, works, serves, and creates." Although favoring dialogue, analectics does not end in a bland consensualism but respects the gap or difference (*dia*) between self and other, between oppressor and oppressed, shunning the temptation of a total-izing synthesis: "I want to develop a philosophy of a dialogue as part of a phi-losophy of liberation of the oppressed, the excommunicated, the excluded, the Other."[19]

For Dussel, liberation of the oppressed does not involve a brute struggle for power—which would only lead to the replacement of one type of oppression by another. In line with the idea of an "ethical hermeneutics," his aim is not only to liberate the oppressed and excluded, but also to liberate the oppressors from their desire to oppress—thus ultimately appealing to a latent ethical po-tential. It is in this respect that Dussel invokes the example of Bartolemé de Las Casas, the Spanish cleric who, at the time of the conquest of the Ameri-cas, denounced the violence of the conquistadors, but without endorsing sim-ple counterviolence or the unleashing of totalizing carnage. As he writes in *The Invention of the Americas*, it was Las Casas who, in traveling in the New World, had a transformative experience: he "underwent tutelage at the hands of the oppressed and learned to admire the beauty, culture, and goodness of the indigenous, the new, the Other." In a Levinasian sense, Las Casas discov-ered in the Americas an ethics which is not abstractly imposed but arises from the concrete encounter with the "face" of indigenous peoples; and "out of his love" for them he launched his critique of their oppression, while pleading for a different, "analectical" mode of interaction. Proceeding to a more general level, the text crisply pinpoints the preconditions of a nonimperialist dialogue applicable to our present time. The idea of such a dialogue, Dussel writes, should not lapse into "the facile optimism of a rationalist, abstract universalism" which merely imposes Eurocentric standards on the rest of the world. At the same, it must steer clear of the quagmire of "irrationality, incommunicability, or incommensurability" which is merely the flip side of Eurocentrism. What is needed instead is the fostering of an alternative or analectical reason open to the traumas of exclusion and oppression, an outlook that should "deny the irrational sacrificial myth of modernity" while simultaneously affirming "the emancipative tendencies of the enlightenment and modernity within a new transmodernity."[20]

The second study cited above—*The Underside of Modernity*—radicalizes the critique of Eurocentric modernity by inserting this critique into the broader parameters of the ongoing process of globalization. Arguing against some recent Western thinkers (like Habermas and Charles Taylor), Dussel insists that the meaning of modernity cannot be solely found in the "discourse of modernity" or in the Western "sources of the self." Despite certain triggering factors operating within the geographical confines of Europe, modernity also has broader connotations—that makes it possible to distinguish between its purely "Eurocentric" and its "global or planetary" significance. What the latter dimension reveals is the role of modernity "as *center* of a global process" where the center elevates itself with reference to the global "periphery" (which is variously called colonial, neocolonial, underdeveloped, "third world," and now South). Notwithstanding the influence of the Reformation, European enlightenment, and revolution, the text asserts, modernity in its broader reach was born "when Europe begins its expansion beyond its historical limits." At this juncture, Europe "arrives in Africa, in India and Japan, thanks to Portugal; in Latin America and from there in the Philippines, thanks to the Spanish conquest." While Europe thus establishes itself as "center" and vanguard, other societies and cultures are deprecated as "immature, barbarous, underdeveloped." It is thus that the "second moment" of modernity—its other side or underside—is inaugurated: no longer as "an emancipatory rational nucleus" but as "an irrational sacrificial myth." Although most empires in the past considered themselves as centers of a certain geographical context, the situation is changed in modernity because of the latter's global reach: "Only *modern* European culture, from 1492 onwards, became the center of a world system, of a global or universal history that confronts (with various forms of subsumption and exteriority) *all the other cultures of the world*—cultures that now will be militarily dominated as its periphery."[21]

According to Dussel, the (Habermasian) notion of a "discourse of modernity" is flawed not only because of its Eurocentric focus, but also because of its very restricted scope of possible "counterdiscourses" (which cannot be limited to Nietzsche and postmodernism). In contrast to the stress on recent, intra-European skirmishes, the text insists that the idea of a "counterdiscourse" to modernity is already five centuries old: it began on the Hispaniola Island "when Anton de Montesinos attacked the injustices that were being committed against the Indians" and from there extended to the classrooms of Salamanca, to the work of Bartolemé de Las Casas and the lectures of Francisco de Vitoria. Here, the importance of the periphery comes into view. For, Bartolemé de Las Casas "would not have been able to criticize Spain without having resided in the periphery, without having heard the cries and lamentations, and without having seen the tortures that the Indians suffered at the hands of the colonizing Europeans." For Dussel, it is the "others" in the periphery that constitute the real source and impetus of modern "counterdiscourses" (even in the European center). Hence, for philosophers and intellectuals, the study of Latin America, of Africa and Asia is not "an anecdotal task" or a residual pastime. Rather, it involves historical "truth and justice"; it is a matter of remembering a history that "*rescues* the nonhegemonic, dominated, silenced, and forgotten counterdiscourse, namely, that of the constitutive alterity or underside of modernity itself." Henceforth, the study of philosophy or the history of ideas can no longer be confined to a Western canon. What is demanded by our time—the age of globalization—is the development of "a new global vision of philosophy," one which will reveal hitherto unsuspected dimensions once the "rich thematic of the *refraction* of the center in or by the periphery" is perceived as the untapped and perhaps inexhaustible heritage or patrimony of the entire world.[22]

As formulated by Dussel, the "philosophy of liberation" is one of the prominent counterdiscourses of our time. It stands in the tradition of "critical philosophy"—though it moves beyond Kant's transcendental formalism in the direction of a greater awareness of its historical and social situatedness. It is a philosophy "born in the periphery" but with "global or planetary aspirations." Such a philosophical outlook, Dussel asserts, must always ask first of all "who is situated in the exteriority of the [dominant] system" or "in the system as an alienated, oppressed segment." In line with negative dialectics and its notion of nonidentity, liberation philosophy rejects all forms of totalizing synthesis, in the realization that "all totalities can be fetishized"—regardless of whether one deals with political totalities (such as imperial regimes) or cultural totalities (such as "Judeo-Christian civilization" or the "American way of life").[23] In support of this outlook, the text repeatedly invokes the teachings of Heidegger and Adorno, supplemented by some Levinasian insights.

Basically, we read, the approach started from "Heideggerian phenomenology" and from "the Frankfurt School at the end of the sixties," and then turned to Levinas because of his stress on "exteriority" and nontotality. More specifically, the point of departure was the "later Heidegger's" concern with "*Lebenswelt*" (world of daily life) and the concrete situatedness of human existence (being-in-the-world). In the case of Adorno, the main sources of inspiration were the notions of "negative dialectics," "myth of modernity," and "dialectic of enlightenment" (all reinterpreted from the angle of periphery). Amplified by some further ideas, what all these precedents bring into view is a difficult course between affirmation and empty rejection. Taking up a central point of the earlier study, Dussel states:

> Liberation philosophy criticizes the "sacrificial myth" of modernity as irrational, albeit presupposing and preserving its "rational emancipatory nucleus," thereby also transcending modernity itself. Our project of liberation can be neither anti- nor pre- nor postmodern, but instead must be transmodern. This is . . . the condition of all possible philosophical dialogue between North and South, because we are situated in an asymmetrical relation.[24]

What Dussel here calls asymmetry is otherwise often called hegemony— or else the onset of a new global imperialism (involving the rule of the "West" over the "Rest"). In such a situation, nothing can be more important and salutary than the cultivation of global critical awareness, of critical counterdiscourses willing and able to call into question the presumptions of global imperial rule. The dangers of such totalizing domination are becoming more evident every day. With the growing technological sophistication of weaponry we are relentlessly instructed about the underside of modernity, about the fateful collusion of power and knowledge in the unfolding of modern enlightenment (as analyzed by Adorno and Horkheimer). Coupled with the globalizing momentum, military sophistication greatly enhances the prospect of global warfare—indeed of global "total" warfare (as envisaged by Heidegger in the 1930s). Such warfare, moreover, is profiled against the backdrop of hegemonic asymmetry (as seen by Dussel): the vastly unequal possession of nuclear and other weapons of mass destruction. In this situation, the goal of global warfare is bound to be the "total" subjugation of less developed or subaltern societies—a subjugation accomplished through long-distance military offensives capable of inflicting maximum casualties on enemies while minimizing the attackers' costs.[25] Given the intoxicating effects of global rule, must one not also anticipate corresponding levels of total depravity and corruption among the rulers? In fact, must one not fear the upsurge of a new breed of "global master criminals" (*planetarische Hauptverbrecher*) whose actions are likely to match those of their twentieth-century predecessors, and perhaps even surpass them (behind a new shield of immunity)? Armed with unparalleled nuclear devices and unheard-of strategic doctrines, global masters today cannot only control and subjugate populations, but in fact destroy and incinerate them (from high above). In the words of the Indian novelist Arundhati Roy, addressed to the world's imperial rulers:

> To slow a beast, you break its limbs. To slow a nation, you break its people; you rob them of volition. You demonstrate your absolute command over their destiny. You make it clear that ultimately it falls to you to decide who lives, who dies, who prospers, who doesn't. To exhibit your capability you show off all that you can do, and how easily you can do it—how easily you could press a button and annihilate the earth.[26]

NOTES

1. Aristotle, *Politics*, 1252b. (Aristotle ascribes the saying to "our poets.") Regarding Kant see his "An Answer to the Question: What Is Enlightenment?" in *Kant's Political Writings*, ed. Hans Reiss, trans. H. B. Nisbet (Cambridge: Cambridge University Press, 1970), pp. 54-60.

2. Horkheimer, *Eclipse of Reason*, p. 97. With regard to fascism, Horkheimer added this important further qualification (p. 121): "In modern fascism, rationality has reached a point at which it is no longer satisfied with simply repressing nature; rationality now exploits nature by incorporating into its own system the rebellious potentialities of nature. The Nazis manipulated the repressed desires of the German people." With proper modification, something similar could be said about contemporary forms of "fundamentalism."

3. Max Horkheimer and Theodor W. Adorno, *Dialektik der Aufklärung* (first published 1947; repr., Frankfurt-Main: Fischer, 1969), pp. 3, 9; translated by John Cumming under the title *Dialectic of Enlightenment* (New York: Seabury Press, 1972), pp. xiii, 3. (In the above and subsequent citations I have slightly altered the translation for purposes of clarity.)

4. Horkheimer and Adorno, *Dialectic of Enlightenment*, pp. 4, 8-10. "Enlightenment," the text continues, "behaves toward things like a dictator toward men: he knows them only insofar as he can manipulate them." Revealingly, the authors draw a parallel between "commanding" and the modern infatuation with "making" or instrumental fabrication—an infatuation which needs to be sharply distinguished from the realm of doing or "praxis," especially political praxis.

5. Horkheimer and Adorno, *Dialectic of Enlightenment,* pp. 7, 14, 29. The insight that modernity, while ostensibly promoting human freedom or emancipation, at the same time tightens the network of social disciplines was later developed in greater detail by Michel Foucault, especially in his *Discipline and Punish: The Birth of the Prison*, trans. Alan Sheridan (New York: Vintage Books, 1979).

6. Horkheimer and Adorno, *Dialectic of Enlightenment,* pp. 24, 39-42. Compare also their comment on the sense of remembrance (p. xv): "The issue is not the con-

servation of the past but the redemption of the hopes of the past." The idea of an "unmanageable" or incalculable future resonates with the title of one of Jean-Luc Nancy's writings: his *La communauté désoeuvrée* (Paris: Bourgeois, 1986), translated by Peter Connor et al. as *The Inoperative Community* (Minneapolis: University of Minnesota Press, 1991). Compare in this context also my "An 'Inoperative' Global Community? Reflections on Nancy," in *Alternative Visions: Paths in the Global Village* (Landham, MD: Rowman & Littlefield, 1998), pp. 277-297.

7. Adorno, *Negative Dialektik* (Frankfurt-Main: Suhrkamp, 1966), pp. 17-18, 36; translated by E. B. Ashton as *Negative Dialectics* (New York: Seabury Press, 1973), pp. 8, 27-28. (In the above and subsequent citations I have slightly altered the translation for purposes of clarity.)

8. Adorno, *Negative Dialectics*, pp. 6-7, 12, 19. As one should note, the above critique does not simply mean a substitution of multiplicity for unity and of particularity for universality. As Adorno adds soberly (p. 158): "Like Kant and the entire philosophical tradition including Plato, Hegel is a partisan of unity. Yet, an abstract denial of the latter would not befit thinking either. The illusion of grasping the manifold directly would mean mimetic regression and a lapse into myth, into the horrors of diffuseness—just as unitary thinking, imitating blind nature through its repression, ends in mythical dominion at the opposite pole. Self-reflection of enlightenment is not its revocation."

9. Adorno, *Negative Dialectics*, pp. 141, 179-180, 191.

10. Compare in this regard my "Adorno and Heidegger," in *Between Freiburg and Frankfurt: Toward a Critical Ontology* (Amherst: The University of Massachusetts Press, 1991), pp. 44-71; also Herrmann Mörchen, *Adorno und Heidegger: Untersuchung einer philosophischen Kommunikationsverweigerung* (Stuttgart: Klett-Cotta, 1981).

11. Heidegger, *Beiträge zur Philosophie*, pp. 38-40, 42. For an English translation (not followed here) see *Contributions to Philosophy (From Enowning)*, trans. Parvis Emad and Kenneth Maly (Bloomington, IN: Indiana University Press, 1999). The critique of worldviews/ideologies was continued and deepened in "Die Zeit des Welbildes" (1938) where Heidegger denounced the increasingly virulent "contest of worldviews" (*Kampf der Weltanschauungen*). See *Holzwege* (Frankfurt-Main: Kostermann, 1950), pp. 69-104, especially p. 87; and for an English translation "The Age of the World Picture," in *The Question Concerning Technology and Other Essays*.

12. Heidegger, *Beiträge zur Philosophie*, pp. 126-132. As one should note, Heidegger always differentiates carefully between *Erlebnis* (emotive feeling) and *Erfahrung* (which *Dasein* has to shoulder or undergo).

13. Heidegger, *Beiträge zur Philosophie*, pp. 50-51, 140, 282. In Heidegger's words (p. 26): "*Ereignis* hands over (*übereignet*) God to humans while dedicating/consecrating (*zueignet*) humans to God."

14. Heidegger, *Besinnung*, ed. Friedrich-Wilhelm von Herrmann (*Gesamtausgabe*, vol. 66; Frankfurt-Main, Klostermann, 1997), pp. 16-17, 122-123. As he adds (p. 123): "Are humans here not definitively fixated as oriented toward the control and mastery of beings (while abandoning and being abandoned by being, *Seinsverlassenheit*)?"

15. Heidegger, *Besinnung*, pp. 16-17, 22, 187-188, 191. According to the text, our time finds itself at a crossroads or parting of ways: a parting that determines "whether *Machenschaft* finally overwhelms humans, unleashing them into limitless power-seekers, or whether being discloses its truth as a need—a need through which the encounter/counterpoint (*Entgegnung*) of God and humans intersects with the chiasm between earth and world" (p. 15). I am indebted to Krzysztof Ziarek for the felicitous rendering of *machtlos* as "power-free."

16. Heidegger, *Die Geschichte des Seyns*, ed. Peter Trawny (*Gesamtausgabe*, vol. 69; Frankfurt-Main: Klostermann, 1998), pp. 46-48, 50, 64, 69, 76-78.

17. Heidegger, *Die Geschichte des Seyns*, pp. 44, 63, 70, 77-78, 180, 209. For a critique of "leaders" (*Führer*) as supreme technicians compare also Heidegger, "Überwindung der Metaphysik" (1936-1946), in *Vorträge und Aufsätze*, part I (Pfullingen: Neske, 1954), pp. 71-99, especially pp. 85-88. For an English translation by Joan Stambaugh see *The End of Philosophy* (New York: Harper & Row, 1973), pp. 103-109.

18. The phrase "ethical hermeneutics" is borrowed from Michael D. Barber, *Ethical Hermeneutics: Rationalism in Enrique Dussel's Philosophy of Liberation* (New York: Fordham University Press, 1998). As Barber elaborates (p. 69): "One who lives out the ethos of liberation locates herself in the 'hermeneutic position' of the oppressed and takes on their interests." Regarding the "preferential option for the poor" see especially Gustavo Gutierrez, *A Theology of Liberation*, trans. Sr. Caridad Inda and John Eagleson (Maryknoll, NY: Orbis Books, 1973).

19. Enrique Dussel, *The Invention of the Americas: Eclipse of the "Other" and the Myth of Modernity*, trans. Michael D. Barber (New York: Continuum, 1995), p. 12; also his *Método para una filosofia de la liberación: Superación analectica de la dialéctica Hegeliana*, 3rd ed. (Guadalajara: Editional Universidad de Guadalajara, 1991), pp. 185-186.

20. Dussel, *The Invention of the Americas*, p. 132. See also Barber, *Ethical Hermeneutics*, pp. 64-65.

21. Dussel, *The Underside of Modernity: Apel, Ricoeur, Rorty, Taylor, and the Philosophy of Liberation*, trans. Eduardo Mendieta (Atlantic Highland, NJ: Humanities Press, 1996), pp. 51-52, 131-131 (translation slightly altered). Arguing specifically against Taylor, Dussel states (p. 131) that "this manner of interpreting modern identity is Eurocentric, that is to say, provincial, regional, and does not take into account modernity's global significance and, hence, the role of Europe's periphery as 'source,' equally constitutive of the modern 'self' as such." The edge against Habermas is particularly evident in the comment (p. 3) that, in Latin America, "we cannot complete or 'realize' fully an incomplete modernity (as Habermas optimistically suggests), because as the 'slave' we have paid with our misery, our actual 'nonbeing' (first, since 1492, as colonized, and then, since 1810, as part of the neocolonial world)." Compare in this context Jürgen Habermas, *The Philosophical Discourse of Modernity: Twelve Lectures*, trans. Frederick G. Lawrence (Cambridge, MA: MIT Press, 1987), and Taylor, *Sources of the Self*.

22. Dussel, *The Underside of Modernity*, pp. 135-137. The text at another point (p. 52) refers to the dispute between Las Casas and Ginés de Sepúlveda in Valladolid

(1550) where the latter argued (in the manner of contemporary Western "hawks") that "European culture is the most highly developed"; that "other cultures exit from their barbaric condition only by means of the modern civilizing process"; and that, whenever underdeveloped cultures oppose this civilizing process, "it is just and necessary to use violence in order to squash such opposition."

23. Dussel, *The Underside of Modernity*, pp. 8, 11, 137. In this context, Dussel also makes reference to the role of religion (from the angle of a "theology of liberation"). Although rejecting an oppressive or totalizing religious system, he notes (p. 11) that one might "affirm the Absolute in the case when it would ground, justify, or give hope to the oppressed in their process of liberation. Symbolically, the Pharaoh-god justified domination; but the Yahweh of the slave of Egypt, led by Moses, gave motives of liberation. . . . If there is an Absolute, it cannot but be the Other of every system, as the breath of life of all that lives. In this case, religion becomes a fundamental moment in the praxis of liberation."

24. Dussel, *The Underside of Modernity*, pp. 3, 20, 53. With regard to Adorno, Dussel carefully distinguishes "negative dialectics" from an empty negativity; to guard against the latter danger he occasionally (pp. 3, 81) invokes the metaphysical positivism of the "old Schelling." While appropriating insights from Levinas, he criticizes the Levinasian approach to otherness as "absolutely abstract with respect to every possible world"; to add a dimension of social concreteness, he turns to Marx's emphasis on "living labor" (pp. 53-54).

25. This strategy was already in place at the time of the conquest of the Americas. In the word of Tomás de Torquemada, commenting on the Spanish conquest of the Aztec empire: "Less than one hundred Castilians died, a few horses. . . . Of the Mexicans one hundred thousand died, without counting the ones who died of hunger and plague." See his *Monarquia Indiana*, cited by Dussel, *The Underside of Modernity*, p. 52. Recent superpower wars against third-world countries reveal a similar scenario.

26. Roy, *The Cost of Living*, p. 79.

Chapter Three

Empire or Cosmopolis?
Civilization at the Crossroads

Not long ago, Saddam Hussein—the former president (or dictator) of Iraq—was captured by Western troops who quickly proceeded to display him, shackled and disheveled, to an avid world press. This display of the former ruler, one observer commented, resembled "pretty much what the Roman Emperors used to do to defeated barbarian kings."[1] The observer was not a simple man in the street, but a distinguished expert in the history and governing norms of international law—norms that had been briskly brushed aside in that particular war (which, in the end, showed itself as one of conquest). According to general agreement, it is the adherence to ethical and legal norms that distinguishes a "civilization" from primitive, lawless, or barbaric forms of life. Thus, the legal expert's statement contained a double indictment. On the one hand, his comment disclosed a dark spot in the Roman imperial edifice: the fact that, in its treatment of alien rulers and peoples, Rome was itself near barbaric and certainly not as civilized as it claimed to be. More important is the second point: that things have remained "pretty much" the same since the time of the Caesars—and this despite two thousand years of "Christian civilization" (which, at its inception, was meant to transform and perhaps replace the Roman Empire). This realization casts a melancholy pall on hopes expressed by Immanuel Kant that the progressive improvement of humankind is not just a dream or "empty chimera."[2] It also lends credence to Mahatma Gandhi's quip about Western culture or civilization: "It *would be* a good idea."

The issue I want to address in the following pages concerns the future of this so-called civilization. Basically, as it seems to me, the events in Iraq throw into relief a dramatic crossroads facing the world: the crossroads between empire and global cooperation, between world dictatorship and an interdependent community of peoples (which can loosely be called "cosmopolis"). A major factor triggering this crossroads is the twilight besetting the so-called Westphalian system, that is, the traditional system of inter-state relations dating back to the Peace of Westphalia. Twilight prevails in this domain because of the unresolved status of that system: the fact that some of its central ingredients are neither defunct nor fully intact. On the one hand, contrary to some premature prognoses, the Westphalian principle of state sovereignty continues to be eagerly championed, especially by powerful nation-states; on the other hand, given the relentless growth of global markets and communication networks (what is often termed "globalization"), no state—no matter how self-contained—can fully escape the inroads of global interdependence. It is precisely this ambivalence, this juncture of radical state autonomy and globalization which gives rise to opposing tendencies: on the one side, the ambitions of empire where globalization is subjected to global sovereignty (a global Leviathan); on the other side, a democratic cosmopolis achieved through the subordination of sovereignty to global interdependence. The following discussion seeks to explore this contemporary crossroads and its divergent paths, mainly with an emphasis on normative and philosophical considerations. I proceed in three steps. While the opening section examines the nature or character of the emerging global empire, the ensuing sections concentrate on normative assessments: rehearsing first arguments which traditionally have been, and continue to be, offered in defense of empire, in order finally to present counterviews of champions of an alternative (cosmopolitan) path or vision.

GLOBALIZING LEVIATHAN

In assessing the nature of "empire," especially in the contemporary context, one needs to recall the hybrid character of the global arena: the odd collusion of sovereignty and interdependence. To some extent or to a lesser degree, a similar hybridity can also be found in earlier periods. However, what lends to the present situation its dramatic novelty is the juncture of unparalleled superpower autonomy and the global reach of that power's effects. The novelty of this global reach can easily lead analysts to dubious conjectures or conclusions: especially the conjecture of an entirely unheard-of and amorphous imperial structure, an edifice without center and periphery, without obedience and command. Thus, under the combined influence of "postmodern" rhetoric and functionalist theories of social complexity, some recent analysts have depicted the emerging empire as a system of intricately interlocking subsystems, of markets and communications networks, of "micro-powers" and "virtualities"—without any trace of a sovereign Leviathan.[3] What is correct in this conjecture is the fact that Leviathan no longer monopolizes the scene but shares the global arena with a vast array of public, nonpublic, and often unaccountable institutions and agencies. To this extent, the Indian novelist Arundhati Roy is undoubtedly on target when, in pondering the nature of empire, she urges us to consider not only the American superpower but also "the World Bank, the International Monetary Fund, the World Trade Organization (WTO), and multinational corporations." As she concludes: "*All* this is Empire."[4]

Yet, the complexity of the global structure does not tempt the novelist for a moment into political naiveté. In fact, the quoted passage is instantly followed by the observation that the vast "confederacy" of imperial networks has also vastly increased the distance "between those who make the decisions and those who have to suffer them." With this insight Roy is in concurrence with American "realists" and "neorealists" (for whom, no doubt, the distance is an occasion for rejoicing). As one such realist observer recently remarked, without embarrassment or subterfuge: "The military, economic, and political power of the United States makes the rest of the world look Lilliputian."[5] To be sure, the emergence of the new, America-centered empire is not the discovery of American realists or neorealists; it was predicted and analyzed more than a decade ago by one of the country's leading cultural critics: Edward Said. Reflecting on "American ascendancy" in his book *Culture and Imperialism*, Said noted at the time that "imperialism did not end, did not suddenly become 'past' once decolonization had set in motion the dismantling of the classical empires"; on the contrary, the rise of the United States "as the last superpower suggests that a new set of force lines will structure the [entire] world."[6] Couched in polemical language, Said's prediction of an emerging new imperialism could be, and was often, dismissed as the rambling of a literary academic out of tune with the complexities of international politics. Even today, the notion of an America-centered empire tends to be denied by well-meaning liberals fondly attached to the old constitutional republic. However, how can nostalgia blind us to obvious facts? Listen to the comments of Michael Ignatieff, a writer not suspect of critical or subversive tendencies, who depicts the United States as

> the only nation that polices the world through five global military commands; maintains more than a million men and women at arms in four continents; deploys carrier battle groups on watch in every ocean; guarantees the survival of countries from Israel to South Korea; drives the wheels of global trade and commerce; and fills the hearts and minds of an entire planet with its dreams and desires.[7]

What these lines reveal is the presence of an immense superpower, a giant super-Leviathan extending its influence into every corner of the earth. This is precisely what the term "empire" signifies. In a nutshell, empire means the extension of political and military power beyond the scope of the metropolitan homeland, that is, the wielding of dominion over foreign territories inhabited by noncitizen populations. As one will note, it is not geographical size per se that is decisive. Thus, although composed of fifty states, the domestic United States is not an empire, because all the (adult) inhabitants of the homeland are at least in principle entitled to political participation.[8] The crucial criterion of empire is rather rule over noncitizens, that is, over alien populations not entitled to participate in the shaping of metropolitan policies. This indicates that "empire" cannot be democratic as an empire (no matter what its domestic practices may be). Simply put: empire and democracy are contradictory terms—an aspect too readily ignored by champions of *pax Americana*. Thus, when Walter Russell Mead observes that America is "the sole global power" relying on a "global consensus" and that it "dominates to an unprecedented degree" the "first truly global civilization," he glosses over (or fails to notice) the incoherence of his concepts—because global superpower collides with global consensus just as full-scale domination militates against global civilization.[9] The same slide or slippage is favored even by distinguished international experts. Thus, in examining "key factors" in contemporary international politics, Zbigniew Brzezinski singles out two: "the primacy of American global power" and "the global appeal of democracy"—but without worrying in the least about their incongruence or about the impact of the latter appeal on the former primacy.[10]

By extending its reach to foreign lands, imperial superpower elides the nexus of civil mutuality and reciprocity. Basically, in setting aside democratic rules of active participation and representation, imperial rule over noncitizen populations amounts to a relation of command and obedience—which, at its core, is a relation of fear. In his recent study of the new imperialism, Benjamin Barber very correctly emphasizes this component of fear by speaking candidly about "fear's empire" or the empire of fear. In his presentation, fear operates in two directions. On the one hand, by amassing an immense arsenal of sophisticated weaponry, the superpower instills fear, and in fact seeks to strike "terror," into the hearts of its adversaries and would-be competitors. On the other hand, being deprived of representation or an active voice, subordinated populations are likely to feel frustrated and hence may resort to violent retaliation or acts of "terrorism"—thereby enmeshing themselves in unending "terror wars." Locked into the cycle of fearful enmity, terror and counterterror reinforce each other over time, progressively eroding all residues of civility both at home and abroad. In Barber's words: the empire of fear in the end becomes "a realm without citizens, a domain of spectators, of subjects and victims whose passivity means helplessness and whose helplessness defines and sharpens fear."[11] His analysis vividly underscores the parallels between empire and the Hobbesian image of Leviathan. As will be recalled, Hobbes's image of domestic peace was profiled against a condition of anarchic warfare, a condition governed or "terrorized" by the fear of violent death. Seeking to escape from this terror, people launch into the construction of a commonwealth—only to find themselves at the mercy of a fear-inspiring potentate whose edicts can nullify the hoped-for personal safety.[12]

During recent years, the fear factor has been vastly intensified on all sides. Partly in response to the attacks of September 11, the superpower has unleashed the "war against terrorism" and then the military offensive in the Near East. It also has abrogated international disarmament agreements and embarked, again unilaterally, on the development of new strategic weapons, including "smart" nuclear bombs. Still more provocatively, the United States has announced to the world a global policy agenda with clearly imperialist features—something previous empires were reluctant to do. The agenda is called the "National Security Strategy of the United States of America" and was formally promulgated on September 20, 2002. The document reflects an ambitious imperial design—whose scope dwarfs the ambitions of all previous empires. A number of features clearly stand out: first, the assertion of America's absolute military supremacy in the world; next, the refusal to allow the emergence of any possible "peer power" capable of challenging imperial rule; and finally, the claimed right to resort to war—if necessary in a preventive or preemptive fashion—against any hostile challenges mounted by "rogue states" or nonstate actors. As a presidential letter prefacing the document blandly affirms: "The United States possesses unprecedented—and unequaled—strength and influence in the world." To ensure the undisputed maintenance of this supremacy, American forces—the letter adds—must remain strong enough "to dissuade a military buildup in hopes of surpassing, or equaling, the power of the United States." In order to forestall any unwelcome surprises, the document finally assigns to America the right to act preventively or preemptively (that is, beyond the traditional confines of self-defense)—a passage that on some readings, includes a nuclear first-strike capability.[13]

Probably the most disturbing feature of the document is the notion of preventive and/or preemptive warfare. In Benjamin Barber's words, the logic of such warfare "relies on long-term prediction and a presumed concatenation of events" vastly exceeding the bounds of self-defense: "By shooting first and asking questions later, it opens the way to tragic miscalculation" and "sets a disastrous example for other nations claiming their own exceptionalist logic."[14] In still more forceful terms, the idea has been criticized by Richard Falk in an essay on "The New Bush Doctrine." By allocating to America powers vastly in excess of international agreements, Falk writes, the new doctrine is willing "to abandon rules of restraint and of law, patiently developed over the course of centuries, rules governing the use of force in relation to territorial states." By claiming preventive and even preemptive prerogatives, the strategic policy amounts in effect to the proclamation of a global absolutism. This is the case, he adds, because the policy is "a doctrine without limits, without accountability to the United Nations or international law, without any dependence on a collective judgment of responsible governments and, what is worse, without any convincing demonstration of practical necessity." For Falk, one of the most problematic aspects of the policy is the fear factor implicit in a global absolutism freed from civic mutuality and accountability. In his words:

> Since the end of the cold war the United States has enjoyed the luxury of being undeterred in world politics. It is this circumstance that makes Bush's "unilateralism" particularly disturbing to other countries. . . . [For] there is every reason for others to fear that, when the United States is undeterred, it will again become subject to the "Hiroshima temptation" in which it might threaten and use such weapons in the absence of any prospect of retaliation.[15]

Surely, it cannot be the objective of a "civilized" country to dominate other peoples through fear and nuclear blackmail. Neither Falk nor Barber limit their arguments to critical indictment but proceed to offer viable alternative agendas (whose fuller discussion I postpone to a later point). Instead of seeking to impose its will on the world and its peoples, Falk asks that America join the world in tackling the ethical-political challenge of promoting a form of "humane global governance" compatible with democratic standards, thus laying the groundwork for a well-ordered global regime (or "cosmopolis").[16] A similar aim is espoused by Benjamin Barber who, in lieu of the policy of preventive and preemptive warfare, advocates the idea of "preventive democracy," insisting that terrorism can be mitigated or stopped "only in a world of peaceful democracies" while imperial strategies are "less than ideal instruments" and in fact counterproductive for equitable global governance.[17]

APOLOGIES FOR EMPIRE

Let me now turn to normative or evaluative assessments by asking these questions: What arguments are used, and have been used in the past, in defense of empire? And what arguments can be marshaled by its opponents? As it happens, in the history of the West, imperialist ventures have invariably been accompanied by ambitious moral and civilizational claims seeking to vindicate these ventures. Differently phrased: despite manifestly brutal and dehumanizing policies, empire-builders in the West have acted, or pretended to act, with a seemingly good conscience (an aspect which may distinguish Western imperialists from their non-Western or Asiatic counterparts).[18] Sometimes famous thinkers and philosophers have lent their name to this moralizing subterfuge. Well known (or notorious) is Aristotle's statement, as recorded in his *Politics*: "Meet it is that barbarians should be governed by the Greeks." The main justification for this claim was the Greeks' (supposed) greater rationality and self-control as compared with the barbarians' dissolute and profligate lifestyle.[19] Aristotle's statement furnished welcome support to his Macedonian pupil Alexander when he embarked on his far-flung military conquests. In due course, Alexander's legacy was taken over by imperial Rome, which extended its military control into all corners of the (then-known) world. In the works of Roman apologists—especially some Stoics and imperial jurists—Aristotle's maxim of justified rule was developed into an elaborate system of moral and legal principles claiming to be anchored in universal human reason and immutable laws of nature.

Following the fall of Rome, roughly one thousand years elapsed before another European power resumed Rome's imperial ambitions.[20] At this point, the claim to rule was raised by monarchical Spain, which, at that historical juncture, was the dominant hegemon or superpower in late-medieval and early-modern European politics. What distinguished Spanish imperialism from earlier precedents were two points. First, the near-global scope of its dominion. Propelled by the voyages of the "Age of Discovery," the new empire was able to establish its control over distant lands, over populations located beyond the "ocean blue" and wedded to vastly different cultural traditions. The second distinctive feature was the infusion of Christian religious doctrines into discussions about conquest and about the rightness of imperial-colonial practices. In large measure, this infusion explains the intensity of claims and counterclaims advanced during this period and the missionary zeal animating many conquistadors (a zeal not found among classical precursors).

A high point in the exchange of claims and counterclaims was a disputation held in 1550 in Valladolid between a prominent defender and an equally prominent critic of empire. The defender was the philosopher-theologian and court historian Ginés de Sepúlveda, a man well trained both in classical (Aristotelian and Stoic) philosophy and in the Christian scholastic tradition. In his defense of empire, Sepúlveda mobilized a broad amalgam of past teachings that, with some ingenuity, could be read as warrants for Spanish imperial rule. In an instructive fashion, the Argentinian-Mexican philosopher Enrique Dussel has summarized the apologist's arguments into five major claims. The first claim is the assertion of Spain's superior rationality, maturity, and cultural sophistication, an assertion buttressed by the maxim that, "in the nature of things," the higher is supposed to rule over the lower, reason over passion, form over matter. Borrowing from Aristotle's teachings (especially his notion of "natural slavery"), Sepúlveda affirmed it as a general principle that "the perfect always ought to dominate and rule over the imperfect, the excellent over its opposite"—a principle which was tailor-made for the cause of Spanish imperialism. For, when comparing Spaniards with native people in the New World, the conclusion was evident: "Being by nature slaves, the barbarians [in the Americas], uncultured and inhuman [or barely human] as they are," ought to submit to superior rule. For Sepúlveda, this was not just a matter of brute power, but a dictate of ethics and justice: "By natural right it is found to be 'just' that matter should submit to form, body to soul, the appetites to reason, animals to humans, women to men, the imperfect to the perfect, the worse to the better, for the common good of all."[21]

Once the premises of this thesis were granted, the other claims followed as a matter of course. The second point was the idea that Spanish rule over the barbarians was exercised generously for the latter's benefit, so as to promote the Indians' cultural and spiritual uplift and advancement. In Sepúlveda's own formulation of this version of "white man's burden": "What better and more salutary thing could occur to these barbarians than to be governed by the imperial rule of those whose prudence, virtue, and religion will convert the barbarians finally . . . into civilized people?" Of course, there were limits to Spanish benevolence—which leads to the third point: the threat of violent coercion and punishment for all those resisting Spain's civilizing mission, a violence proclaimed to be "just and necessary" by natural right. In Sepúlveda's words again: "If they [the barbarians] refuse our empire, they can be compelled by arms to accept it—and this will be a just war in accordance with natural right and law." Whenever the imperial rulers had to resort to such military force or violence—this is the fourth point—they could do so with a perfectly "good conscience," being justified both by classical metaphysics and Christian doctrine: "For, were we not to do it [i.e., exercise violence and coercion], we would fulfill neither the natural law nor the commandment of Christ." This point culminated in the fifth and last claim: namely, that imperial violence is actually instigated by the obstinacy and (terroristic) recalcitrance of native populations who merely reap what they sow. In Dussel's poignant expression: the victims of imperialism in the periphery are finally held "responsible for their own victimization." In their intricate concatenation—he adds—the five claims raised by the Spanish doctor were thoroughly absorbed and reiterated by subsequent imperial elites, from British and French apologists to defenders of *pax Americana*.[22]

To be sure, despite a certain argumentative continuity, the nature of imperial claims underwent important transformations during subsequent centuries.

With the rise of modern science and rational enlightenment, Christian apologetics receded steadily into the background (without being completely erased), making room instead for "secular" ideas of scientific management and technical-instrumental control. As a corollary, the notion of a Christian empire—partially buttressed by classical "natural right"—steadily gave way to artificially designed political structures held together by a combination of contractual or market principles, functional networks, and Leviathan-style sovereignty grounded in human will. Initiated and nurtured first in the empires of Britain and France, these modern changes reached their full fruition in the contemporary period. The basic challenge facing present-day empire—as it faced previous empires—remains justification or legitimation; and the challenge is greatly complicated by comparison with the situation at Valladolid. Simply put: how can one justify imperial domination over subjugated (noncitizen) populations given the retreat of classical metaphysics and Christian theology, and their replacement by modern science and secular rationality coupled with the spreading of democratic aspirations and the global appeal of human rights? As the available evidence suggests, the solution resides in a combination of diverse (sometimes conflicting) argumentative strategies, chiefly the following: civilizational benevolence or "developmentalism"; technocratic scientism and economism; "realist" power politics (relying on thinkers from Machiavelli and Hobbes to Nietzsche and beyond); plus remnants of classical metaphysics and Christian apologetics. Joined together, these strands at times coalesce into a heady agenda of global conversion, an agenda pursued with the same missionary zeal exhibited earlier by the conquistadors.

Among the assorted strategies, developmentalism is the most widely preferred claim, due to its deceptively moralizing appeal. In this domain, the legacy of Sepúlveda is very much alive. In a speech delivered to Congress shortly after September 11 and announcing a worldwide "war on terrorism," the American president declared: "This is the world's fight. This is civilization's fight. This is the fight of all who believe in progress and pluralism, tolerance and freedom." With this statement, America proclaimed itself the guardian of "civilization," and in fact the standard-bearer of a mission to preserve civilization by spreading its benefits worldwide (what the French used to call "*mission civilisatrice*"). In the same speech, the president denounced America's opponents as enemies of genuine (American-style) civilization, as people who "hate *our* freedoms—*our* freedom of religion, *our* freedom of speech, *our* freedom to vote and assemble and disagree with each other."[23] Following the logic of the "war on terrorism," opponents of civilization have to be forced militarily to change their ways, unless they can be pressured or converted by other means to submit to the global mission. What is new in this developmental concept by comparison with Sepúlveda is mainly the goal: instead of spreading Christianity to the New World the objective now is to spread "our freedoms" and "our culture," that is, the benefits of Western modernity. This kind of developmentalism is a cherished notion not only of politicians but also of academic social scientists. According to a prominent American expert, writing during the cold war period, global advancement involves in essence a form of modernization, that is, a process in which "tradition-bound villages or tribal-based societies are compelled to react to the pressures and demands of the modern, industrialized and urban-centered world." As he added candidly:

> This process might also be called Westernization, or simply advancement and progress; it might, however, be more accurately termed the diffusion of a world culture—a world culture [or civilization] based on advanced technology and the spirit of science, on a rational view of life, a secular approach to social relations. . . . At an ever-accelerating rate, the direction and volume of cross-cultural influences has become nearly a uniform pattern of the Western industrial world imposing its practices, standards, techniques, and values upon the non-Western world.[24]

At a closer look, developmentalism actually is a jumble of diverse facets, not all of which share the same moralizing appeal. While some facets—the core of *"mission civilisatrice"*—are purposive or intentional in character, other aspects seem to operate in a more anonymous and quasi-automatic fashion, beyond the range of direct political control. Most prominent among the latter are modern industry, the economy, and advanced technology. In their combination, these features are central components of modern Western society, and their evolution seemingly obeys a logic of its own. Yet, despite this appearance, none of these features are free of deliberate impulses; nor are they outside the range of fear's empire. This is clearly evident in the case of the capitalist market economy whose global reach renders it a crucial instrument of developmentalism—but an instrument severely marred by its domineering effects. Falk speaks in this context of "predatory globalization" and "predatory capitalism." As he points out, at least since the fall of the Soviet Union, the energies of governing elites in the United States have been directed toward "globalizing the world economy," in the direction of a "predatory globalization" under the auspices of a minimally regulated, neoliberal form of capitalism known as the "Washington consensus." The overall effect of this policy has been the tendency "to widen income gaps between North and South, as well as to ignore persisting poverty and longer-term environmental decay." As Falk adds, this policy—seemingly self-propelled and self-generating—has more recently been placed more tightly under political control. In the aftermath of September 11, he notes, the "nerve center of empire building" has, for the time being, "decisively shifted back to the state, with the political discourse moving from 'globalization,' an economistic framing of the new reality, to 'war' and 'security.'"[25]

A similar role is played by modern science and technology. Although seemingly nonpolitical or extra-political, science and technology have increasingly been placed in the service of political and military-industrial elites—to the point that (in the view of a prominent philosopher) the entire world is being transformed into a giant artifact bent on reducing everything into a mere resource for domineering power.[26] Given steady advances in sophistication, contemporary technology readily lends itself to techniques of social surveillance and control beyond the predictions of George Orwell and the dreams of earlier totalitarian rulers (like Hitler and Stalin). With the extension of surveillance techniques into outer space, human life around the globe is tendentially placed into a grand "Panopticon" where every move is tracked by a global overseer. Richard Falk paints a grim picture of the evolving scenario. As part of the "fundamental American project of global domination," he writes, the ongoing "weaponization of space" yields (or is meant to yield) "an unlimited capability to destroy at a moment's notice a point of resistance or hostility anywhere on the planet. . . . If this project aiming at global domination is consummated, or nearly so, it threatens the entire world with a kind of subjugation, and risks encouraging frightening new cycles of megaterrorism as the only available and credible strategy of resistance." Undeterred by such prospects, the American secretary of defense (Donald Rumsfeld) has already initiated major programs to develop laser and kinetic-kill weapon systems on battle stations in outer space, asserting that America must "have the means to exert force in, through, and from space."[27]

Clearly, a policy of this nature seems far removed from any kind of developmentalism or "*mission civilisatrice*." Some defenders of empire—especially so-called neorealists (Falk speaks of "war thinkers" or "Pentagon warriors")—completely dismiss the missionary idea, placing themselves squarely on the ground of sheer power politics (or superpower politics). Some even show openly their contempt for ethics and civility. When some European leaders remonstrated against a war launched in violation of global norms, the mentioned secretary of defense ridiculed such moral scruples as signs of weakness and senility, as the whimpers of an "old Europe" unable to keep up with the strides of a youthful (or better: juvenile) America. Another "war thinker"—a renowned expert in international politics—ventured into planetary mythology by likening cautious and recalcitrant Europe to a feminine Venus as contrasted with America's mighty-armed and truculent Mars.[28] Given their obsession with sheer power, (neo)realist defenders of empire are unlikely to be deeply steeped in philosophy, especially the tradition of political philosophy; nevertheless, remnants of that tradition may on occasion provide welcome support. Thus, Pentagon warriors may find congenial Machiavelli's preference for a politics of fear over a politics of consensus. Likewise, they are bound to relish portions of Thomas Hobbes's *Leviathan*, especially his argument regarding the primacy of the "sword" over mere words. Among more recent philosophers, some of Nietzsche's teachings are prone to attract the warriors' attention—just as they have attracted the attention of earlier imperialists. Among these teachings, notions like "grand politics" and "will to power" inevitably hold great fascination, given their intimation of a global hierarchy or rank order based on command and obedience. With some transatlantic correction, sympathy may also greet Nietzsche's futurist scenario when, in response to external threats, Europe would "resolve to become menacing too, namely, to acquire *one will* by means of a new caste that would rule Europe—a long, terrible will of its own that would be able to cast its goals millennia hence."[29]

More philosophically inclined partisans of imperial dreams are unlikely to be satisfied with mere snippets of the intellectual tradition. In their effort to find a deeper warrant for rank order or hierarchy, such partisans often delve into older (premodern) philosophical or metaphysical teachings. It is in this context that remnants of classical "natural right" are retrieved, where natural right means the affirmation of an essential status hierarchy differentiating between higher and lower, superior and inferior, rational and irrational. In large measure, this effort of retrieval is the hallmark of the camp of (so-called) neoconservatves whose members wield considerable influence both inside and outside the American government today. To be sure, in an age of liberal democracy and civic equality, the defense of rank order must be cautious or circumspect—which explains the frequent resort to verbal subterfuge and camouflage (or what is called "esoteric" discourse). Politically, this camouflage is paralleled by the tendency of neoconservatives to rule not directly but quietly and behind the scenes (perhaps in the fashion of Plato's "nocturnal council"). A main problem encountered by partisans is the remoteness of classical metaphysics: the fact that the assumption of "natural" rankings is not only rejected by democrats, but also no longer fully believable to devotees themselves. It is for this reason that classical nostalgia is often supplemented by a very modernist type of voluntarism: especially by resort to the recreation and imposition of rank order through a Nietzschean "will to power." The end result is a Platonic-Nietzscheanism— incongruous on philosophical grounds, but rendered congruous by its political aims.[30]

As for neoconservative thinkers, sheer power politics is unsatisfactory also for religious supporters of "grand politics." Curiously, our time has seen the recovery not only of classical teachings, but also of Christian politics on a grand scale—in a Protestant variation on Sepúlveda's Catholic discourse. Intermingled with Machiavellian and Nietzschean phrases, religious rhetoric is routinely employed by American politicians and religious leaders alike. Thus, during the election campaign in 2000, the leading candidate called Jesus his "favorite political philosopher," and on the eve of launching the Iraq war, the same leader proclaimed the attack to stand in "the highest moral [and religious] tradition of our country."[31] Religious sermonizing of this kind is a stock-in-trade of clerical defenders of imperial policies, led by well-known Protestant televangelists. In many ways, Christian televangelists have been the most fervent and virulent missionaries of empire. Joining the "war on terrorism" (and converting it implicitly into a crusade), several have not hesitated to denounce Islam as an "evil religion" and its prophet as a vile impostor. Some of them have even proclaimed the terror war as the opening salvo in the final battle between good and evil (Armageddon), a battle to be won by preemptive nuclear strikes (with Christ possibly returning on a mushroom cloud).[32] Even Sepúlveda would have been stunned.

EMPIRE REBUKED

Just as defense of empire can look back to a long intellectual pedigree, opposition to empire can claim its own (more illustrious) lineage extending to the ancients. Emperor Alexander was snubbed by Diogenes, while imperial Rome nurtured in its womb non-imperial thinkers like Seneca as well as recalcitrant religious movements, which ultimately could not be absorbed. It is well to remember that Christianity first emerged in the shadow of the Roman Empire, and not as a welcome guest or accomplice. In fact, the birth of Christian religion heralded something vastly different from imperial domination: namely, the promise of a reign of justice, goodness, and genuine peace. Although infiltrated and partly obscured by imperial ambitions, the evolving Christian "civilization" always preserved a recessed memory of these beginnings, a memory that could be activated (and was activated) at crucial moments of Western history. One such crucial moment was the formation of the Spanish Empire, at the onset of the modern age. At this point, the Gospel's non-imperial or anti-imperial promise was invoked powerfully by Bartolemé de Las Casas who met and disputed Sepúlveda in Valladolid.

A Dominican friar and at one point bishop of Chiapas, Las Casas had no difficulty in rebutting the arguments of his opponent. For one thing, in contrast to Sepúlveda's mere book learning, Las Casas had firsthand experience of the effects of Spanish rule in the Americas. Having spent many years in the New World, he was intimately acquainted with the atrocities inflicted by so-called Christian armies on the native inhabitants. As he wrote in his "Very Brief Account of the Destruction of the Indies": "Among these gentle sheep [the Indians], the Spaniards entered like wolves, tigers, and lions which had been starving for many days, and for forty years they have done nothing else . . . than outrage, slay, afflict, torment, and destroy them." And in his posthumous "History of the Indies" he added bitterly: "I leave, in the Indies, Jesus Christ our God scourged and afflicted and buffeted and crucified, not once but millions of times, on the part of the Spaniards who ruin and destroy these people and deprive them of the space they require to live."[33] In addition to his firsthand experience, Las Casas was also a highly educated scholar, a man steeped in scriptures and classical texts—and apparently better able to understand their meaning than his opponent. Thus, without denying "natural" rankings and different human aptitudes or talents, he was able to disconnect these rankings from claims to political domination by simply remembering Jesus' words as reported in Mark's Gospel: "Whosoever wishes to be first among you, must first be the servant of all" (Mark 10:44). In a similar manner, he was able to debunk the invocation of classical authorities in support of Spanish rule by showing the incompatibility of that rule with classical conceptions of politics. For, when properly read (or read "against the grain"), Aristotle defined politics as a relation between equal citizens and not as a "household" relationship (with Indians clearly not being part of the Spanish household). Moreover, Aristotle's distinction between just and unjust types of government implied that Spanish despotism, wielded solely for the benefit of Spain, could not claim to be a just regime, as it violated the freedom and equality shared by indigenous peoples.[34]

Among the claims advanced by Sepúlveda in Valladolid, those most readily demolished by Las Casas were the assertions of Spanish superiority and of their moral benevolence displayed in their effort to bring their culture and religion to the Indians (*"mission civilisatrice"*). For, how could one attach moral of "civilizing" claims to an enterprise carried out with so much violence and brutality? In Las Casas' own lifetime, hundreds of thousands, perhaps millions of Indians perished due to Spanish actions. As his "Very Brief Account" relates: "Whereas there were more than three million souls whom we saw in Hispaniola, there are today not two hundred of the native population left." Devastation on such a scale—he rightly complained—left an indelible stain on Western "civilization" and made a mockery of Christian religion. In terms of his "History": "The Spaniards who traverse the land with their violence and wicked example . . . make the name of Christ into a blasphemy."[35] Far from educating or "civilizing" native (or non-European) peoples, the example of the Spanish conquest was likely to have the very opposite effect, by producing stubbornness and violent resistance. Here is a

passage from his famous *"Del Único Modo"* ("The Only Method of Attract-
ing All People to the True Faith") which deserves to be quoted in full:

> A rational creature has a natural capacity for being moved, directed and drawn
> to any good gently, because of his freedom of choice. But if natives find them-
> selves first injured, oppressed, saddened, and afflicted by the miseries of wars,
> the loss of their children, their goods, and their own liberty . . . how can they be
> moved voluntarily to listen to what is proposed to them about faith, religion, jus-
> tice, and truth [we might add today: freedom and democracy]? If it is true that a
> soft word multiplies friends while "an ill-tempered man stirs up strife"
> (Proverbs 15:18), how many enemies will not such bitter words and deeds
> make? Therefore, if man ought to be guided and persuaded to good, gently and
> mildly, while warfare compels in a harsh, bitter and violent manner, it is clear
> that the latter means—unnatural and opposed to the condition of human nature—
> will produce contrary effects.[36]

Las Casas has been called the "protector of the Indians"—and with good
reason. Not only was he passionately committed to their well-being and just
treatment, but his pleas (at least for a time) also exerted a definite influence
on imperial and church policies.[37] Beyond the immediate context of the Spanish conquest, his example retains an important lasting significance: by inti-
mating an alternative course for Western civilization (and civilization in general), away from imperialism and "grand" power politics. In his *The
Underside of Modernity*, Enrique Dussel credits Las Casas with having orig-
inated an alternative or "counterdiscourse" to the story of European expan-
sionism. This initiative would not have been possible for Las Casas, he
writes, "without [his] having resided in the periphery, without having heard
the cries and lamentations, and without having seen the tortures that the Indians suffered at the hands of the colonizing Europeans. That [experience of
the] Other is the origin of the European counterdiscourse." In a similar vein,
Gustavo Gutierrez—a chief spokesman of contemporary "liberation theology"—acknowledges the continuing importance of Las Casas through the
centuries, and especially in our own time. Emphasizing the religious dimension, Gutierrez states that the friar's chief task consisted above all "in letting
it be known in the Indies that there is a God, and that God is the God of Abraham, Isaac, Jacob, and Jesus" who is an enemy of injustice and oppression.
Given the persistence of large-scale oppression and injustice in the world—
he adds—it is obvious "why the figure of Las Casas is of such striking universality: here we have someone who, still today, issues a challenge to people at various corners of the planet." In struggling for an alternative path, his
example is "invested with characteristics of prophetic denunciation that maintain all their validity today."[38]

To be sure, as previously indicated, (Western) modernity has introduced many changes, and the strategies of contemporary apologists of empire are no longer quite the same as Sepúlveda's. To this extent, the arguments of Las Casas need to be supplemented and amplified—but surely not discarded. One area where his example remains eminently fruitful relates to the handling of traditional teachings and practices, including the teachings of classical metaphysics and scholastic theology. By proceeding carefully but reading "against the grain," his example illustrates the possibility of retrieving the best and most promising aspects of older legacies rather than succumbing to their worst and most oppressive features. Aristotle is a case in point. Instead of insisting on invidious rankings and the "naturalness" of slavery, Las Casas preferred to accentuate "the philosopher's" contributions to a politics of freedom, equality, and friendship. The same approach guided his treatment of Roman Stoics and scholastic theologians. With some modification, a similar approach can be applied to modern writers or thinkers with whom Las Casas was not or could not be familiar. Thus, in the case of Machiavelli—a favorite author of (neo)realists—a proper reading involves deemphasizing the politics of fear and center staging the "republican" Machiavelli, that is, the champion of the Roman republic (vis-à-vis the empire). With regard to Hobbes, a reading faithful to the Spanish friar entails a decentering of the Leviathan coupled with a foregrounding of the consensual and normative dimensions of his work. The task is made particularly easy in the case of Nietzsche—the mentor of many hardline neoconservatives—because of the sprawling multidimensionality of his work. Thus, as a counterpoint to grand politics and will to power (with their war-mongering implications), Nietzsche himself provides the antidotes of self-overcoming and infinite longing for goodness, for those "blessed isles where my friends are dwelling." Here are some lines from *Zarathustra*, completely unpalatable to contemporary realists: "I am driven out of fatherlands and motherlands. Thus, I now love only my *children's land*, yet undiscovered, in the farthest sea: for this I bid my sails search and search."[39]

The point where Las Casas' example remains most clearly pertinent today is in the debunking of imperial benevolence (*mission civilisatrice*)—what more recently is called "developmentalism." As he pointedly remarked: how can indigenous or non-Western populations trust the "good intentions" of colonizers or missionaries, if at the same time their lands are being confiscated, their possessions plundered, and their families and compatriots either killed or thrown into dungeons (or internment camps)? Under such circumstances, civilization itself is turned into a cloak for violent domination and oppression—an outcome bound to trigger violent resistance as well as an upsurge of worldwide cynicism. There are obvious lessons here for our own time of endless "terror wars." As Falk remarks, denouncing the deceptive mask of developmental beneficence (evident in such slogans as "Operation Enduring Freedom"): "It is difficult for the international public not to think that power politics alone is what counts, at least for the strongest and most imperial of sovereign states."[40] Most damaging for the credibility of Western civilization, conceived as a "Christian civilization," is the complicity of Christian clerics and televangelists in imperial power politics. Clearly, when Christ is turned into a stand-in (or "mascot") for a country's national security policies, something has gone terribly wrong. When the message of the "prince of peace" is converted into an agenda for war-mongering and imperial aggrandizement, then—in Las Casas' terms—the name of Christ becomes a "blasphemy," with the result that religion itself becomes suspect and objectionable in the eyes of well-meaning and peace-loving people. In the words of a prominent contemporary theologian—still mindful of the friar's legacy—the collusion of God-talk with empire building is a "sin of pride," a failing incompatible with and destructive of genuine faith.[41]

There remains a further lesson from the past. Apart from denouncing the violence of imperial policies, Las Casas in his writings and actions also intimated another path for the future: the path of a commonwealth of free and equal peoples based on mutual respect and sympathy. In our time, his vision has to be expanded and globalized—which brings into view the notion of a global commonwealth or "cosmopolis" embracing different cultures and societies and held together not by a central Leviathan but by lateral connections and bonds of cultural and political interdependence. Benjamin Barber stresses this vision when he opposes to preventive warfare the agenda of "preventive democracy" with global implications. In Barber's presentation, preventive democracy is not a missionary doctrine imposed by an imperial center, but rather a practice nurtured at the grassroots level—that is, at local and national levels—and radiating out from there to regional and global arenas. A similar view is endorsed by Falk when he writes that "we must [first] rescue shipwrecked democracy here at home and find the path that leads away from American empire-building toward humane global governance." The alternative path of cosmopolis is not anti-American or anti-Western, although it is clearly opposed to American imperial ambitions. Actually, given its domestic diversity and multiculturalism, American society—cleansed of these ambitions—might well serve as a model or prototype for an interdependent and multicultural cosmopolis. In Barber's words:

> A multicultural nation whose majority will soon comprise a host of minorities and whose society looks more and more like the world it paradoxically refuses to join can, if it wishes, promote its diversity as a model for others. A society of global cities is well suited to global democratic leadership; tolerance, humility,

inventiveness and a belief in self-government . . . are values that others can emulate without feeling like they are being colonized.[42]

As to the concrete structure of the future cosmopolis, much is left to human ingenuity, practical experimentation, and political prudence and good judgment (*phronesis*). Given the dangers of empire, the structure cannot or is unlikely to be that of a world government or even a world federation. More promising are looser forms of interconnection between nation-states and regions, involving (importantly) not only governments but also people as citizens (that is, as potential global or transnational citizens).[43] More crucial than formal structures are the spirit and motivation animating cosmopolitan institutions, that is, the cultivation of global civility, civic engagement, and responsibility. Here we are back at "civilization," but now seen as a civilizing or educational effort from the ground up—admittedly a difficult and laborious undertaking. As Joseph Nye has correctly noted, cultivating this kind of civility can require "years of patient, unspectacular work, including close civilian cooperation with other countries."[44] Despite its difficulty, this is the only viable path open and acceptable to people aspiring to the status of "civilization." The first thing people embarking on this path have to learn is to forgo the "power trip": to realize that genuine change does not result from domination, manipulation, or will to power. Basically, a precondition for turning away from empire is another kind of turnabout (*periagogé*): a turning from power lust to ethics and civility, from violence to peace. It is at this point that we encounter again Nietzsche's "blessed isles," his longing for the "children's land" unspoiled by adult corruption. In a way it is the same land that is invoked by Arundhati Roy when she writes that we cannot and should not oppose empire with empire. All we can do is "to lay siege to it, to shame it, to mock it: with our art, our music, our literature, our stubbornness, our joy, our brilliance, our sheer relentlessness—and our ability to tell our own stories."[45]

NOTES

1. Comment of Francis Boyle, professor of international law at the University of Illinois, December 17, 2003; see www.democracynow.org/article.pl?sid=03/12/17/1611203. For a recent text by the same professor see Francis A. Boyle, *Destroying World Order: U.S. Imperialism in the Middle East Before and After September 11* (New York: Clarity Press, 2004).

2. Immanuel Kant, "Perpetual Peace: A Philosophical Sketch," in *Kant's Political Writings*, pp. 114, 130. Regarding the recent escalation of global violence and its relation to "civilization" compare, e.g., Shadia B. Drury, *Terror and Civilization* (New York: Palgrave/Macmillian, 2004).

3. For recent assessments of the global arena in terms of functional networks compare, e.g., John Keane, *Global Civil Society* (Cambridge, UK: Cambridge University Press, 2003); and Saskia Sassen, *Global Networks, Linked Cities* (New York: Routledge, 2002). To some extent, traces of functionalist and postmodern imagination are also evident in Michael Hardt and Antonio Negri, *Empire* (Cambridge, MA: Harvard University Press, 2000). For extensive comments on the latter book see Paul A. Passavant and Jodi Dean, eds., *Empire's New Clothes: Reading Hardt and Negri* (New York: Routledge, 2004).

4. Arundhati Roy, "Confronting Empire," in *War Talk* (Cambridge, MA: South End Press, 2003), pp. 103, 107. The talk was first presented at the closing rally of the World Social Forum in Porto Alegre, Brazil, January 27, 2003.

5. Tim Wiener, "Mexico's Influence in Security Council Decision May Help Its Ties With U.S.," *New York Times*, November 9, 2002, p. A11.

6. Edward W. Said, *Culture and Imperialism* (New York: Alfred A. Knopf, 1993), p. 282. Compare in this context also Stanley Aronowitz and Heather Gautney, eds., *Implicating Empire: Globalization and Resistance in the 21st Century* (New York: Basic Books, 2003), and Chalmers Johnson, *Blowback: The Costs and Consequences of American Empire* (New York: Henry Holt and Co., 2000).

7. Michael Ignatieff, "The Burden," *New York Times Magazine*, January 5, 2002, p. 22.

8. In the same manner, imperial Rome was not an empire over Romans, just as imperial Britain was not an empire for its citizens. This does not mean that imperial rule abroad will not affect domestic politics; in fact, some contamination seems almost inevitable. Referring to Socrates' opposition to Athenian imperial ventures, Dana Villa writes: "An imperial democracy cannot stay a democracy for long, since the basis of democratic justice—equal shares for all—demands a self-restraint directly at odds with the energies and ambitions of imperialism." See *Socratic Citizenship* (Princeton, NJ: Princeton University Press, 2001), p. 34.

9. Walter Russell Mead, *American Foreign Policy and How It Changed the World* (New York: Alfred A. Knopf, 2002), p. 10.

10. Zbigniew Brzezinski, "Epilogue: Democracy's Uncertain Triumph," in *Globalization, Power, and Democracy*, ed. Marc F. Plattner and Aleksander Smolar (Baltimore, MD: Johns Hopkins University Press, 2000), p. 149.

11. Benjamin R. Barber, *Fear's Empire: War, Terrorism, and Democracy* (New York: Norton, 2003), p. 216. Regarding the rampant erosion of civility, dramatically illustrated by torture videos, see Rosa Ehrenreich Brooks, "A Climate that Nurtures Torture," *Los Angeles Times*, May 9, 2004, and Susan Sontag, "What Have We Done?" *The Guardian*, May 24, 2004.

12. In his introduction, Barber quotes the maxim from Machiavelli's *The Prince* that "it is better to be feared than loved." See *Fear's Empire*, p. 15. The maxim also applies to the sovereign in Hobbes's *Leviathan*. The difference, of course, is that for Hobbes the commonwealth is founded on contractual agreement—which makes room for at least a measure of civic mutuality.

13. For the text of the National Security Strategy paper, see http://www.whitehouse.gov/nsc/nss.html. Regarding nuclear capability see Mike Allen and Bar-

ton Gellman, "Strike First, and Use Nuclear Weapons if Necessary," *Washington Post, National Weekly Edition,* December 16-22, 2002.

14. Barber, *Fear's Empire,* p. 81.

15. Richard Falk, "The New Bush Doctrine," *The Nation,* July 15, 2002. See also Falk, *The Great Terror War* (New York: Olive Branch Press, 2003), and Clyde Prestowitz, *Rogue Nation: American Unilateralism and the Failure of Good Intentions* (New York: Basic Books, 2003).

16. Falk, *The Great Terror War,* pp. 27, 36.

17. Barber, *Fear's Empire,* pp. 176, 205. Barber (pp. 209-211) also cites a "Declaration of Interdependence," sponsored by the "global citizens' campaign" and patterned on the American Declaration of Independence, according to which the "people of the world" recognize their "responsibilities to the common goods and liberties of humankind as a whole."

18. Thus, it is hard to imagine that Genghis Khan or Timur (Tamerlane) would have defended their actions on moral or civilizational grounds. By contrast, there are important Asian rulers denouncing empire on moral grounds: e.g., King Darius of Persia and Emperor Ashoka of India.

19. Aristotle, *Politics,* 1295b7; see also Ernest Barker, *The Politics of Aristotle* (Oxford: Clarendon Press, 1946), p. 181.

20. I bypass here the so-called Holy Roman Empire, which—apart from the adventures of the crusades—was not an expansionist "empire" (in the sense used here); nor was it a centralized or monolithic imperial structure.

21. Dussel, *The Underside of Modernity,* pp. 52, 60n22. The citations are from Juan Ginés de Sepúlveda, *Tratado sobre las justas causas de la guerra contra los Indios* (Mexico City: Fondo de Cultura Economica, 1987), pp. 83, 153.

22. Dussel, *The Underside of Modernity,* pp. 52, 60–61nn23–25; Sepúlveda, *Tratado sobre las justas causas de la guerra contra los Indios,* pp. 133, 135, 137. Compare in this context also Edward W. Said and Christopher Hitchens, eds., *Blaming the Victims* (London: Verso, 1988).

23. Cited in Falk, *The Great Terror War,* pp. 57, 74. For the attachment of many American neoconservatives to "*mission civilisatrice*" or "white man's burden" see Ari Shavit, "White Man's Burden," *Haaretz,* February 12, 2004. As Shavit indicates, the attachment is amplified (and complicated) through borrowings from "realist" political thinkers like Machiavelli and Thomas Hobbes.

24. Lucian W. Pye, *Aspects of Political Development* (Boston: Little Brown, 1966), pp. 8-9, 44-45. Compare also S. N. Eisenstadt, *Modernization: Protest and Change* (Englewood Cliffs, NJ: Prenctice-Hall, 1966); and my "Modernization and Postmodernization," in Dallmayr, *Beyond Orientalism: Essays on Cross-Cultural Encounter* (Albany, NY: State University of New York Press, 1996), p. 149-174.

25. Falk, *The Great Terror War,* pp. xii-xiii, 32. In Falk's view, the roots of this empire building can actually be traced back before September 11. In his words (pp. 31-32): "Even prior to September 11 there were good reasons to believe that the United States was seeking to achieve an imperial grip on the *new* geopolitics of globalization: by controlling the technological frontiers of information technology; by shaping the

world economy along neoliberal lines as articulated through the medium of such subordinate actors as the IMF, World Bank, and the WTO; by presiding over an innovative 'humanitarian' diplomacy of selective intervention; by aspiring to and demonstrating military dominance in 'zero casualty warfare' . . . ; and by pursuing new generations of nuclear weaponry and quietly moving ahead with plans to militarize space."

26. Martin Heidegger, "The Question Concerning Technology," in *Martin Heidegger: Basic Writings*, pp. 283-317.

27. Falk, *The Great Terror War*, p. xxvii. For the reference to Donald Rumsfeld see Rear Admiral Eugene J. Carroll, Jr., "Unilateralism Amok," *Inforum* (Fourth Freedom Forum), no. 29 (Fall 2001): p. 3.

28. Robert Kagan, *Of Paradise and Power: America and Europe in New World Order* (New York: Alfred A. Knopf, 2003). See also Kagan, "Power and Weakness," *Policy Review* 113 (June-July 2002): pp. 3-28, and in a similar vein, Thomas L. Friedman, "Ah, Those Principled Europeans," *New York Times*, February 2, 2003, sec. 4, p. 15.

29. See Friedrich Nietzsche, *Beyond Good and Evil*, trans. Walter Kaufmann (New York: Random House, 1966), paragraph 208. As he continues: "The time for petty politics is over; the twentieth century will bring with it the struggle for world domination, the *compulsion* of grand politics." For an explicit American defense of world conquest and global domination see David Frum and Richard Perle, *An End to Evil: How to Win the War on Terror* (New York: Random House, 2003). The point of the above comments is not to reduce Machiavelli, Hobbes, or Nietzsche to a narrow power-political reading, but only to note that certain aspects of their works can be and have been used (or abused) for imperial purposes.

30. For probing efforts to discern the combination of Platonic and Nietzschean elements in the neoconservative (sometimes called "Straussian") camp see, e.g., Laurence Lampert, *Leo Strauss and Nietzsche* (Chicago: University of Chicago Press, 1996); Shadia B. Drury, *Leo Strauss and the American Right* (New York: St. Martin's Press, 1997); Harald Bluhm, *Die Ordnung der Ordnung: Das politische Philosophieren von Leo Strauss* (Berlin: Akademie Verlag, 2002); James Atlas, "A Classicist's Legacy: New Empire Builders," *New York Times*, May 4, 2003 (Week in Review); James Lobe, "Strong Must Rule the Weak, said Neo-Conservatives' Muse," *Inter Press Service*, May 8, 2003; Alain Frachon and Daniel Vernet, "The Strategist and the Philosopher: Leo Strauss and Albert Wohlstetter," trans. Norman Madarasz, *Counter Punch*, May 24, 2003; and Joshua Muravchik, "The Neoconservative Cabal," *Commentary*, September 1, 2003. As in the case of Machiavelli, Hobbes, and Nietzsche, I need to add a disclaimer: the above comments in no way seek to hold Leo Strauss responsible for the policies of his neoconservative followers. For a thoughtful essay on Nietzsche, see Strauss, "Note on the Plan of *Beyond Good and Evil*," *Studies in Platonic Political Philosophy* (Chicago: University of Chicago Press, 1983), pp. 174-191.

31. The statements are reported respectively in "Bush Wears Religion on his Armored Sleeve," *The Washington Spectator* 29, no. 10 (May 15, 2003): p. 1; and "President's Corner," *The Light* (Newsletter of the Interfaith Alliance), Spring 2003, p. 2. In the latter publication, the Rev. Welton Gaddy asks sharply (p. 2): "How dare any politician, including the president, even implicitly suggest that God is a kind of mascot of the nation?"

32. For derogatory remarks of prominent televangelists on Islam and its prophet, see Akbar S. Ahmed, "The Perfect Christmas Gift," in *Religion News Service* (Washington, DC: December 2003). Compare in this context also Kimberly Blaker, ed., *The Fundamentals of Extremism: The Christian Right in America* (New Boston, MI: New Boston Books, 2003), and Emran Qureshi and Michael A. Sells, eds., *The New Crusades: Constructing the Muslim Enemy* (New York: Columbia University Press, 2003). One wonders how and to what extent Christian rhetoric is palatable to hardcore Pentagon warriors and Nietzchean-style neoconservatives. One suspects that hardline neoconservatism is meant for a restricted circle of experts and "war thinkers," while Gospel-talk is designed to enlist the loyalty of the "masses."

33. Bartolemé de las Casas, *Historia de las Indias*, in *Obras escogidas*, ed. Juan Perez de Tudela (Madrid: Biblioteca de Autores Españoles, 1957-58), vol. 2, p. 511; and *Brevissima Relacion*, in *Obras escogidas*, vol. 5, pp. 136-137. The translation of the passage from the "Very Brief Account" is taken from George Sanderlin, ed., *Bartolemé de las Casas: A Selection of His Writings* (New York: Alfred A. Knopf, 1971), p. 166. Compare also Las Casas, *A Short Account of the Destruction of the Indies*, trans. Nigel Griffin (New York: Penguin, 1992), p. 11; and *The Devastation of the Indies: A Brief Account*, trans. Herma Briffault (Baltimore, MD: Johns Hopkins University Press, 1992), p. 29.

34. Invoking the teachings of "the philosopher" (Aristotle), Las Casas in his *Historia* tried to show that American Indians were not "barbarians" and hence could not be treated simply as slaves. Moreover, relying both on Aristotle and Cicero, he argued that Indians were rational human beings like Europeans and hence were entitled to freedom and equality. To quote passages from *Historia*: "As Cicero sets it down in *De Legibus*, Book I, all the races of the world are men, and of all men and of each individual there is but one definition, and this is that they are rational. All have understanding and will and free choice, as all are made in the image and likeness of God. . . . And consequently, all have the power and ability or capacity . . . to be instructed, persuaded, and attracted to order and reason and laws and virtue and all goodness. . . . They are likewise prudent and endowed by nature with the three kinds of prudence named by the philosopher [Aristotle]: solitary, economic, and political. . . . And in following the rules of natural reason, they have even surpassed by not a little those who were the most prudent of all, such as the Greeks and Romans." *Historia*, vol. 3, pp. 3-4, 165-166; vol. 4, pp. 433-434; translation taken from Sanderlin, *Bartolemé de las Casas: A Selection from His Writings*, pp. 115, 143, 200-202.

35. See "Very Brief Account," in *Obras escogidas*, vol. 5, pp. 136-137; and *Historia*, in *Obras escogidas*, vol. 2, p. 511.

36. Bartolemé de las Casas, *Del Único Modo de Atraer a Todos los Pueblos a la Verdadera Religión*, ed. Augustin Millares Carlo (Mexico City: Fondo de Cultura Economica, 1942), pp. 400-401. For the English translation see Sanderlin, *Bartolemé de las Casas: A Selection of His Writings*, pp. 162-163. Compare also Las Casas, *The Only Way*, ed. Helen R. Parish, trans. Francis P. Sullivan, S. J. (New York: Paulist Press 1992), p. 118.

37. Partly due to the friar's pleas, Emperor Charles V in November 1542 promulgated a series of laws ordering the fair and equal treatment of the Indians and prohibiting their

enslavement. Unfortunately, the laws were not fully enforced. In June 1537, Pope Paul III had already issued a bull (*"Sublimis Deus"*) ordering that Indians "are by no means to be deprived of their liberty or their property . . . nor should they be in any way enslaved." See Lewis Hanke, *The Spanish Struggle for Justice in the Conquest of America* (Boston: Little Brown, 1965), p. 73; Sanderlin, *Bartolemé de las Casas: A Selection of His Writings*, pp. 16, 157; also *Indian Freedom: The Cause of Bartolemé de las Casas*, ed. and trans. Francis P. Sullivan (Kansas City: Sheed & Ward, 1995), pp. 248-252.

38. See Dussel, *The Underside of Modernity*, p. 136; Gustavo Gutierrez, *Las Casas: In Search of the Poor of Jesus Christ*, trans. Robert R. Barr (Maryknoll, NY: Orbis Books, 1993), pp. 9-11.

39. See Walter Kaufmann, ed., *The Portable Nietzsche* (New York: Viking Press, 1968), pp. 196-197, 233 ("Thus Spoke Zarathustra").

40. Falk, *The Great Terror War*, p. 11. As he adds, pointing to the consequences of the sanctions imposed on Iraq since the Gulf War of 1990 (p. xiv): "According to reliable and objective estimates, these sanctions have by now been responsible for almost a million civilian deaths and widespread societal suffering"—a situation further aggravated by the subsequent Iraq war.

41. Rev. Marty Martin, as reported in *The Washington Spectator* 29, no. 10 (May 15, 2003): p. 3.

42. Barber, *Fear's Empire*, p. 214; Falk, *The Great Terror War*, p. 36. To be sure, the significance of American multiculturalism is contested. For many neoconservatives, American multiculturalism is not the harbinger of cosmopolis but a threat to the maintenance of traditional American "identity" and exceptionalism. See, e.g., Samuel P. Huntington, *Who Are We? The Challenges to America's National Identity* (New York: Simon & Schuster, 2004).

43. The dangers of a unified or homogenized cosmopolis devoid of local and regional arenas of political contestation have been eloquently underscored by Danilo Zolo, especially in his *Cosmopolis: Prospects for World Government*, and *Invoking Humanity: War, Law and Global Order*, trans. Federico and Gordon Poole (London and New York: Continuum, 2002). As he writes in the latter book (pp. ix-x): "After the hiatus of the Cold War and the formal liberation of the colonized countries of Africa and Asia, the West's ancient mission to control, occupy, and 'civilize' the non-Western world is returning with full force and can only provoke, as a bloody counterpoint, a 'global terrorism' that is ever more ruthless and effective. . . . Now more than ever, [Hans] Kelsen's formula 'peace through law,' looks like an Enlightenment illusion, with its prescriptive optimism and naïve cosmopolitan universalism."

44. Joseph S. Nye, Jr., *The Paradox of American Power: Why the World's Only Superpower Can't Go it Alone* (New York: Oxford University Press, 2002), p. xv; cited in Barber, *Fear's Empire*, pp. 203-204. On "transnational" citizenship see specially Etienne Balibar, *We, The People of Europe? Reflections on Transnational Citizenship* (Princeton: Princeton University Press, 2004).

45. Roy, *War Talk*, p. 112.

Chapter Four

Confronting Empire:
A Tribute to Arundhati Roy

Sometimes one feels like "tuning out." Faced with the incessant noise of war-planes and propaganda machines, one sometimes feels like stopping up one's ears in order to shut out the world. The impulse is particularly strong in the "developed," industrial North—given the fact that development almost in-variably means a ratching up of the noise level. Although amply motivated, the attempt for many of us does not quite succeed. For, in muffling the roar of military-industrial noises, our ears become available for and attuned to a different kind of sound: the recessed voices of the persecuted and exploited, the anguished cries of the victims of development and military power. A great philosopher of the last century vividly described the tendency of modern lives to become submerged in societal noises, in the busy clamor of social con-formism (what he called "*das Man*"). But he also indicated a different possi-bility, a different path involving a kind of turning-around or a movement lead-ing from "tuning out" to a new kind of "tuning in." In his portrayal, this attunement or tuning in meant an opening of heart and mind to recessed voices drowned out by societal pressures: above all to the voice of "con-science" which calls us into mindfulness, into a new mode of careful being-in-the-world.[1]

As one will note, conscience here does not call one into a solipsism far re-moved from the world, but rather onto a road leading more deeply into the world, into its agonies and hidden aspirations. Not long ago, such a call struck me somewhat unexpectedly. It happened in the midst of a new war, while fire-bombs were dropping on distant cities and the roar of warplanes rocked that part of the world. At that time I began reading a book called *The God of Small Things*—and was transported beyond surface events into the deeper recesses of human agonies. The book is from the pen of a writer I had not encountered before (I shamefully confess) by the name of Arundhati Roy. She hails from the "South," more specifically from Kerala in India, and now lives in Delhi. Happening in the midst of a war ostensibly launched by the North, the encounter for me had a special significance: by awakening me again to the enormous rifts tearing apart our world and by urging on me a renewed mindfulness. In the meantime, I have read several of Arundhti Roy's other writings, including a series of essays collected in her books *The Cost of Living*, *Power Politics*, and *War Talk*. The following pages are meant as a tribute to her: as an expression of gratitude to her for serving in many ways as a voice of conscience calling on people everywhere, but especially people in the North, to step back from the pretense of cultural superiority and to return to the cultivation of our shared humanity.

A WRITER-ACTIVIST?

Paying tribute to a writer like Arundhati Roy is risky and difficult—especially for a nonwriter (or a nonliterary writer) like me. The difficulty is particularly great in the case of a novel like *The God of Small Things*, an outstanding work of fiction, which deservedly has received the distinguished Booker Prize.[2] Not being a novelist or a literary critic, how could I possibly do justice to the vast richness of this book, the immense subtlety of its nuances, its stories within stories and echoes within echoes? How could I fathom its depth of imagination and the intense agonies of its characters? Famous writers East and West have celebrated her work: John Updike has compared it to a Tiger Wood story, while Salmon Rushdie has praised her combination of passion and intellectual verve. My own approach has to be somewhat different. Having spent most of my adult years mulling over ponderous philosophical texts, I have to link her work with my own background that, in the main, has always hovered between philosophy and politics or between theory and praxis.

The aspect I want to pick up first of all is the title of her prize-winning novel. The very phrase "The God of Small Things" is in a way counterhegemonic if not seditious. Traditional religion, especially in the West, has always associated "God" with bigness or greatness. Of all the things in the world, and of all the big things, God was held to be the biggest or greatest; among all the many causes and moving engines in the world, God was seen as the first or primary cause or engine. Due to the traditional linkage of "throne and altar," the bigness of God has tended to rub off on the status of princes, kings, and political rulers. This fascination with bigness has proven to be hard to shake, and in some form even persists today. Thus, when "world leaders" or presidents claim to be mouthpieces or "stand-ins" for God, their power appears to be wielded by "divine right" (which is a very big right). To be sure, this pretense of leaders is contested and debunked by modern democracy with its emphasis on the importance of ordinary people and ordinary lives. As it happens, these ordinary lives—although seemingly small if compared with the power of potentates—are by no means "small" in terms of dignity and moral-spiritual significance. For grown-up people in democracies, God no longer has need of pomp and circumstance but is content to remain sheltered in ordinary phenomena and inconspicuous places and events. As Walter Benjamin has remarked (and I have had occasion to mention before), ordinary lives at any moment can become the narrow gate through which the Messiah suddenly and without fanfare enters. Thus, it is a small, nearly imperceptible change that changes everything.[3]

In Arundhati Roy's novel, the change is so unobtrusive that it is not specifically elaborated or thematized. However, on some other occasions she has shed light on the book's title. In her essay "The Greater Common Good" of 1999 (reprinted in *The Cost of Living*), we find some tantalizing lines. "Perhaps," she writes,

> perhaps that's what the twenty-first century has in store for us: the dismantling of the Big. Big bombs, big dams, big ideologies, big contradictions, big countries, big wars, big heroes, big mistakes. Perhaps it will be the Century of the Small.

And she adds: "Perhaps right now, this very minute, there's a small god up in heaven readying herself for us."[4] As we know, of course, this "small god" (if she comes) will be up against all the old bigness: the big old God associated with the biggest country, the biggest superpower, the biggest wealth, the biggest arsenal of weapons of mass destruction, the biggest bigness. If the small god were to come, she would certainly not arrive in a mammoth conflagration or on top of a nuclear mushroom cloud—as some devotees of Armageddon now predict and propagate. She would come on the wings of a dove, as the consoler of the desolate, the healer of the wounded, the liberator of the oppressed. As Arundhati Roy herself stated in a recent interview, commenting on the title of her novel:

> To me the god of small things is the inversion of God. God is a big thing and God's in control. The god of small things . . . whether it is the way children see things or whether it is the insect life in the book, or the fish or the stars—there is no accepting of what we think of as adult boundaries. This small activity that goes on is the underlife of the book. All sorts of boundaries are transgressed upon.[5]

In many quarters, and not without reason, Arundhati Roy is considered a political activist and public intellectual—in addition to, or apart from, being a writer. Yet, as the preceding passages make clear, her activism does not subscribe to any "big ideology" or overarching platform seeking to mold and reshape social life; she also does not favor mass organizations wedded to rigid marching orders or agendas. As she remarked coyly about her childhood in Kerala: she grew up in a state where different "religions coincide" and coexist, where "Christianity, Hinduism, Marxism and Islam . . . all live together and rub each other down."[6] The point of her remark was not simply to debunk these "religions," but rather to relativize them slightly and thus to prevent them from becoming ideological straitjackets. As it seems to me, a main feature of Roy's work is that it escapes ready-made formulas or pigeonholes. In a nimble way, she refuses to accept the rubrics offered by contemporary society: the options of ivory-tower retreat (literature for literature's sake) or of mindless street activism—or else the superoption of the writer-intellectual as the architect of grand social platforms. She is celebrated as a writer; but she is also known as a political activist. What is intriguing and even dazzling is the manner in which she is both—the manner in which writing and doing, thinking and acting in her case are neither radically separated nor fused in an ideological stew. As she remarked in an interview given at the World Social Forum in early 2003: "When I write, I don't even think consciously of being political—because I *am* political. I know that even if I wrote fairy stories, they would be political." As she added, literature and politics (contrary to widespread belief) are not "two separate things"—which does not mean that there is not a world of "difference between literature and propaganda" (where the latter instrumentalizes the former for extrinsic goals). For Roy, writing and acting are not at odds but reflective of a "way of being"—reflective of the writer's distinctive way of being-in-the-world.[7]

In a fashion reminiscent of Edward Said, Roy asks a question which is too often sidestepped by contemporary intellectuals: the question regarding the social responsibility of literature and art (and one might add: philosophy). "What is the role of writers and artists in society?" she queries in *Power Politics*. "Can it be fixed, described, characterized in any definite way? Should it be?"[8] In a poignant way, this question had been raised by Edward Said in his Reith Lectures of 1993, subsequently published as *Representations of the Intellectual*. At the time of his lectures, Said was renowned as a writer; but he was also suspect in many quarters as a political activist. As he noted in his introduction: "I was accused of being active in the battle for Palestinian rights and thus disqualified for any sober or respectable platform at all." His lectures pinpointed the public role of the intellectual as that of a peculiar insider-outsider, in any case of an "amateur and disturber of the status quo." If intellectuals were complete "outsiders," they would enjoy the alibi or refuge of an ivory tower, far removed from Julien Benda's "*trahison des clercs*"—what Said calls "Benda's uncritical Platonism." But if they were complete "insiders," they would become accomplices and sycophants of the ruling power, thus robbing the intellect of its critical edge. "Insiders," he writes, "promote special interests, but intellectuals should be the ones to question patriotic nationalism, corporate thinking, and a sense of class, racial or gender privilege." For Said, the "principal duty" of intellectuals, writers, and artists resides in the search for "relative independence" from societal pressures—an independence that justifies his characterization of the intellectual "as exile and marginal, as amateur, and as the author of a language that tries to speak the truth to power."[9]

Without implying any direct influence, Arundhati Roy's outlook broadly concurs with Said's. In *Power Politics* she lays down two guideposts for writers: first, "there are no rules"; and secondly, "there are no excuses for bad art"—where the second guidepost severely complicates the first. The absence of formal, externally fixed rules does not mean that everything is left to arbitrary whim. "There is a very thin line," she writes, "that separates the strong, true, bright bird of imagination from the synthetic, noisy bauble." The point is that the writer (or the intellectual) constantly has to search for that line and allow herself to be measured by its standard: "The thing about this 'line' is that once you learn to recognize it, once you see it, it's impossible to ignore. You have no choice but to live with it, to follow it through." (In his introduction, Said observed likewise that there are no fixed "rules" by which intellectuals can know "what to say or do," but that it is crucial nonetheless to uphold standards of conduct.) Regarding the public role of writers or intellectuals this means that there cannot be fixed rules dictating either specific social obligations or else mandating radical exile. The rub is again the peculiar inside/outside position of writers or intellectuals: they have to know sufficiently the language of their community in order properly to address it; and they have to be sufficiently dislodged to contest that language. Whichever way they choose—inside or outside—there is no real escape: "There's no innocence; either way you are accountable." As Roy concedes, a good or great writer "may refuse to accept any responsibility or morality that society wishes to *impose* on her." Yet, the best and greatest also know that if they abuse their freedom—by joining the ivory tower or else becoming "palace entertainers"—they inevitably damage their art: "There is an intricate web of morality, rigor, and responsibility that art, that writing itself, imposes on a writer. It's singular, it's individual, but nevertheless it's there."[10]

Roy's entire work is a testimonial to the stringent demands of the "thin line." In her writings and in her public conduct she has resisted both radical politicization or political co-optation and retreat into the haven of *belles let-ters*. Like every thoughtful writer or intellectual, Roy does not like to be conscripted into ideological agendas or be submerged in mindless activism. As a reflective person, she relishes subtle nuances and the open-endedness of many issues. In her own words: "I am all for discretion, prudence, tentativeness, subtlety, ambiguity, complexity. I love the unanswered question, the unresolved story, the unclimbed mountain, the tender shard of an incomplete dream." But she adds an important caveat: "Most of the time." Problems may be so urgent, public policies so threatening or destructive that even the most pensive person cannot remain uninvolved—without becoming an accomplice. Are there not occasions, she asks, when prudence turns into "pusillanimity" and caution into cowardice? Can a writer or intellectual afford to be "ambiguous about everything," and is there not a point where circumspection becomes "a kind of espousal"? No one can accuse Arundhati Roy of being pusillanimous or cowardly. Whatever pressing issues or lurking disasters there may be in this world, she has never hesitated to speak out—and to do so forcefully and without equivocation. In her words again:

> Isn't it true, or at least theoretically possible, that there are times in the life of a people or a nation when the political climate demands that we—even the most sophisticated of us—overtly take sides? I believe that such times are upon us. And I believe that in the coming years intellectuals and artists in India will be called upon to take sides.[11]

Not only in India, one might add, but all over the world.

THE MILITARY-INDUSTRIAL COMPLEX

The issues on which Arundhati Roy has most frequently and most forcefully spoken are two: big corporate business and the war machine—whose interconnection or collusion President Dwight Eisenhower had termed the "military-industrial complex." This interconnection has been steadily tightening since Eisenhower's time. Basically, the war machine is designed to keep markets stable and safe for business investments; in turn, corporate business finances the maintenance of the war machine. For Roy, the most glaring and preposterous manifestations of this collusion in India are the development of the nuclear bomb and the construction of "big dams" or mega-dams. Some of her sharpest attacks have been leveled at these targets. Although not intuitively evident, she has neatly pinpointed the linkage between the two phenomena—while inserting both in the broader framework of globalization. From a global angle, dam construction is part of the global market dominated by Western corporate business; on the other hand, nuclear bombs are compensatory devices meant to provide domestic security and to pacify volatile masses. As she noted in an interview with David Barsamian (in 2001), it is crucial to perceive the links between "privatization, globalization, and [religious] fundamentalism." For when, in constructing dams, a country like India is "selling its entire power sector" to foreign business firms (like Enron), pressure is placed on the government to compensate people by building a bomb or else by erecting a "Hindu temple on the site of the Babri mosque." So, this is the trade-off one has to understand: "With one hand, you are selling the country out to Western multinationals; and with the other, you want to defend your borders with nuclear bombs."[12]

Dam construction has been a major preoccupation of modern India. Just as, for Lenin, electrification held the key to Russia's future, dams—in particular mega-dams—were touted as springboards of India's rapid economic development. In a famous speech in 1948, Prime Minister Jawaharlal Nehru had proclaimed "dams are the temples of modern India" (a phrasing he himself came to regret later). In the period following independence, the country embarked on a craze of dam constructions, one more ambitious and extensive than the other. As Roy notes in *The Cost of Living*, India is "the third largest dam-builder in the world," having constructed since 1948 a total of roughly 3,300 big dams. The latest and most ambitious undertaking along these lines is the Sardar Sarovar Dam, a monumental megadam that is being built on the Narmada River in central India—the same river which, according to government plans, is going to provide sites in the future for some additional three thousand dams. Although heralded as developmental marvels, the human and social costs of big dams have so far vastly outstripped any economic benefits. In Roy's words, the reservoirs of these dams have "uprooted millions of people" (perhaps as many as thirty million). What is worse: "There are no government records of how many people have actually been displaced" and there is a total lack of anything resembling a "national rehabilitation policy." Against the backdrop of this grim scenario, the Sardar Sarovar Dam is now taking its toll. As the waters at the dam's reservoir are rising every hour, she writes, "more than ten thousand people face submergence. They have nowhere to go."[13]

Dam construction in India is complicated and aggravated by the impact of globalization—which today is closely linked with the panaceas of neoliberalism, structural adjustment, and (above all) privatization. The latter policy is particularly grievous when it involves the privatization of water resources in third-world countries. In this case, the policy does not just mean an innocuous "structural adjustment," but the transfer of effective control over the daily lives of millions of people. This transfer, one should note well, does not signify the end of "power" but rather the replacement of public power—the role of democratically elected leaders—by the unaccountable power of executives of private (chiefly foreign or multinational) businesses. Keeping one's focus on water-generated or electrical power, the deeper meaning of "power politics," in Roy's usage, becomes clear. As she states: "Dam builders want to control public water policies" just as "power utility companies want to draft power policies, and financial institutions want to supervise government investment." In this context, Roy offers one of the most trenchant definitions of "privatization" that one can find in the literature anywhere. "What does privatization really mean?" she asks, and answers:

> Essentially, it is the transfer of productive public assets from the state to private companies. Productive assets include natural resources: earth, forest, water, air. These are assets that the state holds in trust for the people it represents. In a country like India, seventy percent of the population lives in rural areas. That's seven hundred million people. Their lives depend directly on access to natural resources. To snatch these away and sell them as stock to private companies is a process of barbaric dispossession on a scale that has no parallel in history.[14]

The consequences of the privatization of natural resources are today no longer left to guesswork or conjecture. In 1999—Roy recalls—the government of Bolivia privatized the public water supply system in the city of Cochabamba and signed a forty-year lease with a consortium headed by Bechtel, the giant U.S. engineering firm: "The first thing Bechtel did was to raise the price of water; hundreds of thousands of people simply couldn't afford it any more." Something similar may be in store for people in India. With regard to water resources there, the prime advocates and beneficiaries of privatization have been General Electric and Enron. Typically, concerned state governments in India have been induced to sign so-called Power Purchase Agreements with big companies, preferably foreign or multinational companies—agreements which transfer basic control over water and electric power to the purchasers. When such agreements break down or run into trouble with local agencies, they tend to be renegotiated—often at rates of return still more beneficial to the purchasing companies. In Roy's words: "The fish bowl of the drive to privatize power, its truly star turn, is the story of Enron, the Houston-based natural gas company." The first Power Purchase Agreement between Enron and the state of Maharashtra was signed in 1993. Due to changes in political leadership at the state level, the contract had to be repeatedly rewritten and renegotiated, leading to steadily higher costs to the state. While the initial contract pegged the annual amount owed to Enron in the neighborhood of 400 million dollars, the latest "renegotiated" agreement compels Maharashtra to pay to Enron a sum of 30 billion dollars. As Roy comments: "It constitutes the largest contract ever signed in the history of India. . . . Experts who have studied the project have called it the most massive fraud in the country's history."[15]

To be sure, the costs of dam constructions and the sale of water resources are not only borne by local governments, but also (and even principally) by the masses of poor people victimized by "power politics." Despite the huge fanfare boosting big dams and big companies, the results for these masses have been disheartening. After the construction of thousands of dams, Roy notes, some 250 million people have no access to safe drinking water, while over 80 percent of rural households still do not have electricity. The deprivation is experienced most acutely by the Adivasis (indigenous tribal people) and the Dalits (formerly called "Untouchables") who are also most seriously affected by big dams. In the case of the Sardar Sarovar Dam on the Narmada River, more than half of all the people displaced are Adivasis; and another large segment is made up of Dalits. Here power politics joins the grim story of ethnic conflict and caste discrimination. "The ethnic 'otherness' of these victims," Roy comments, "takes some of the pressure off the 'nation builders.'" It is like having an expense account whereby India's poorest people are "subsidizing the lifestyles of her richest." Thus, despite appeals to the "greater common good" (supposedly advanced by big dams), a good part of the "cost of living" of the upper crust of society is charged to the meager fortunes of the poor. When faced with inequities or injustices of such proportions, Roy's language tends to become stirring and nearly biblical—reminiscent of Lincoln's fulmination against a "house divided." "The millions of displaced people in India," we read in *The Cost of Living*,

> are nothing but refugees of an unacknowledged war. And we, like the citizens of White America and French Canada and Hitler's Germany, are condoning it by looking away. Why? Because we are told that it's being done for the sake of the Greater Common Good. That it's being done in the name of Progress, in the name of the National Interest (which, of course, is paramount) . . . We believe what it benefits us to believe.[16]

As previously mentioned, the construction of megadams is closely linked with militarism or the advancement of military power—which, in our age, means the development of nuclear bombs and weapons of mass destruction. In India, the big event happened in May 1998 with the detonation of the first nuclear bomb—an explosion that, according to government reports, made "the desert shake" and a "whole mountain turn white." For Arundhati Roy—voicing the sentiments of millions of people in India and elsewhere—the event was an ominous turning point steering the country and the rest of the world in a perilous and potentially disastrous direction. As she noted, the case against nuclear weapons had been made by thoughtful people many times in the past, often in passionate and eloquent language; but this fact offered no excuse for remaining silent. Despite a certain fatigue induced by the need to repeat the obvious, the case had to be restated clearly and forcefully: "We have to reach within ourselves and find the strength to think, to fight." As with regard to megadams and their social consequences, Roy lent her pen to the vigorous denunciation of militarism and nuclear megapolitics. In language designed to infuriate Indian chauvinists and especially devotees of "Hindutva" (India for Hindus), an essay published in the aftermath of the explosion asserted bluntly: "India's nuclear tests, the manner in which they were conducted, the euphoria with which they have been greeted (by us) is indefensible. To me, it signifies dreadful things: the end of imagination; the end of freedom actually." In still bolder language, the same essay exposed the linkage between megabombs and the ruling military-industrial complex which, in India and elsewhere, constitutes the major threat to the survival of democratic institutions: "India's nuclear bomb is the final act of betrayal by a ruling class that has failed its people [that is, failed to nourish and educate the people]. The nuclear bomb is the most anti-democratic, anti-national, anti-human, outright evil thing that man has ever made."[17]

One of the most valuable features of Roy's antinuclear essay is its realist candor: its unblinking willingness to look at the horrors of nuclear devastation. This candor is particularly important in view of recent attempts—again by ruling elites—to downplay these horrors by throwing over them the mantle of relative normalcy or else of strategic inevitability (given the global dangers of "terrorism"). Most prominent among these ruses is the rhetoric of "smart nuclear bombs" and (even more hideously) of "preemptive nuclear strikes." Piercing this fog of deception, Roy's essay offers a stark description of "ground zero": "If there is a nuclear war, our foes will not be China or America or even each other. Our foe will be the earth herself; the very elements—the sky, the air, the land, the wind and water—will all turn against us." Readers who still remember Hiroshima and Nagasaki will find their memories joltingly refreshed by Roy's stark portrayal:

> Our cities and forests, our fields and villages will burn for days. Rivers will turn to poison; the air will become fire; the wind will spread the flames . . . Temperatures will drop to far below freezing and nuclear winter will set in. Water will turn into toxic ice. Radioactive fallout will seep through the earth and contaminate groundwater. Most living things, animal and vegetable, fish and fowl, will die.

Faced with catastrophes of this magnitude, the head of an atomic research center in Bombay (Mumbai) recommended that, in case of nuclear attack, people retire to the basements of their homes and take iodine pills. As Roy scathingly remarks, governmental (so-called) preparedness is a sham; it is "nothing but a perilous joke in a world where iodine pills are prescribed as a prophylactic for nuclear irradiation."[18]

The reasons given by Indian officials for the development of nuclear capability have been primarily three: the looming danger of China; the ongoing conflict with Pakistan; and the Western example of nuclear power politics. None of these reasons stand up to scrutiny. Regarding China, Roy comments, the last military confrontation happened over three decades ago; since that time, conditions have by no means deteriorated but rather "improved slightly between us." Relations between India and Pakistan are more tense and perilous, especially when the focus is placed on Kashmir. However, here the geographical proximity itself undermines nuclear programs on both sides. In Roy's words: "Though we are separate countries, we share skies, we share winds, we share water. Where radioactive fallout will land on any given day depends on the direction of the wind and the rain." Hence, any nuclear attack launched by India against Pakistan will be "a war against ourselves." Somewhat more tricky—but ultimately equally fallacious—is the reference to Western power politics and the obvious hypocrisy involved in Western nuclear policies ("bombs are good for us, not for you"). Although containing more than a kernel of truth, the charge of hypocrisy and duplicity does not vindicate India's nuclear arsenal. "Exposing Western hypocrisy," Roy asks mockingly, "how much more exposed can they be? Which decent human being on earth harbors any illusions about it?" While protesting self-righteously against nuclear proliferation, Western regimes have in fact amassed the largest arsenal of nuclear devices and other weapons of mass destruction; and they have never hesitated to use this arsenal for their own political advantage: "They stand on the world's stage naked and entirely unembarrassed, because they know that they have more money, more food, and bigger bombs than anybody else. They know they can wipe us out in the course of an ordinary working day."[19]

As one should note well, Roy's point here is to criticize India's nuclear program, not to shield Western hypocrisy and warmongering. Her book *Power Politics* contains stirring passages condemning the spread of warmongering all over the world, but especially the kind of belligerence unleashed by the so-called war on terrorism (what Richard Falk has called "the great terror war"). Roy is adamantly opposed to the high-handed and unilateral definition of "terrorism" by state governments—especially governments whose own policies may have the effect of "terrorizing" large populations at home and abroad. Here is a memorable statement on behalf of the victims of governmental warmongering: "People rarely win wars; governments rarely lose them. People get killed; governments molt and regroup, hydra-headed. They [governments] first use flags to shrink-wrap peoples' minds and smother real thought, and then as ceremonial shrouds to bury the willing dead." In our time of unprecedented media manipulation, Roy's denunciation of chauvinistic flag-waving and brainwashing surely deserves close attention. One of her main concerns is the unpredictable outcome of nationalist belligerence: the fact that, in pursuing national glory, governments or ruling elites may unleash or exacerbate "huge, raging human feelings" present in the world today. What warmongering typically ignores are the underlying sources of conflict: especially the misery of common people whose sufferings cannot be alleviated by warfare. At the time of the war in Afghanistan (2001), Roy penned a passage whose salience has further increased in light of subsequent military adventures:

> Put your ear to the ground in this part of the world, and you can hear the thrumming, the deadly drumbeat of burgeoning anger. Please. Please, stop the war now. Enough people have died. The smart missiles are just not smart enough. They are blowing up whole warehouses of suppressed fury.[20]

INDIA AND THE FUTURE

Roy's forthrightness—her role as writer-activist pleading on behalf of common people—has not earned her universal applause. Although celebrated by some literary figures and academic intellectuals, her readiness to "speak truth to power" has irked and infuriated chauvinists, warmongers, and acolytes of "bigness," both at home and abroad. As she remarked once to an Indian reporter: "Each time I step out, I hear the snicker-snack of knives being sharpened. But that is good; it keeps me sharp." There can be no doubt that, despite and in the teeth of great power politics, Arundhati Roy has maintained her "sharpness" and intellectual integrity—not out of spite or meddlesomeness, but out of a deep commitment to humanity at large, to a world inhabited and sustained by the "god of small things." In this respect, her work has served as a beacon of hope to the persecuted and oppressed, to the victims of military-industrial complexes everywhere. The presence of such a beacon—or a series of beacons—is crucial today in a world dominated or contaminated by globalizing neoliberalism, structural downsizing, and privatization. In this context, one may usefully recall a phrase she used in her conversation with David Barsamian: "The only thing worth globalizing today is dissent." To be sure, globalizing dissent does not mean the construction of grand ideological panaceas or the formulation of general marching orders. Rather, dissenters are called upon to resist in very concrete contexts and for a very specific purpose: the alleviation of injustice and misery. "Each person," she commented to Ben Ehrenreich at the World Social Forum in Brazil (2003), "has to find a way of staying his or her ground. It's not that all of us have to become professional activists. All of us have to find our particular way."[21]

As Roy fully realizes (perhaps better than many "progressive" thinkers), the obstacles to resistance are formidable and nearly overwhelming. Her portrayal of conditions in India and the rest of the world is exceedingly grim—a grimness which has placed her on the "index" of domestic and global ruling elites. Take the example of India first. Her book *Power Politics* opens with passages that are deeply shocking and disheartening. "As Indian citizens," she writes there, "we subsist on a regular diet of caste massacres and nuclear tests, mosque breakings and fashion shows, church burnings and expanding cell phone networks, bonded labor and the digital revolution, female infanticide and the Nasdaq crash." As these lines indicate, the country is torn apart by the conflicting pulls of traditionalist fundamentalism and high-tech modernity; at the same time, society exhibits a widening gulf between a small globalizing elite and the large masses of people victimized by megadams and big bombs. "It is," she adds, "as though the people of India have been rounded up and loaded onto two conveys of trucks, a huge big one and a tiny little one"— with the tiny convey heading toward a "glittering destination somewhere near the top of the world," while the large one "melts into darkness." The picture becomes even move disturbing when Roy turns to her immediate environment: the metropolis of Delhi. "Close to forty percent of Delhi's population of twelve million (about five million people)," she comments, "live in slums and unauthorized colonies. Most of them are not serviced by municipal services—no electricity, no water, no sewage systems. About fifty thousand people are homeless and sleep on the streets." Joined by a large army of "informal" laborers, the latter people are the "noncitizens" of Delhi, surviving "in the folds and wrinkles, the cracks and fissures, of the 'official' city."[22]

To be sure, conditions in India are not autonomous or unique, but merely an outgrowth or reflection of conditions in the world today—a world dominated by the West and its only remaining megapower, America. Roy's denunciation of Western colonial, neocolonial, and imperial machinations has never been reticent or subdued. As she wrote on the West's domineering impulses: "These are people whose histories are spongy with the blood of others. Colonialism, apartheid, slavery, ethnic cleansing, germ warfare, chemical weapons—they virtually invented it all. They have plundered nations, snuffed out civilizations, exterminated entire populations." What aggravates the situation further is that the plundering of nations has usually been carried out with a "good conscience": for the sake of progress, modernization, or (simply) freedom. In this respect, Americans have an unequaled record of missionary zeal. *Power Politics* offers a long list of countries that America has attacked or been at war with since World War II—a list ranging from China and

Korea to Vietnam, El Salvador, and Nicaragua, and finally to Afghanistan and Iraq. In nearly all instances, military action was justified by the rhetoric of freedom or the defense of Western (superior) values. Referring to America's self-description as "the most free nation in the world," Roy raises the question: "What freedoms does it uphold?" And answers: "Within its borders the freedoms of speech, religion, thought; of artistic expression; food habits, sexual preferences (well, to some extent), and many other exemplary, wonderful things. Outside its borders the freedom to dominate, humiliate, and subjugate— usually in the service of America's real religion, the 'free market.'" Turning specifically to the labels attached to the wars against Afghanistan and Iraq— Operation Infinite Justice, Operation Enduring Freedom—she comments: "We know that Infinite Justice for some means Infinite Injustice for others. And Enduring Freedom for some means Enduring Subjugation for Others."[23]

As it happens, and as Roy fully realizes, the situation is still more complex and hazardous: the neat separation between "freedom at home" and "nonfreedom abroad" cannot be maintained for long. Sooner or later, militarism and the insatiable demands of the military-industrial complex are bound to undermine domestic liberties as well. This tendency is well illustrated by the ongoing "war on terrorism" and the prioritization of domestic or "homeland" security. In Roy's words: "Operation Enduring Freedom is ostensibly being fought to uphold the American Way of Life. It will probably end up undermining it completely." The erosion of domestic liberties may proceed slowly and with all kinds of rhetorical subterfuges. However, security demands will ultimately prevail—with far-reaching consequences. The American government and governments all over the world, Roy continues, will use the climate of war as an excuse "to curtail civil liberties, deny free speech, lay off workers, harass ethnic and religious minorities, cut back on public spending, and divert huge amounts of money to the defense industry." Considering the latter consequence, there almost seems to be a subterranean complicity between the terrorists and the military-industrial complex, both pulling in the direction of increased defense spending and global militarization. The net result of this collusion is the emergence of a kind of a global "empire" wedded to megapower politics, with potentially totalitarian implications. The sheer scale of surveillance necessary in such an empire is likely to produce "a logistical, ethical, and civil rights nightmare," with public freedom being the first casualty. For Roy, an imperial or ruthlessly hegemonic world is "like having a government without a healthy opposition. It becomes a kind of dictatorship. It is like putting a plastic bag over the world and preventing it from breathing."[24]

The enormity of the danger—a danger that literally takes one's breath away—may be conducive to discouragement and despair. In some occasional passages, Roy herself seems ready to concede defeat and throw in the towel.

Reflecting on her native India and its recent infatuation with big dams and big bombs, she sometimes appears willing to beat a retreat or escape into purely imaginary realms. "If protesting against having a nuclear bomb implanted in my brain," she writes in *The Cost of Living*, "is anti-Hindu and antinational, then I secede. I declare myself an independent, mobile republic." This republic, she adds a bit playfully, so far has "no flag" and its policies are simple: "I am willing to sign any nuclear nonproliferation treaty or nuclear test ban treaty" and "immigrants are welcome." Playfulness, however, is only a thin disguise here for a deep sadness: "My world has died; and I write to mourn its passing." As it happens (fortunately), loss and mourning are not Roy's final words. Even when tempted by despair, she quickly remembers the need to distinguish between oppressive governmental policies and the genuine concerns of common people living ordinary lives, both at home and abroad. Counterbalancing her sharp critique of American megapolitics, she assures ordinary American people "that it is not them, but their government's policies that are so hated." The same trust in ordinary lives also applies to India. Here too, the sparks of common decency have not yet been entirely extinguished, despite massive assaults by ruling elites. Friends of India and friends of democracy are likely to relish the following lines Roy penned in *Power Politics*:

> India's redemption lies in the inherent anarchy and factiousness of its people, and in the legendary inefficiency of the Indian state . . . Corporatizing India is like trying to impose an iron grid on a heaving ocean and forcing it to behave. My guess is that India will not behave. It cannot. It's too old and too clever to be made to jump through hoops all over again. It's too diverse, too grand, too feral, and—eventually, I hope—too democratic to be lobotomized into believing in one single idea, which is ultimately what globalization really is: Life is Perfect.[25]

In the end, Roy's writings exude not despair, but hope and commitment to a better—more just, more humane—future. Hope in her case—one should note well—is not born from wishful thinking, but from a sober readiness to "stay one's ground" in the face of seemingly overwhelming odds. Although severely tested, this readiness is not entirely whimsical or unfounded because, ultimately, hope is sustained by a love that will not quit. "There is beauty yet," we read, "in this brutal, damaged world of ours—hidden, fierce, immense. Beauty that is uniquely ours and beauty that we have received with grace from others. . . . We have to seek it out, nurture it, love it." Commitment to a better future surely requires active engagement, but—and here is the rub—an engagement that exceeds willful activism. The reason is that the "good life" (so-called) cannot be engineered or fabricated in the manner in which devotees of "empire" construct or fabricate their imperial edifice. Although involving praxis, commitment to a better future also requires a certain reticence, a refusal to dominate, coerce, or construct—hence a willingness to allow the good life to happen when it "comes." In this respect, Roy's outlook bears a certain resemblance to Jacques Derrida's notion of a "democracy to come"—about which he writes that such a democracy must have "the structure of a promise—and thus the memory of that which carries the future, the to-come, here, and now." No one has been better able than Roy to capture the sense of this promise and to artic-ulate it in moving language. Here are the closing lines of "Come September," an address she presented in Santa Fe on September 18, 2002: "Perhaps there is a small god up in heaven readying herself for us. Another world is not only pos-sible, she is on her way. Maybe many of us won't be here to greet her; but on a quiet day, if I listen very carefully, I can hear her breathing."[26]

NOTES

1. Martin Heidegger, *Being and Time*, pp. 250-258.

2. Arundhati Roy, *The God of Small Things* (New York: Random House, 1997).

3. Benjamin, "Theses on the Philosophy of History," in *Illuminations*, p. 266. The notion of a sheltered or disguised god is also invoked in the famous biblical passage (Luke 9:48) where Jesus says: "Whoever receives this child in my name receives me, and whoever receives me receives him who sent me; for who is least among you is truly great."

4. Roy, *The Cost of Living*, p. 12.

5. See "On Writing," http://website.lineone.net/~jon.simmons/roy/tgost4.htm.

6. Arundhati Roy, "A Life Full of Beginnings and No End"; see http://www.aroy .miena.com.

7. Interview with Ben Ehrenreich, "Happiness is a Weapon: Indian Author Arundhati Roy at the World Social Forum in Brazil," *Los Angeles Weekly*, February 21-27, 2003; see http://www.laweekly.com/ink/03/14.

8. Arundhati Roy, *Power Politics*, 2nd ed. (Cambridge, MA: South End Press, 2001), p. 4.

9. Edward W. Said, *Representations of the Intellectual: The 1993 Reith Lectures* (New York: Pantheon Books, 1994), pp. x, xiii-xvi. As he adds courageously (pp. xvii–xviii): "The romance, the interest, the challenge of intellectual life is to be found in dissent against the status quo at a time when the struggle on behalf of the under-represented and disadvantaged groups seems so unfairly weighted against them. . . . But there is no dodging the inescapable reality that such representations by intellec-tuals will neither make them friends in high places nor win them official honors. It is a lonely condition, yes, but it is always a better one than a gregarious tolerance for the way things are." Compare also Ian Maclean, Alan Montefiore, and Peter Winch, eds., *The Political Responsibility of Intellectuals* (Cambridge, UK: Cambridge University Press, 1990).

10. Roy, *Power Politics*, pp. 5-9; Said, *Representations of the Intellectual*, p. xiv.

11. Roy, *Power Politics*, pp. 11-12.

12. Interview with David Barsamian, *The Progressive Magazine*, April 2001; see http://www.progressive.org/intv0401.html.

13. Roy, *The Cost of Living*, pp. ix-x, 13.

14. Roy, *Power Politics*, p. 43. Compare also her comment in the same text (p. 50): "Essentially, privatization is a mutually profitable business contract between the private (preferably foreign) company or financial institution and the ruling elite of the third world"—where "ruling elite" is not synonymous with the democratically elected representatives of the state.

15. Roy, *Power Politics*, pp. 44, 53-55. As she adds (p. 55): "The project's gross profits work out to between twelve and fourteen billion dollars. The official return on equity is more than thirty percent. That's almost double what Indian law and statutes permit in power projects."

16. Roy, *The Cost of Living*, pp. ix, 18-19, 21. Compare also her spirited comments on another facet of the Narmada project (p. 63): "The same political formation that plunged a whole nation into a bloody, medieval nightmare because it insisted on destroying an old mosque to dig up a nonexistent temple, thinks nothing of submerging a hallowed pilgrimage route and hundreds of temples that have been worshipped in for centuries. It thinks nothing of destroying the sacred hills and groves, the places of worship, the ancient homes of the gods and demons of the Adivasi."

17. Roy, *The Cost of Living*, pp. 94, 110, 123, 125. As Roy adds (pp. 125-126): "If you are religious, then remember that this bomb is Man's challenge to God. It is worded quite simply: *we have the power to destroy everything that You have created.* If you are not (religious), then look at it this way. This world of ours is four thousand six hundred million years old. It could end in an afternoon."

18. Roy, *The Cost of Living*, pp. 95-96, 99.

19. Roy, *The Cost of Living*, pp. 111-112.

20. Roy, "War is Peace," in *Power Politics*, pp. 126, 137, 140. See also Richard Falk, *The Great Terror War*.

21. See "Happiness is a Weapon," *Los Angeles Weekly*, February 21-27, 2003; also David Barsamian, "Arundhati Roy," in *The Progressive Magazine*, April 2001.

22. Roy, *Power Politics*, pp. 2-3, 20-21.

23. See Roy, *Power Politics*, pp. 128-129; *The Cost of Living*, p. 112.

24. Roy, *Power Politics*, pp. 118-119, 131, 138. Regarding the complicity between terrorism and "state terror," Roy insists (p. 130) that freedom-loving people do not have to choose between the Taliban and the U.S. government, between American hawks and the "mad mullahs": "All the beauty of human civilization—our art, our music, our literature—lies beyond these two fundamentalist, ideological poles." Regarding the danger of imperialism see also Roy's "Confronting Empire," in *War Talk* pp. 103-104. This is the address she delivered at the World Social Forum in Porto Allegre, Brazil, on January 27, 2003. For the text see *War Talk*, pp. 103-112.

25. Roy, *Power Politics*, pp. 31, 108; *The Cost of Living*, p. 109.

26. Roy, "Come September," Lensic Performing Arts Center, Santa Fe, New Mexico; see *War Talk*, p. 75. Compare also *The Cost of Living*, p. 123, and Jacques Derrida, *The Other Heading: Reflections on Today's Europe*, trans. Pascale-Anne Brault and Michael B. Naas (Bloomington, IN: Indiana University Press, 1992), p. 78.

Chapter Five

Speaking Truth to Power:
In Memory of Edward Said

At the dawn of Western civilization stands a figure that has never ceased to intrigue subsequent generations. As we know, Socrates was not an academic philosopher, but an ordinary person speaking to ordinary people in the marketplace. Yet, his way of being ordinary was extraordinary because he reminded people he met of their deeper potential, of the call of conscience waiting to be heard. He did not speak to people from above, from the height of superior knowledge as opposed to popular ignorance or prejudice. After he was condemned to death, he did not choose to leave his native place even when offered the chance—because he did not wish to become a mere outsider judging from afar. It is precisely through these local commitments that his life and death have acquired more-than-local significance: by bearing witness to the perennial demands of justice and truth, as opposed to oppressive political power. No doubt, power-holders have never been enamored with such witness; more often than not, they have sided with the Athenian jury or else manipulated "public opinion" to serve their needs. In our own time, manipulation has reached unprecedented degrees. Aided by the media and novel surveillance techniques, people even in nominally "free" societies are subjected to modes of thought control unimagined by George Orwell. Not surprisingly, the old slogans of "patriotism" and "national security" have emerged again as the great "silencers": that is, as weapons designed to silence dissent and the ability to "speak truth to power."

Here the example of the Athenian thinker acquires particular importance by showing the distance between the parochial chauvinism of power elites and the potential of a deeper loyalty or "patriotism": namely, loyalty to the voice of conscience which is the genuine "patrimony" of civilized communities. Fortunately, our time is not completely devoid of this patrimony or voices of dissent struggling to be heard even against great odds. Until his death in September of 2003, Edward Said was a beacon of constructive dissent and intellectual courage. To be sure, in an age of globalization, Edward Said's concrete loyalties could no longer be quite the same as those of the Athenian thinker. Given global dislocations and vast population shifts, his attachments had to be local-global, that is, navigate between local and global commitments. Throughout his life, his writings and actions remained faithful to his Palestinian background (he was born in Jerusalem in 1935); in fact, he served as one of the most eloquent and steadfast defenders of Palestinian rights through several decades. At the same time, as an emigrant to and later citizen of the United States, he assumed the difficult role of public intellectual in the broader (near-global) American context. In both dimensions or on both levels, Said exemplified the stance of responsible criticism, a stance prompting him with growing intensity to remind both his American hosts and his Palestinian friends of the nonnegotiable standards of justice and fairness. The following discussion can only convey glimpses of Said's lifework. Three aspects are singled out. First, attention is given to Said's own understanding of the role of the public intellectual or reflective critic in our time. Next, this role is projected onto a global scale, leading to an examination of Said's famous conception of "Orientalism" and of his broader views on North-South relations. Finally, an attempt will be made to probe Said's underlying philosophical guideposts or motivations, an attempt that in the end points back in the direction of Athens.

REPRESENTATIONS OF THE INTELLECTUAL

On numerous occasions, Said has commented on the role of public intellectuals in modern society; invariably, his comments bore clear overtones of self-scrutiny and self-reflection. The most sustained discussion of the topic can be found in his famous Reith Lectures delivered in London (for the BBC) in 1993. Titled "Representations of the Intellectual," the lectures offered both an overview of prevailing arguments and a forceful plea for a distinctive conception or role: that of the intellectual as social critic or (Socratic) gadfly bent on disturbing social prejudices, especially prejudices fostered by ruling power elites. As the opening pages unequivocally assert, the intellectual in his/her public role should be viewed as an "outsider," an "amateur," a "disturber of the status quo"—especially a disturber of the "stereotypes and reductive categories" circulating in society. In contrast to the host of apologists and sycophants readily recruited by ruling powers, genuine intellectuals in Said's view should be people willing "to question patriotic [or chauvinistic] nationalism, corporate thinking, and a sense of class, racial or gender privilege." In order to shoulder this task of questioning, intellectuals firmly need to cultivate a certain independence of mind and a distance from the pervasive contagion of power. It is this independence and distance that ultimately provide a warrant for the characterization of the intellectual "as exile and marginal, as amateur, and as the author of a language that tries to speak the truth to power."[1]

As Said knew well from personal experience, cultivating such independence involves risks and dangers—dangers that have been immensely increased during the past decade (and especially since September 11). In his prescient words: "Both in the West and the Arab world the fissure separating haves and have-nots deepens every day, and among intellectuals in power it brings out a smug heedlessness that is truly appalling." What is not quite clear from the passages cited so far is the meaning of such terms as "outsider" or "exile" and the corollary distinction between inside and outside. A central chapter of the published lectures deals precisely with this issue. The chapter juxtaposes two prominent conceptions of the intellectual's role: those formulated respectively by Antonio Gramsci and Julien Benda. For Gramsci, the preferred role was that of socially engaged and functioning individuals—what he called "organic intellectuals"—contrasted with socially aloof gurus or mandarins. As Said states: "Gramsci believed that organic intellectuals are actively involved in society, that is, they constantly struggle to change minds and expand markets"—a struggle distinguishing them from disengaged sages. On the other hand, Benda accentuated the role of socially disengaged guardians of higher wisdom, of "a tiny band of super gifted and morally endowed philosopher-kings who constitute the conscience of mankind." For Benda, real intellectuals necessarily constitute a tiny elite whose task it is to uphold "eternal standards of truth and justice that are precisely *not* of this world"—hence his designation of them as "clerics" (*clercs*). What troubled and upset Benda at the time of his writing—between the two World Wars—was the pliant surrender of intellectuals to the blandishments of mass ideologies or movements, that is, their abdication of moral authority to what he called "the organization of collective passions" such as sectarianism, mass sentiment, nationalist belligerence, and class interests.[2]

Said's own conception of the role of intellectuals does not coincide fully with either of the two prototypes. Basically, the issue for him was not whether intellectuals are socially embedded or disembedded, whether they are "inside" or "outside" the (social) world. Rather, the paramount question was *how* they are embedded or disembedded, that is, *how* they are in the world. Said's lectures indicate a certain distance from Gramsci's perspective—at least to the extent that the notion of "organic intellectuals" implies that they are fully embedded functionaries or mouthpieces of collective movements. This role dovetails too neatly with the recent upsurge of intellectuals as managers and bureaucrats in the so-called knowledge industries. At the same time, the lectures reveal a certain (qualified) sympathy for Benda's "uncompromising view" of the intellectual's mission. "There is no doubt in my mind," he writes, "that the image of a real intellectual as generally conceived by Benda remains an attractive and compelling one." What is particularly compelling is the refusal of Benda-style intellectuals to be co-opted or instrumentalized by nationalist, corporate, or religious power elites. As Said adds admiringly: deep in the "combative rhetoric" of Benda's work is to be found "this figure of the intellectual as a being set apart, someone able to speak the truth to power—a crusty, eloquent, fantastically courageous and angry individual for whom no worldly power is too big and imposing to be criticized and pointedly taken to task."[3]

Yet, despite these gestures of sympathy or solidarity, the difference cannot be overlooked. Said speaks at various points cryptically of Benda's "uncritical Platonism" and "quite impossible absolutism"; but the issue lies deeper. For, conceived as radically disengaged, how can intellectuals take a meaningful stand on anything? When speaking grandly about justice and truth, against whose injustice and untruth are they protesting? When speaking about oppression and domination, whose oppressive power and whose oppressed condition are they seeking to expose? The fact is that, thrown back upon themselves, mandarins tend to speak only for themselves (and have traditionally done so). It is here that Said's critically engaged perspective intervenes. In his view, intellectuals can surely not be mere social functionaries; but neither can they claim a special alibi. As he makes abundantly clear, public intellectuals must indeed uphold justice and truth; but in doing so, they necessarily take the side (reflectively) of those suffering from injustice and untruth, of the multitude of poor and marginalized people victimized by oppression. What this means is that the public intellectual stands at the cusp of inside and outside, of embeddednes and disembeddedness—but not in a neutral way, because the relation between the powerful and the powerless, the oppressors and the oppressed is never equal or in balance. As Said notes (echoing the "preferential option for the poor"): "There is no question in my mind that the intellectual belongs on the same side with the weak and unrepresented." And here is a passage in the same chapter of the text that deserves to be lifted up at length:

> The central fact for me is, I think, that the intellectual is an individual endowed with a faculty for representing, embodying, articulating a message, a view, an attitude, philosophy or opinion to, as well as for, a public. And this role has an edge to it, and cannot be played without a sense of being someone whose place it is publicly to raise embarrassing questions, to confront orthodoxy and dogma (rather than produce them), to be someone who cannot easily be co-opted by governments and corporations, and whose *raison d'être* is to represent all those people and issues that are routinely forgotten or swept under the rug.[4]

These observations are directly pertinent to Said's own public role—and especially his role as an expatriate Palestinian intellectual. As indicated before, Said at no point denies the intellectual's contextual embeddedness. "All of us live in a society," he writes, "and are members of a nationality with its own language, tradition, historical situation." Born into a distinct language every intellectual (just like other people) for the most part "spends the rest of his or her life in that language which is the principal medium of intellectual activity." However, what needs to be noticed—and what is crucial for critical intervention—is the fact that language communities are not monolithic blocs but rather complex fabrics exhibiting multiple strands and internal rifts. Partly due to social inertia, language communities over time tend to foster certain "habits of expression" which, supported by ruling elites, function to insure conformism and preserve the status quo. Said approvingly cites George Orwell to the effect that dominant political languages are designed "to make lies sound truthful and murder respectable, and to give an appearance of solidity to pure wind." A main ambition of dominant "habits of expression" is to excise internal dissent or contestation and to inculcate a pliant consensus. Said gives an example from the first Gulf War—but his comments are even more pertinent in our post-September 11 situation. "During the Gulf War," he states, "public discussion of the crisis, especially on television but also in print journalism, assumed the existence of a national 'we'—which was repeated by reporters, military personnel, and ordinary citizens alike, such as 'when are *we* going to begin the ground war,' or 'have *we* incurred any casualties?'" Critical intellectuals here have to be on their guard and resist being co-opted by power elites; they need to decide whether to support "the weaker, the less well represented, the forgotten or ignored" or to side with the powerful—remembering Walter Benjamin's words: "Whoever has emerged victorious participates to this day in the triumphal procession in which the present rulers step over those who are lying prostrate."[5]

Celebration of a triumphal "we" readily gives rise to Manicheism: to the polarization between "us" and "them" and the demonization of "them" (or the other). In recent Western opinion, "them" has tended to be identified with "Islam"—neglecting the inner diversity and multiplicity of the Islamic world. For, as Said states, Islam is after all "a religion and culture, both of them composite and very far from monolithic." Neglect of internal diversity, however, is not only the hallmark of Western media, but frequently also of Muslim leaders—especially leaders of so-called fundamentalist or militant movements. Here too, critical intellectuals need to remonstrate. Especially in countries where Islam is the faith of the vast majority, Said observes, the job of the intellectual is not simply "to go in for choruses praising Islam," but rather to introduce into the din some sober reminders: first of all, an interpretation of

Islam stressing "its complex, heterodox nature," and secondly, the demand addressed to Islamic authorities "to face the challenges of non-Islamic minorities, women's rights, of modernity itself, with humane attentiveness and honest reappraisals, not dogmatic or pseudo-populist chants." To be sure, in crisis situations when entire Muslim populations are oppressed and threatened with political and even physical extinction, intellectuals need to remember their own embeddedness and come to the defense of the persecuted (as Frantz Fanon did during the Algerian war of liberation). Yet, even in these cases, intellectuals need to remain soberly responsible: instead of fanning populist passions, they need to remind people that the goal is not simply to replace foreign with native oppression, but rather to open up new spaces for living (in Aimé Césaire's terms: for "the invention of new souls"). Echoing Fanon and Césaire, Said pens this memorable passage: although it is important for intellectuals to support their community's struggle during crisis times,

> loyalty to the group's fight for survival cannot draw in the intellectual so far as to narcotize the critical sense, or reduce its imperatives, which are always to go beyond survival to questions of political liberation, to critiques of the leadership, to presenting alternatives that are too often marginalized or pushed aside as irrelevant to the main battle at hand.[6]

One would only wish that a similar sobriety were exemplified by intellectuals on different sides of the battle line. In fact, one would wish that the number of critical intellectuals were not in such dismally short supply around the world. In the concluding chapters of his text, Said reflects on this plight and its significance particularly for Western society. Concurring with Russell Jacoby, he notes that public or "nonacademic" intellectuals have for all practical purposes disappeared in America, leaving in their place nothing "except a whole bunch of timid and jargon-ridden university dons, to whom no one in society pays very much attention." In contrast to an earlier generation of writers and thinkers, concentrated mostly in New York's Greenwich Village, all one finds today is an array of mandarins—chiefly of "closeted literature professors with a secure income and no interest in dealing with the world outside the classroom." To the extent that intellectuals still enter the public domain, they tend to be either social functionaries (employed by the media) or else "neoconservative" acolytes of the powers-that-be. To underscore the retreat into ivory-tower academicism, Said introduces the distinction between "professionals" and "amateurs" (the latter term here meaning lovers of ideas and their public display and discussion). "By professionalism," he writes, "I mean thinking of your work as something you do for a living, between the hours of nine and five with one eye on the clock, and another cocked at what is considered to be proper, professional behavior"—that is, "not rocking the boat" but rather "making yourself marketable and above all, presentable, hence un-controversial and unpolitical and 'objective.'" By contrast, "amateurism" in-volves the desire "to be moved not by profit or reward but by love for and un-quenchable interest in the larger picture, in making connections across lines and barriers, in refusing to be tied down to a specialty, in caring for ideas and values despite the restrictions of a profession."[7]

The pertinence of Said's distinction must be obvious to anyone teaching or studying in American (and for that matter European) universities today. Everywhere—in public as well as private educational institutions—one finds the relentless ascendancy of "professionalism," coupled with growing bureau-cratization and the rise of corporate business standards. Said lists several fac-tors which contribute to this development. One is the growing compartmen-talization of knowledge, that is, the increasing specialization of academic inquiry. "The higher one goes in the education system today," he writes, "the more one is limited to a relatively narrow area of knowledge." Inevitably con-nected with this trend is the sidelining of broader, possibly disturbing ques-tions and the steady confinement of the specialist within a rigid type of "methodism" (evident in the sway of impersonal theories and methodologies). Another inevitable corollary is the cult of "expertise" or the certified expert whose professional pronouncements are liable (and meant) to silence or dele-gitimize "unprofessional" public dissent or contestation. This silencing brings into view the most salient feature of the discussed change: the drift toward ap-athetic conformism, toward pliant submission to ruling powers in the name of nationalism or national security. Said reminds readers of "research" agendas like "Projet Camelot" (undertaken by social scientists for the Army beginning in 1964) and of a host of similar agendas supported by governmental agencies with the aim of promoting political, military, and economic objectives. For Said, all these enterprises are far removed from the genuine vocation of an "amateur" public intellectual whose activities and commitments are fueled "by care and affection rather than by profit and selfish, narrow specialization."[8]

ORIENTALISM AND BEYOND

One kind of professionalism or presumed expertise to which Said has devoted special attention throughout his career is the expert knowledge claimed by Western academics with regard to non-Western, especially Islamic, societies and cultures. As is well know, he has articulated his views on this topic under the broad label of "Orientalism." What has troubled him in this field is not ac-ademic inquiry or the desire to know as such; rather, the problem for him was the unequal or hegemonic structure of "Orientalist" discourse: the fact that—

following Bacon's equation of knowledge and power—Western academics assigned to themselves a superior vantage point and hence a kind of mastery over the Orient seen as a passive and backward subject matter. It was this kind of asymmetry which, in Said's view, called for the intervention of public intellectuals and their critical acumen. As he wrote in his introduction to his book (first published in 1978): Orientalism can be "analyzed as the corporate institution for dealing with the Orient—dealing with it by making statements about it, authorizing views of it, describing it, settling it, ruling over it: in short, Orientalism as a Western style for dominating, restructuring, and having authority over the Orient." As an academic expertise, Orientalist discourse has always been closely connected with real political modes of domination. As Lord Curzon remarked at the establishment (in 1909) of the school of Oriental Studies in London: such studies are "an imperial obligation . . . part of the necessary furniture of Empire." In more lofty terms, Lord Balfour roughly at the same time justified Britain's imperial presence in Egypt as part of the West's civilizing mission, based on superior knowledge, maturity, and expertise: "We are in Egypt not merely for the sake of the Egyptians, though we are there for their sake; we are there also for the sake of Europe at large."[9]

This is not the place to review in detail the many historical analyses and observations contained in Said's study—something which has been done extensively in the literature. Still, looking at the book in retrospect or by hindsight, one cannot fail to be struck by the perceptive and uncannily prescient comments offered in its concluding section titled "Orientalism Now." As Said recognizes there, Orientalism in its traditional, mainly European form has passed from the scene; but this has not put an end to the old knowledge-power equation: a new kind of asymmetry or East-West hegemony has come to hold sway. "France and Britain no longer occupy center stage in world politics," he writes; "the American imperium has displaced them. A vast web of interests now links all parts of the former colonial world to the United States, just as a proliferation of academic subspecialties divides (and yet connects) all the former philological and European-based disciplines like Orientalism." The main innovation introduced by American-style Orientalism is a shift from philological and literary concerns to a focus on social science and administrative management; as a result, it is the social scientist and managerial expert on whose shoulders the "mantle of Orientalism" has come to rest. As in previous periods, expertise is again closely connected with strategic policy objectives, now on a global scale. Partly for geopolitical and partly for religious reasons, Orientalist discourse in the post-Cold War period tends to give primacy to Islam and the Arab world—and usually in hostile or derogatory terms. In fact, Said notes, hosts of books and articles are published "that represent absolutely no change over the virulent anti-Islamic polemics of the Middle Ages and the Renaissance." Despite various changes in accent, the "principal dogmas" of traditional Orientalism still persist, and particularly in studies dealing with the Near East. Among these dogmas is the presumed difference between the West that is "rational, developed, humane, superior," and the Orient which is "aberrant, undeveloped, inferior." A close corollary is the idea that the Orient is incapable of knowing or defining itself, hence requires Western managerial expertise—a view linked with the further dogma that the Orient is "at bottom something to be feared" (the Yellow Peril, the Mongols, terrorism) or "to be controlled" (through conquest, pacification, or occupation).[10]

Since the book's first publication, the issues raised in it have not come to rest; in fact, given the upsurge of neocolonialism and neoimperialism, the book's significance has increased over time. Unsurprisingly, its author felt compelled to revisit its issues repeatedly, for the sake of both clarifying and expanding his argument. An essay written half a decade later (in 1985), entitled "Orientalism Reconsidered," offered a response to some critical rejoinders while also profiling more clearly the basic thrust of the earlier study. As Said indicates, his original aim was to articulate a kind of "imaginative geography" by both tracing the line separating Orient from Occident and the multiple intrusions and collusions complicating their respective meanings. Appealing to Giambattista Vico's teachings, he insists that Orient and Occident are "facts produced by human beings" and hence must be studied as "integral components of the social, and not the divine or natural, world." The chief animus fueling the book, he confesses, was the pervasive structure of asymmetry and hegemony, a structure generating the need to speak truth to power. At its core, the challenge to Orientalism involved "a challenge to the muteness imposed upon the Orient as object." By operating as a "science of incorporation and inclusion," Orientalism functioned as "scientific [or academic] movement whose analogue in the world of politics was the Orient's colonial accumulation and acquisition by Europe." Regarding critical rejoinders, Said distances himself mainly from "nativist" readings—which view his text as an anti-Western tract promoting nativist nostalgia—and also from "nationalist" readings reducing the issue to a power-political contest. The essay is particularly careful in differentiating the critique of Orientalism from an uncritical endorsement of "Islamism" and everything done by Arabs or Muslims: "Far from being a defense either of the Arabs or of Islam—as my book was taken by many to be—my argument was that neither existed except as 'communities of interpretation' and that, like the Orient itself, each designation represented interests, claims, projects, ambitions, and rhetorics" which need to be carefully scrutinized by applying "methodological vigilance."[11]

Diffuse and impressionistic in character, the essay could not, and did not, constitute the author's last word. Barely a decade later, Said added an "Afterword" to his study, which was at pains to elucidate more fully its central objective and to ward off misreadings. A crucial point is again the power differential and the obfuscation of this difference by Orientalist discourse. "My [enduring] objection" to Orientalism, Said observes, is not that it is "just the antiquarian study" of Oriental languages and cultures, but that "as a system of thought" it approaches a heterogeneous and complex human reality from an "uncritically essentialist standpoint," and moreover from a supposedly superior standpoint. This approach disregards historical change and, more importantly, it "hides the *interests* of the Orientalist"—for, despite the distinction between scholarship and politics, these interests can never be fully detached "from the general imperial context that begins its modern global phase with Napoleon's invasion of Egypt in 1798." As Said recognizes, in light of the immense power differential, his book was often perceived as, and indeed constituted to some extent, "a kind of testimonial to subaltern status," to "the wretched of the earth talking back." Expressed differently, it represented "a sort of testament of wounds and a record of sufferings, the recital of which was felt as a long overdue striking back at the West." While remonstrating against a reductively political (and especially anti-Western) reading, he does not disown certain agonistic political overtones. Against its long confinement to a professional specialty, the afterword states, I have tried to show the application and existence of Orientalism "in the general culture, in literature, in ideology, and social as well as political attitudes." Without in any way claiming that Orientalism is "evil or sloppy" in every instance, "I do say that the *guild* of Orientalists has a specific history of complicity with imperial power, which it would be Panglossian to call irrelevant."[12]

Yet, despite these agonistic overtones, the afterword is emphatic in rejecting narrowly polemical construals. The chief edge of the afterword is directed against "essentializing" and polarizing interpretations, which would approximate *Orientalism* to Samuel Huntington's "clash of civilizations" scenario. As Said insists, this reading ignores the pervasive "anti-essentialism of my arguments," the fact that the book was meant to be "a study in critique, not an affirmation of warring and hopelessly antithetical identities." Although allowing the subaltern to speak, he adds, "I never felt that I was perpetuating the hostility between two rival political and cultural monolithic blocs, whose construction I was describing and whose terrible effects I was trying to reduce." More specifically, the book's intent was thoroughly misconstrued if it was read as an assault on the Occident and a simplistic apology for "Islamism or Muslim fundamentalism." As on previous occasions, Said is eloquent in refuting this charge. *Orientalism*, he writes, is "mistakenly read as a surreptitiously anti-Western work," a work that seeks to elevate "the image of an innocent and aggrieved Islam." Skeptical about all categorical designations, he adds, the book was in fact "painstakingly careful about *not* 'defending' or even discussing the Orient and Islam." Despite egregious misrepresentations, penned both by Zionists and radical Arabs, the book's point was not to substitute for an arrogant Orientalist discourse an equally arrogant and aggressive nativism: "The picture of Islam that I represented was not one of assertive discourse and dogmatic orthodoxy, but was based instead on the idea that communities of interpretation exist within and outside the Islamic world, communicating with each other in a dialogue of equals." With regard to the raging conflict in the Middle East, this means "only a negotiated settlement between the two communities of suffering, Arab and Jewish, would provide respite from the unending war."[13]

As we all know, this respite has not happened. On the contrary, the failure of the Oslo peace process and the outbreak of the second intifada have intensified the Middle East conflict—an intensification further compounded by September 11 and the war on Iraq. In the midst of this turmoil, in 2003, Said wrote a new preface to the twenty-fifth anniversary edition of *Orientalism*. As the preface observes somberly, political conditions in the world, and especially in the Near East, have steadily gone from bad to worse during the last quarter century. On the heels of suicide bombings and collective reprisals "the illegal and unsanctioned invasion and occupation of Iraq by Britain and the United States" has taken place, "with a prospect of physical ravagement, political unrest, and more invasions that are truly awful to contemplate." Events of this kind seem to vindicate Huntington's cultural logic—a logic "unending, implacable, irremediable." To make things worse, American-style Orientalists or neo-Orientalists have exerted a powerful influence on American foreign policy by deliberately fostering a climate of "culture clash" and Islamophobia, premised on "such preposterous phenomena as the 'Arab mind' and centuries-old Islamic decline that only American power could reverse." In Said's account, the effectiveness of this neo-Orientalist discourse must not be underestimated; in collusion with government and media it has successfully accomplished the "demonization" of a large part of humanity. Remonstrating firmly against this propaganda, the preface draws this lesson: "Without a well-organized sense that these people over there were not like 'us' and did not appreciate 'our' values—the very core of traditional Orientalist dogma as I describe its creation and circulation in this book—there would have been no war."[14]

As on previous occasions, critique of American Orientalism and foreign policy does not translate into an endorsement of anti-Westernism or a simplistic "Islamism." The preface wishes to have no truck with "an easy anti-Americanism that shows little understanding of what the United States is really like as a society." It also wants to have no truck with nostalgic complacency and a retrograde traditionalism that turns a blind eye to forms of domestic oppression, exploitation, and corruption. In many parts of the Muslim world, Said complains pointedly, constructive agendas of social and political regeneration have been overtaken "by failure and frustration" as well as "by an Islamism built out of rote learning, the obliteration of what are perceived to be other, competitive forms of secular knowledge, and an inability to analyze and exchange ideas within the generally discordant world of modern discourse." One of the most disabling features plaguing the Muslim world, in terms of the preface, is the suppression of religious freedom and freedom of conscience by self-appointed clerical elites, a suppression going hand in hand with the denial of the right to interpret scripture (*ijtihad*) granted in earlier times. "The gradual disappearance of the extraordinary tradition of Islamic *ijtihad*," Said states, "has been one of the major cultural disasters of our time, with the result that critical thinking and individual wrestling with the problems of the modern world have simply dropped out of sight. Orthodoxy and dogma rule instead."[15]

In boldly rebuking both Western-Orientalist arrogance and self-centered nativist *ressentiment*, Said clearly displays his mettle as a public intellectual willing to unsettle both deeply engrained cultural stereotypes and political animosities. In eloquent language, the preface of 2003 pinpoints the basic gist of Said's work as articulated in *Orientalism* and beyond. "My idea in *Orientalism*," we read, "is to use humanistic critique to open up the fields of struggle, to introduce a longer sequence of thought and analysis to replace the short bursts of polemical, thought-stopping fury that so imprison us in labels and antagonistic debate." In appealing to "humanistic critique," the preface aligns itself explicitly with the tradition of "humanism" and the cultivation of the "humanities." As one should note, however, "humanism" in Said's usage is far removed from human self-glorification or a myopic egocentrism. "By humanism," he writes, "I mean first of all attempting to dissolve Blake's mind-forged manacles so as to be able to use one's mind historically and rationally for the purposes of reflective understanding and genuine disclosure." More pointedly, affirming humanism involves an exit from self-enclosure in favor of fostering "a sense of community with other interpreters and other societies and periods"—which means, in the end, that "there is no such thing as an isolated [or unilateral] humanist." In application to the contemporary global situation, and especially the raging conflict in the Near East, a humanist perspective implies a basic change of direction: away from mayhem and destructiveness toward a recognition of mutual dependency and responsibility. In Said's words:

> The point I want to conclude with now is to insist that the terrible reductive conflicts that herd people under falsely unifying rubrics like "America," "the West,"

or "Islam" and invent collective identities for large numbers of individuals who are actually quite diverse, cannot remain as potent as they are, and must be opposed, their murderous effectiveness vastly reduced in influence and mobilizing power. . . . Rather than the manufactured clash of civilizations, we need to concentrate on the slow working together of cultures that overlap, borrow from each other, and live together in far more interesting ways than any abridged or inauthentic mode of understanding can allow.[16]

HUMANISM AND POWER

Written a few months before his death, the preface of 2003 in many ways brings together crucial themes pervading Said's entire sprawling opus. Apart from addressing concrete topics relating to the global North-South conflict (as reflected especially in the Near East), the preface also points up deeper theoretical and philosophical issues sheltered behind the glare of daily news items. A central philosophical issue concerns the relation between truth and power and the meaning of the motto "speaking truth to power"—a motto that has been the guiding motif of Said's work from beginning to end. Several alternatives present themselves. Is truth a superior wisdom removed from worldly contests, an esoteric kind of knowledge entrusted to a select group of mandarins? Or is truth a kind of counterforce or counterpower, a weapon wielded by subalterns in defiance of ruling power elites? Or else, finally, is truth a kind of transformative agency, a peculiar possibility or potency—a power/nonpower—slumbering in power relations reminding contestants of the "truth" of their relationship: which is the truth of mutuality or mutual recognition? This last alternative seems to be implied in the preface's assertion "that every human domain is linked to every other one, and that nothing that goes on in our world has ever been isolated and pure of any outside influence."[17]

Closely connected with the power-truth (or power-knowledge) nexus are a number of other issues having to do with the meaning of human agency, of social identity formation, and of history or historical change. Needless to say, these are difficult questions, and in tackling them, Said had to struggle to find his bearings. As it seems to me, it is possible to detect in his writings a subtle learning process, involving a shift from an earlier preoccupation with power and power contestation toward a steadily deepening appreciation of mutuality and humanistic understanding as an antidote to conflict. The early preoccupation with power and power conflicts is evident, to some degree, in the original version of *Orientalism*: in its emphasis on the sheer power differential between Orientalist discourse and the Orient as subject matter, between imperial imposition and subaltern subjection, and also in the accent on purely "strategic" forms of reading whereby texts are said to acquire "mass, density, and referential power."[18] The preoccupation is more clearly visible in the book *Covering Islam* (published a few years later), and especially in its chapter titled "Knowledge and Power." In discussing the role of interpretation, especially regarding Islamic societies, the chapter asks rhetorically: "What is it that makes a topic of interest out of what might otherwise be an academic or antiquarian concern if not power and will, both of which in Western society (as in all others in differing degrees) tend to be organized, to be capable of certain kinds of implementation?" Elaborating on this point, Said notes that interpretation always depends on "who the interpreter is, who he or she is addressing, what his or her purpose is in interpreting, at what historical moment the interpretation takes place"—all of which is unexceptionable except for the added statement that interpretation "acquires the status of knowledge by various means, some of them intellectual, many of them social and political" and that interpreting is "first of all a form of making: that is, it depends on the willed intentional activity of the human mind, molding and forming the objects of its attention with care and study." The upshot of this statement is that it is ultimately "this conscious willed effort of overcoming distances and cultural barriers that makes knowledge of other societies and cultures possible."[19]

The accent on "willed" (unilateral) interpretation finds a close parallel in the discussion of identity formation and historical change. With regard to the latter, Said is fond of invoking the testimony of Vico, as found especially in his *New Science*. The "Introduction" to *Orientalism* states expressly: "we must take seriously Vico's great observation that men make their own history, that what they can know is what they have made." The invocation is repeated in the "Afterword" of 1994, which declares it to be "the central point of all this" that "as Vico taught us, human history is made by human beings" and that, "as the struggle for control over territory is part of that history, so too is the struggle over historical and social meaning." What is neglected or deemphasized here is that, for Vico, "men" not only "make" history, but are in turn also shaped and molded by the latter as part of what he called the "*corsi e recorsi*" of the "world of nations." From the making or fabrication of history it is only a short step to the fabrication of the agents of historical change, that is, to the idea of constructed social identities. Building on earlier comments, the "Afterward" asserts unequivocally that "human identity is not only not natural and stable, but constructed and occasionally even invented outright." As Said adds, identity formation is inevitably agonistic or antagonistic, for the notion of self-identity involves "the construction of opposites and 'others' whose actuality is always subject to the continuous interpretation and reinterpretation of their differences from us." Hence, "each age and society recreates its 'Others.'" What aggravates matters is that identity constructions are not merely "mental processes" but "urgent social contests" involving concrete political issues. In short, the afterword affirms, identity construction is "bound up with the disposition of power and powerlessness, and is therefore anything but mere academic woolgathering."[20]

Little reflection is required to perceive the difficulty of this view: taken literally, it jeopardizes the entire undertaking of *Orientalism*. For, if others' identities are always and inevitably constructed at will, how could one possibly take exception to the Orientialists' hateful and pejorative construction of the Orient? What alternative would have been available to them? It is with respect to all these related issues that Said's later work, and especially this 2003 preface, show signs of considerable seasoning and deepened circumspection. The preface complains sharply about the blatant constructivism of American neo-Orientalists and their presumed expertise. The present and future lives of entire populations, Said notes, are redesigned in American think tanks thousands of miles away from their fields of application. With "breathtaking insouciance" hosts of experts and "jejune publicists" who have "no live notion" of the language of people on the ground proceed to fabricate "an arid landscape ready for American power to construct an *ersatz* model of free market 'democracy.'" The critique of identity fabrication is accompanied by a rethinking of historical change, away from simple "making" in the direction of a greater appreciation of memory work. "What our leaders and their intellectual lackeys seem incapable of understanding," the preface observes, "is that history cannot be swept clean like a blackboard, clean so that 'we' might inscribe our own future there and impose our own forms of life for these lesser people to follow." What is repressed or mutilated in these hegemonic erasures, in these imperial strategies of "changing the map" of regions, are "the uncountable sediments of history, which include innumerable histories and a dizzying variety of peoples, languages, experiences, and cultures."[21]

Perhaps the most significant marks of seasoning concern the relation between interpretation and domination or between humanism and power. The preface draws a clear line between unilateral and dialogical (or hermeneutical) modes of reading. There is a difference, we read, between "knowledge of other peoples and other times that is the result of understanding, compassion, careful study and analysis for their own sakes," and on the other hand, "knowledge—if that is what it is—that is part of an overall campaign of self-affirmation, belligerency, and outright war." Basically, what surfaces in this contrast is the distinction between "the will to understand for purposes of co-existence and humanistic enlargement of horizons" and "the will to dominate for purposes of control and external dominion." It is precisely this distinction which enables a humanistic scholar and public intellectual to "speak truth to power" by reminding it of a different possibility. As one should note, the turn to humanism and dialogical understanding does not mean a neglect of domination and hegemonic power differentials. The important thing is that one should not just "speak power to power" but rather appeal to the horizon of an enabling and possibly transformative truth. Here is a remarkable passage where Said brings together the demand of humanism and the critique of domination. Adopting a humanist perspective, he writes,

> is not to say that we cannot speak about issues of injustice and suffering, but that we need to do so always within a context that is amply situated in history, culture, and socioeconomic reality. Our role is to widen the field of discussion, not to set limits in accord with the prevailing authority. I have spent a great deal of my life during the past thirty-five years advocating the rights of the Palestinian people to national self-determination, but I have always tried to do that with full attention paid to the reality of the Jewish people and what they suffered by the way of persecution and genocide. The paramount thing is that the struggle for equality in Palestine/Israel should be directed toward a humane goal, that is, co-existence, and not further suppression and denial.[22]

In a telling fashion, the discussed change of accents is revealed also in a subtle modification of chosen mentors. Said's early work showed a preference for agonistic writers emphasizing sociopolitical struggle and conflict. In his own account, the original version of *Orientalism* bore the strong imprint of Gramsci and Michel Foucault; it was particularly Foucault's notion of "discourse" (as articulated in *Discipline and Punish* and other writings) that was used in order "to identify Orientalism."[23] Without ever being fully eclipsed or replaced, these mentors over the years were supplemented by, or made room for, a host of more "humanistic" writers whose common field of endeavor was the cultivation of philology, literature, and the "humanities." The 2003 preface refers explicitly to this "alternative" inspiration. Most prominent among the listed mentors is a string of German authors and thinkers, starting with Johann Gottfried Herder and later followed "by Goethe, Humboldt, Dilthey, Nietzsche, Gadamer" and still later by "the great twentieth-century Romance philologists Erich Auerbach, Leo Spitzer, and Ernst Robert Curtius." Auerbach's book *Mimesis*—published in 1946 and written while he was in wartime exile—is singled out as "a testament to the diversity and concreteness of the reality represented in Western literature from Homer to Virginia Woolf." A particularly glowing tribute, however, is paid in the preface to Goethe, especially his genuine interest in Islamic poetry (evident in the composition of *West-Östlicher Diwan*) and his later ideas about "*Weltliteratur*" (world literature) meaning the study of all the literatures of the world as a symphonic whole while preserving the individuality of each work. *Weltliteratur* for Goethe, Said comments, involved "a profound humanistic spirit deployed with generosity and, if I may use the word, hospitality. Thus the interpreter's mind actively makes a place in it for a foreign Other."[24]

To be sure, Said's set of mentors is not limited to German authors but, in truly cosmopolitan fashion, ranges from America and Europe to Africa, the Near East, and Asia. Among French mentors, the preface might have included the philosopher-writer Maurice Merleau-Ponty for whom Said held a lifelong sympathy (even when not often mentioning his name). After all, there are remarkable affinities. Like Said, Merleau-Ponty was a public intellectual navigating a difficult course between mandarin aloofness and partisan conscription. At the onset of the Cold War, he wrote an important book on one of Said's central themes—the relation of truth and power—which warned against all kinds of false complicities while vindicating the integrity of intellectual engagement.[25] Early on in his career (in 1967), Said wrote an essay on the French thinker that celebrated him as exemplar of a whole generation of *engagé* writers. "Whether it calls itself Marxism, existentialism, or phenomenology," he states, "the thought of this period almost always concerns itself with *concrete situations* rather than abstractions, with precise methodology not universal principles." Seen from this existential-phenomenological angle, philosophy "ceases to be a privileged, professional activity to which only initiates are admitted" and emerges as a reflective undertaking available to all—for we are all "amateurs together, subjected to contingency, to the 'metamorphoses of fortune,' to 'facticity,' and to death." Sharing and deepening this perspective, Merleau-Ponty nurtured a strong dislike for mandarin philosophy that is "practiced as an elevated survey," preferring instead to investigate "man's preconscious history, his natal attachments to the world." The French thinker's central insight, Said adds, was "that we are in and of the world before we can think about it" and that it is only by taking seriously this involvement that we may be able to catch glimpses of truth.[26]

The tribute paid here to Merleau-Ponty points to a deeper affinity of which Said was perhaps only dimly aware and which touches the core of their respective endeavors. Throughout his life, Said was an *engagé* public intellectual rooted chiefly in literary sources; but the nature of his engagement resonated with the philosopher's distinctive quest. As an intellectual he was preeminently engaged in critique—but not in mandarin fashion judging from a presumed superior vista. His writings contain critical assessments—sometimes sharply worded—of both America or the "West" and of Arab or Muslim societies. But the point of his critiques was not to dismiss either side as hopelessly corrupt or depraved, but rather to trigger a reflective or transformative process—a process allowing each party to develop its better potential (or to become better themselves). In this respect, his critical distance was actually a mode of closeness or affiliation. These comments lead me back to the figure of Socrates—to whom Merleau-Ponty has devoted some of his most stirring pages. Viewed in the Socratic mold, Merleau-Ponty writes in his famous *Eloge de la philosophie*, philosophy is a "strange" enterprise and understands its own "strangeness"; for it is "never entirely in the world" (like a partisan doctrine) nor fully "outside the world" (as an esoteric privilege). When condemned by the Athenian jury, Socrates does not ridicule the city nor does he choose to abscond, but instead remains as a critical witness or teacher: "The same philosophy obliges him to appear before the judges and makes him different from them; the same freedom that brings him in their midst frees him from their prejudices." Thus, it is clear—Merleau-Ponty concludes—that philosophy "limps": for "it dwells in history and in life, but it wishes to dwell at their center, at the point where they come into being with the birth of meaning"—or the birth of truth.[27] These are lines Edward Said might have written.

NOTES

1. Said, *Representations of the Intellectual*, pp. x, xiii, xvi.

2. Said, *Representations of the Intellectual*, pp. xvii, 3-6. The chief references here are Antonio Gramsci, *The Prison Notebooks: Selections*, trans. Quintin Hoare and Geoffrey Nowell-Smith (New York: International Publishers, 1971), and Julien Benda, *The Treason of the Intellectuals*, trans. Richard Aldington (1928; repr. New York: Norton, 1969).

3. Said, *Representations of the Intellectual*, pp. 7-8.

4. Said, *Representations of the Intellectual*, pp. xiv, 6, 11, 22.

5. Said, *Representations of the Intellectual*, pp. xv, 27-29, 32-35. For the citation see Benjamin, *Illuminations*, pp. 255-256. For a more recent plea for national consensus see, e.g., Huntington, *Who Are We? The Challenges to America's National Identity*. In the post-September 11 climate in the United States, critical dissent tends to be labeled "extremist" if not "terrorist."

6. Said, *Representations of the Intellectual*, pp. 39-41.

7. Said, *Representations of the Intellectual*, pp. 70-71, 74, 76. See also Russell Jacoby, *The Last Intellectuals: American Culture in the Age of Academe* (New York: Basic Books, 1987).

8. Said, *Representations of the Intellectual*, pp. 76-77, 80-82. As he adds (pp. 86-87): "The intellectual, properly speaking, is not a functionary or an employee completely given up to the policy goals of a government or a large corporation, or even a guild of like-minded professionals. In such situations the temptations to turn off one's moral sense, or to think entirely from within the specialty, or to curtail skepticism in favor of conformity are far too great to be trusted." As an example of the cult of expertise, Said mentions the dominance of "development" experts in the social sciences during the

Cold War. During that period, he notes (p. 78), "the official American idea held that free-dom in the Third World meant simply freedom from communism: it reigned virtually unchallenged; and with it went the notion endlessly elaborated by legions of sociolo-gists, anthropologists, political scientists, and economists, that 'development' was non-ideological, derived from the West, and involved economic takeoff, modernization, an-ticommunism, and a devotion among some political leaders to formal alliances with the United States."

9. Edward W. Said, *Orientalism* (New York: Vintage House, 1979), pp. 3, 33. As Said elaborates (p. 32): "Knowledge to Balfour means surveying a civilization from its origins to its prime to its decline—and, of course, it means *beings able to do that* . . . To have such knowledge of such a thing is to dominate it, to have authority over it. And authority here means for 'us' to deny autonomy to 'it'—the Oriental country—since we know it and it exists, in a sense, *as* we know it." For the statement by Lord Curzon, see J. L. Methta, *Philosophy and Religion: Essays in Interpretation* (New Delhi: Indian Council of Philosophical Research and M. Manoharlal Publishers, 1990), p. 69.

10. Said, *Orientalism*, pp. 285, 287, 290, 300-301. Regarding the shift of Orien-talism from Europe to the United States, compare especially the book's sequel: Said's *Culture and Imperialism*.

11. Said, "Orientalism Reconsidered," in *Reflections on Exile and Other Essays* (Cambridge, MA: Harvard University Press, 2002), pp. 199, 201-203. The essay ap-peared first in *Race and Class* 27 (Fall 1985). Regarding the charges of anti-West-ernism and uncritical pro-Islamic bias, see especially Bernard Lewis, *The Muslim Discovery of Europe* (New York: W. W. Norton, 1982), and Daniel Pipes, *In the Path of God: Islam and Political Power* (New York: Basic Books, 1983). Compare also Lewis, *Islam and the West* (New York: Oxford University Press, 1993) and *The Cri-sis of Islam* (New York: Modern Library, 2003).

12. Said, "Afterword" in *Orientalism* (New York: Vintage Books, 1994), pp. 333, 335-336, 340-341.

13. Said, "Afterword," pp. 331, 334-335, 337-338. As he adds (p. 337): "Neither in this book, nor in the two that immediately followed it, *The Question of Palestine* (1980) and *Covering Islam* (1981), did I want only to suggest a political program of restored identity and resurgent nationalism." The reference is to *The Question of Palestine* (New York: Vintage Books, 1980), and *Covering Islam: How the Media and the Experts Determine How We See the Rest of the World* (New York: Pantheon Books, 1981). Samuel Huntington had presented his scenario a year before the After-word; see "The Clash of Civilizations?" *Foreign Affairs*, vol. 72 (Summer 1993), pp. 22-49.

14. Said, "Preface to the Twenty-Fifth Anniversary Edition," in *Orientalism* (New York: Vintage Books, 1994), pp. xvii-xviii, xx. As he adds sharply (pp. xxi, xxvi): "There always is a chorus of willing intellectuals to say calming words about benign or altruistic empires, as if one should not trust the evidence of one's eyes watching the destruction and the misery and death brought by the latest *mission civilisatrice* . . . Speaking both as an American and as an Arab, I must ask my reader not to underestimate the kind of simplified view of the world that a rel-

ative handful of Pentagon civilian elites have formulated for U.S. policy in the entire Arab and Islamic worlds, a view in which terror, preemptive war, and unilateral regime change—backed up by the most bloated military budget in history—are the main ideas debated endlessly and impoverishingly."

15. Said, "Preface," pp. xvii-xxviii.

16. Said, "Preface," pp. xxii-xxiii, xxviii-xxix. For a detailed defense of humanism see Said, *Humanism and Democratic Criticism* (New York: Columbia University Press, 2004), a text which goes back to a series of lectures held in 2000 and 2003 in New York and Cambridge, England, respectively.

17. Said, "Preface," p. xxiii. Truth in this last sense resonates, in my view, with Gandhi's notion of *"satya"* (and *satyagraha*) and also with Heidegger's notion of truth as *"aletheia."* The view of general interconnectedness is captured in the Buddhist notion of "dependent co-arising" (*pratitya samutpada*).

18. Said, *Orientalism*, p. 20.

19. Said, *Covering Islam*, pp. 155-156. What is problematic in these statements is not the concern with interpretation as such, but the emphasis on unilateral "will" and purpose. It is true that the chapter also lists as a condition of interpretive understanding that "the student must feel that he or she is answerable to and in uncoercive contact with the culture and the people being studied" (p. 155)—but the relation between this responsibility and interpretive will is not clarified. At an earlier point I remonstrated (gently, I believe) against a certain shortfall of hermeneutical reflection in Said's early work. See Dallmayr, "The Politics of Nonidentity: Adorno, Postmodernism, and Edward Said," in *Alternative Visions: Paths in the Global Village*, pp. 47-69.

20. Said, *Orientalism*, pp. 4-5, 331-332. Regarding Vico, see especially *The New Science of Giambattista Vico*, trans. Thomas G. Bergin and Max H. Fisch (Garden City, NY: Anchor Books, 1961), pp. 351-373.

21. Said, "Preface," pp. xviii-xix. As Said adds (p. xxi), the worst aspect of these policies is that "human suffering in all its density and pain is spirited away. Memory and with it the historical past are effaced in the common, dismissively contemptuous American phrase, 'you are history.'"

22. Said, "Preface," pp. xix, xxiii-xxiv.

23. Said, *Orientalism*, pp. 3, 14, 22. For a later attempt to distance himself somewhat from Foucault see, e.g., the interview of spring 1993 titled *"Orientalism and After,"* reprinted in *Power, Politics, and Culture: Interviews with Edward W. Said*, ed. Gauri Viswanathan (New York: Vintage Books, 2002), pp. 213-215. Compare also the memorial essay "Michel Foucault, 1927-1984," in *Reflections on Exile*, pp. 187-197.

24. Said, "Preface," pp. xxiv-xxv. Compare in this context Erich Auerbach, *Mimesis: The Representation of Reality in Western Literature*, trans. Willard R. Trask (Princeton: Princeton University Press, 1953); and regarding Goethe, my chapter "West-Eastern Divan: Goethe and Hafiz in Dialogue," in *Dialogue Among Civilizations: Some Exemplary Voices* (New York: Palgrave/Macmillan, 2002), pp. 147-65. Another German-language author greatly admired by Said was Theodor W. Adorno whom he describes at one point as "a forbidding but endlessly fascinating man, and

for me, the dominating intellectual conscience of the middle twentieth century." See Said, *Representations of the Intellectual*, p. 54.

25. Merleau-Ponty, *Humanism and Terror: An Essay on the Communist Problem.*

26. Said, "Labyrinth of Incarnations: The Essays of Maurice Merleau-Ponty," in *Reflections on Exile*, pp. 1-2, 4, 6.

27. Merleau-Ponty, *In Praise of Philosophy*, pp. 30, 37, 58. As he adds (p. 36): Socratic philosophy "does not exist as a sort of idol of which he would be the guardian and which he must defend. It exists rather in its living relevance to the Athenians, in its absent presence, in its obedience without respect."

Chapter Six

Critical Intellectuals in a Global Age: Toward a Global Public Sphere

(For Jacques Derrida)

So long as it remains true to itself, philosophy partakes in the lived experience of its time, including its traumas and agonies. Among the most prominent features of our age is the process of globalization, that is, the perceived shrinkage of the globe into a commonly shared space. Although acutely felt in the domains of economics and information technology, the significance of this process is not always sufficiently acknowledged by philosophers and social theorists. Sometimes geographical labels are attached to perspectives or schools of thought, like "Continental philosophy," "Frankfurt School," and so on—labels whose meaning is often belied by what is happening on the ground. Thus, travelers in distant lands may find there more vibrant resonances of "Continental" thought than can be found in Europe today, just as seminal ideas of the early "Frankfurt School" are sometimes more intensely discussed in Asia or Latin America than in their native city. This does not mean that European perspectives are simply disseminated across the world without reciprocity or reciprocal learning. Nor does it mean that local origins are simply erased in favor of a bland universalism (since local origins are often inscribed with concrete and singular sufferings). What it does mean is that landscapes and localities undergo symbolic metamorphoses, and that experiences once localized at a given place increasingly find echoes or resonance chambers among distant societies and peoples.

Symbolic migration today is characteristic of several intellectual or theoretical perspectives—including, perhaps most prominently, the perspective of "analytical" or "Anglo-American" philosophy (whose teachings sometimes exert hegemonic claims around the world). However, a similar outreach also marks Continental-European thought and social theory. No doubt, the latter perspective exhibits a great variety of distinct orientations and emphases. Yet, for purposes of the present discussion, I want to highlight what I consider the chief common traits of Continental-European thought as it developed (roughly) during the past century. As it seems to me, the central common trait of this thought—especially when compared with the "analytical" perspective—is its close attention to the theory-praxis connection, that is, the connection of thinking and doing. This entails an opposition to "pure" theory or a purely spectatorial theorizing which, aiming at objective knowledge, distances the spectator or analyst rigidly from the targets of his/her analysis. The basic underpinnings of this spectatorial approach can be found in the modern Cartesian worldview which, in separating subject and object (*cogito* and extended matter), provided the engine for the rise of modern science and technology (and generally the replacement of quality by quantity). The difference of outlooks has social implications: while spectatorial theory is congenial to, and favored by, people satisfied on the whole with "the way things are" and "the powers that be," practical theorizing appeals mainly to people alienated from the way of the world and bent on some kind of transformation. Seen in this light, Continental-European thought (in its different versions) has tended to be mostly critical and self-critical—by mounting a sustained critique of the modern cult of science, technology, and the market and, more broadly, of the "underside of modernity." In the following I shall first highlight the "critical" dimension pervading Continental-European thought in recent times. Next, I shall discuss parallel critical arguments advanced in the content of non-Western societies, with special attention to Indian social thought. In doing so, I follow in a way the lead of Ulrich Beck who, not long ago, called for "a new critical theory with a cosmopolitan intent."[1] By way of conclusion, I offer some comments on the prospects of a global critical theory and public sphere.

EUROPEAN CRITICAL THOUGHT

As indicated, Continental-European thought (as the term is used here) comprises a number of distinct strands. For present purposes I shall refer to three main perspectives: critical theory (Frankfurt School); phenomenology and hermeneutics (Freiburg School); and deconstruction (French School). Early critical theory provides us with a document that, in instructive fashion, highlights both the practical (or praxis-related) and critical dimensions of European thought of the period: Max Horkheimer's programmatic essay on "Traditional and Critical Theory" (of 1937). In this essay, Horkheimer sharply opposes to each other two kinds of theory: namely, "traditional" theory (corresponding to what I have called a purely spectatorial mode of theorizing) and a critical outlook steeped in practical social engagement. Following the

French philosopher of science, Henri Poincaré, Horkheimer defines the gist of traditional theory as "the sum total of propositions about a subject, the propositions being so linked with each other that a few are basic and the rest derive from these." The definition contains two components: the propositional and the factual. While the validity of such a theory depends on the correspondence of propositions with actual facts or states of affairs, the propositions themselves aim at the greatest possible parsimony and logical transparency. Following again Poincaré, Horkheimer adds that traditional (or scientifically verifiable) theory constitutes a matrix of "stored-up knowledge, put in a form that makes it useful for the closest possible description of facts." In line with the "unified science" movement popular at the time (and supported by Poincaré), the ultimate perfection of pure theory consists in a limited set of highly abstract propositions whose validity extends to the largest possible number of data, and in the end to all phenomena in the world: "The general goal of all theory is a universal systematic science, not limited to any particular subject matter but embracing all possible objects" (although we are still "rather far from such an ideal situation").[2]

As Horkheimer points out, the origins of this mode of theorizing are not of recent date but can be traced to "the beginnings of modern philosophy," and particularly to the Cartesian worldview with its division of subject and object, *cogito* and extended matter, where the former is placed in the analytical judgment seat. In accord with Descartes' conception of method, knowledge properly speaking resides in a set of "clear and distinct" ideas, linked together through chains of deductive reasoning, and ultimately translatable into mathematical formulas. Insofar as this conception of theory shows a tendency, the essay states, it is "toward a purely mathematical system of symbols"—a tendency which by logical necessity progresses from the natural sciences to the human and social sciences as well. In more recent times, the Cartesian worldview has been continued especially by positivists and logical positivists whose overall emphasis has been on transforming philosophy (or theorizing) into a "handmaiden" of science. Although more attentive to practical and social concerns, even the so-called pragmatists followed the positivist lead by construing praxis in a purely "instrumental" sense, thereby subjecting it to the efficiency criteria of existing society. What persists from Descartes to positivism and pragmatism is the predominance of the Cartesian paradigm (with its "dualism of thought and being"), which assigns to the theorizing scholar an extramundane or purely spectatorial position—although this position on closer inspection turns out to be illusory. For, no matter how "independent" and "detached" the expert's knowledge may claim to be, the scholar and his/her theorizing remain "incorporated into the [existing] apparatus of society." To this extent, the scholar's achievements and "original" contributions are "a factor in the conservation and continuous renewal of the existing state of affairs, no matter what fine names s/he gives to what s/he does."[3]

By contrast to this spectatorial outlook, "critical" theorizing presupposes the participatory engagement of the theorist in his world. In Horkheimer's account, the task of critical intellectuals is not to be pliantly supportive of an existing state of affairs, but to problematize and call into question this state from an existential and normative angle; hence, the relation between such intellectuals and their society is necessarily "marked by tension" and this tension characterizes "all the concepts of the critical mode of thinking." Given its accent on participatory engagement, critical theorizing clearly departs from the Cartesian worldview with its separation of *cogito* and nature, observer and target of analysis. In the words of the essay: "The inability to grasp in thought the unity of theory and praxis, and the limitation of the concept of necessity to inevitable [causal] events are both due, from the epistemological viewpoint, to the Cartesian dualism of thought and being"—a dualism which is "congenial both to nature and to bourgeois society insofar as the latter resembles a natural mechanism." In the traditional mode of theorizing—this is for Horkheimer the "decisive" point—the targets of analysis are not at all affected by the theorist's endeavors, nor are these endeavors in turn affected by, or responsive to, dilemmas in the "external world." Being a part of the prevailing "mode of production," the traditional mainstream scholar simply registers and acknowledges existing social conditions (which seem to be ineluctable like forces of nature) without taking a stand. Critical intellectuals are unable to operate in this fashion. In their case, theorizing responds to and inserts itself in the ongoing dilemmas and agonies of social life, from a practical and normative perspective. Simply put: "Critical theory of society is, in its totality, the unfolding of a single existential judgment."[4]

The notion of an "existential judgment" brings into view the conception of a social ethics that is not purely cognitive but rooted in historical experience—without being merely subjective or arbitrary. Proceeding from a broadly Marxian vantage, Horkheimer sees modern Western history as exhibiting a dialectic of progress and regress, of growing emancipation and domination. As he writes, the kind of commodity economy on which modern history rests "contains in itself all the internal and external tensions of the modern era; it generates these tensions in an increasingly heightened form, and after a period of progress . . . [may drive] humanity into a new barbarism." Deviating from even a nonorthodox Marxian ideology, Horkheimer does not find any historical assurance that the decline into barbarism can be averted—except for the efforts of resistance on the part of critical intellectuals who at all times are in short supply. "The idea of a transformed society," he writes soberly, "does not have the advantage of widespread acceptance."

In the general course of events, "truth [meaning: existential-ethical truth] may reside with numerically small groups of people." Yet, he adds, "history teaches us that such groups, hardly noticed even by those opposed to the status quo, outlawed but imperturbable, may at the decisive moment become the leaders because of their deeper insight." Returning to the notion of existential judgment, Horkheimer concludes his essay by stressing the crucial importance of such judgment whose place cannot be usurped by pure theory, formal logic, or mathematical algorithms: For all its insight into social life and social change

> critical theory has no specific influence on its side, except the abolition of social injustice. This negative formulation, if we were to express it abstractly, is the materialist content of the idealist concept of reason.[5]

Despite a diversity of philosophical and political premises, many of the basic points of Horkheimer's essay find a parallel in both Continental phenomenology and deconstruction. A major affinity resides in the effort to overcome traditional "metaphysics" (or pure theory), and especially the predominance of the Cartesian egocentric worldview. In the latter respect, Edmund Husserl's lifework constitutes a crucial way station in the formation of contemporary Continental thought. From the time of his early writings, Husserl's central aim was to breach the Cartesian subject-object split through the accent on the "intentional" directedness of human consciousness, captured in the motto "to the things themselves" (*zu den Sachen*). Far from celebrating the pure self-confinement of reason in a kind of metaphysical narcissism, his practice of "phenomenology" urged reason to venture into the world of phenomena and to allow itself to be nurtured and enriched by this experience. To be sure, despite his principled remonstrations, Husserl's approach in many ways remained heir to the Cartesian (and neo-Kantian) paradigm—a fact evident in his attachment to "transcendental idealism" and his fondness for mathematical logic. Nevertheless, his later writings amply testify to his dissatisfaction with this legacy. A major text of that period is entitled *Cartesian Meditations*—a magisterial work showing the phenomenologist wrestling with the spirit (or ghost) of the Cartesian method. Still later, his disenchantment with positivism and logical empiricism led Husserl to launch a sustained assault on the rootlessness of the modern scientific enterprise, that is, its growing divorce from practical engagement and the concrete experiences of the social "life-world."[6]

Husserl's lifework was carried forward in novel directions by Martin Heidegger's "hermeneutical phenomenology" with its accent on "worldliness"—human existence being defined as "being-in-the-world"—and a further move away from metaphysical theorizing. In his *Being and Time* (of

1927), Heidegger offered a sustained critique of modern metaphysics, insisting on the implausibility or untenability of both the Cartesian *cogito* and Kant's transcendental consciousness. In turning to the linkage of "being" and "time," the text underscored the importance of the experience of finitude or mortality—stylized in the expression of "being-toward-death." At the same time, the central trademark of being human was shifted in the text from "reason" (or animal with reason, *animal rationale*) to the dimension of "care" (*Sorge*)—a shift that marks a decisive move from cognition to praxis. In fact, it is possible to argue that all of Heidegger's central terms—from "being" to language to "*Ereignis*"—should be seen not as nouns (amenable to pure theorizing) but as verbs calling for a transformative praxis. As in the case of Husserl, it is true that Heidegger himself did not always draw the required conclusions from his thought (and at least in one instance drew precisely the wrong conclusion). Nevertheless, the practical as well as critical-social implications of his work can hardly be denied. In terms of praxis-orientation, many observers have pointed to certain affinities with Aristotelian ethics as well as a certain noninstrumental form of pragmatism. As Lawrence Hatab observes correctly, for Heidegger human existence "*is*" what it *does*," disclosing itself in "its living dealings and movements"; to this extent, Heideggerian ethics is released from the subject-object and fact-value binaries of the Cartesian paradigm while approximating the Aristotelian notion of the self as "essentially an activity, not a static essence." In terms of social-historical critique, Heidegger's work is well known for its sharp denunciation of the modern cult of science and technology, especially the cult of giant control mechanisms (*Gestell*) from whose vantage human beings appear as mere cogs in a machine.[7]

The practical orientation of (Freiburg-style) Continental thought is even more pronounced in the case of Hans-Georg Gadamer whose "philosophical hermeneutics" is basically centered on engaged praxis—where the latter means an engagement with texts, with fellow-beings, and with social-historical constellations. As Gadamer notes in an essay specifically titled "Hermeneutics as Practical Philosophy," hermeneutics or the endeavor to make sense of texts and experiences is indeed "philosophical," but in the sense of what traditionally has been called "practical philosophy." This means that, seen as an ongoing effort to understand, hermeneutical interpretation cannot be stabilized in an abstract metaphysical system, nor can it be reduced to a mere technical skill or a mechanically applied recipe. Rather, given the variety of concrete contexts, understanding has to remain constantly open and responsive to situational challenges, precisely in the way of an engaged social praxis. In Gadamer's words, there is a "mutual implication" between understanding and practical action—and it was Aristotle who first thought through this implication "with complete lucidity" in his ethics with its central category of *phronesis*. This outlook stands again in complete contrast with the modern Cartesian worldview with its emphasis on spectatorship and the instrumental mastery of nature through technical fabrication or construction. This "ideal of technical production" implicit in the concept of mechanics, Gadamer states at another point, has had a triumphant ascendancy in modern times and has in fact "become an arm prolonged to monstrous proportions"—a development which has made possible "the nature of our machines, our transformation of nature, and our outreach into space" for purposes of planetary control. What is eclipsed and threatened with erasure in this development is the domain of practical engagement in collaborative understanding, that is, "the realm of all that transcends utility, usefulness, and instrumental calculation."[8]

The practical and social-critical components were further intensified in French existential phenomenology, particularly the writings of Jean-Paul Sartre and Maurice Merleau-Ponty. Especially memorable in the case of Sartre was his denunciation of orthodox Marxism—and of any comprehensive ideology—for celebrating an abstract "scholasticism of the totality," while neglecting the inevitably "heuristic" character of every inquiry and the praxis-orientation of social theorizing.[9] In the case of Merleau-Ponty, critique of dominant ideologies was from the beginning part and parcel of his "genetic" phenomenology (concerned with the "becoming" of phenomena) and extended from Communist to liberal political doctrines. His book *Humanism and Terror* (1947) contains this startling passage (whose relevance has only increased with time): "An aggressive liberalism exists which is a dogma and already an ideology of war. It can be recognized by its love for the empyrean of principles, its failure ever to mention the geographical and historical circumstances to which it owes its birth, and its abstract judgment of political systems without regard for the specific conditions under which they develop." Turning to the praxis-dimension of political life, the book added: "It is not just a question of knowing what the liberals have in *mind* but what in reality is *done* by the liberal state [or the state professing to defend freedom] within and beyond its borders" (italics added). For Merleau-Ponty, the relation to praxis was endemic not only to political thought but to philosophy in general—despite an acknowledged need to avoid narrow partisanship. Far from allowing the philosopher to abscond into an ivory tower, his *Éloge de la Philosophie* ascribed to theoretical reflection a practical task: "One must be able to withdraw and gain distance in order to become truly engaged, which is also, always, an engagement in the truth." Yet, "the very detachment of the philosopher assigns to him a certain kind of action among fellow men."

Here is a passage from the same text that eloquently captures the gist of critical Continental thought:

> At the conclusion of a reflection which at first isolates him, the philosopher, in order to experience more fully the ties of truth which bind him to the world and history, finds neither the depth of himself nor absolute knowledge, but a renewed image of the world and of himself placed within it among others.[10]

Despite a certain intellectual sea change—which happened around 1968—many of the discussed accents of hermeneutics and phenomenology continue to reverberate in late twentieth-century European thought, including French post-structuralism and deconstruction. To some extent, this persistence can even be detected in the writings of Jacques Derrida—a thinker whose work is often associated with radical rupture and a complete dismissal of social agency. What is correct about this reputation is Derrida's undeniable radicalization of the critique of the Cartesian *cogito* and his dismantling of human self-identity in favor of a resolute openness to the "Other's" initiative. Yet, precisely in light of this dismantling, a transformed kind of agency comes into view bent no longer on predatory mastery but on a generous hospitality toward others (akin to Heidegger's "letting be"). In his famous "Reflections on Today's Europe," Derrida urged Europeans (and people in the West more generally) to open themselves up to the rest of the world more hospitably than was the case in the past (when colonialism and "white man's burden" were the preferred policies). In the same text, he also encouraged liberal democrats, comfortably ensconced in "lands of the free," to ponder the possibility of a more generous mode of democratic life—what Derrida called a "democracy to come" or a "democracy that must have the structure of a promise" (thus cannot now be cognitively mapped or managed). For Derrida, the same openness or generosity is also the hallmark of philosophical thinking as such—a thinking that is neither the privilege of mandarins nor the monopoly of self-appointed experts but a general human birthright in need of practical cultivation. As he stated at one point (echoing Merleau-Ponty): "The right to philosophize becomes increasingly urgent," as does the call for philosophers to evaluate and critique perspectives that "in the name of a technical-economic-military positivism," tend to reduce the field and the chances of an "open and unrestricted philosophizing" both in colleges and in international life.[11]

NON-WESTERN CRITICAL THOUGHT

Derrida's call for a critical kind of theorizing or philosophizing—one opposed to the hegemonic "positivism" (in technological, military, and economic domains)—obviously is not restricted to the confines of Europe but has a "cosmopolitan intent." The French philosopher's cosmopolitan or cosmopolitical leanings are well known—having been voiced on numerous occasions, including his text *On Cosmopolitanism* (of 1997).[12] As it happens, his summons today finds echoes or resonances in many parts of the world, from Asia to Africa and Latin America. Actually, given the intrusive and oppressive effects of the reigning "positivism" in most non-Westerns societies, critical theorizing tends to be widespread and at a premium precisely in those parts of the world. In the following, I shall be able to give only a very limited sample of non-Western critical intellectuals voicing their opposition to mainstream positivism as well as to a purely spectatorial (and ethically irresponsible) mode of theorizing. In view of my own frequent and extended visits to India, I shall concentrate my discussion first on theoretical initiatives on the subcontinent, before extending my review to other parts of the world.

In postindependence India, the closest parallel to the outlook of the early Frankfurt School—as articulated in Horkheimer's programmatic essay—can be found in the Centre for the Study of Developing Societies (CSDS) operating in Delhi since 1963. In its structure and design, the Delhi Centre from the beginning resembled its German counterpart: particularly in its emphasis on interdisciplinary cooperation (comprising scholars from the humanities, the social sciences, and psychology) and its concerted effort to bridge the theory-praxis divide. As a result of its interdisciplinary character, studies sponsored or published by the Centre have dealt with a broad spectrum of topics ranging from the ethnic and social-psychological components of social change to problems of rural development and ethno-agriculture to the role of science and technology in the modern world. In terms of theoretical orientation, a primary role has always been played by Rajni Kothari, the initial founder and longtime director of the Centre.[13] Trained both in India and the West, Kothari has distinguished himself (like Horkheimer) as a scholar and institution builder; in addition he has been an activist on all levels (local, national, and international) of politics. About ten years after founding the Centre, he was instrumental in launching the quarterly *Alternatives*, a journal that soon emerged as a leading forum in India for the discussion of issues relating to social change and global transformation. Both his scholarly and his practical-political talents coalesced in 1980 when, together with other Centre colleagues, he inaugurated the movement "*Lokayan*" (meaning "dialogue among people"), designed as an arena for the meeting of academics, policymakers, and activists concerned with grassroots initiatives. His moment of greatest public visibility came in 1989 when, following the defeat of Rajiv Gandhi, he joined the National Front government as a member of the National Planning Commission.

Among Kothari's prolific writings, I want to single out for present purposes these four: *State Against Democracy* (1988), *Transformation and Survival* (1988), *Rethinking Development* (1989), and *Growing Amnesia* (1993). Subtitled "In Search of Humane Governance," the first volume was written mainly in protest against the policies of Indira and Rajiv Gandhi whose regimes were denounced for their attempt to marshall state power—what Derrida might have called state positivism—against the democratic aspirations of the people. In large measure, the book was meant as a challenge to the relentless process of centralization that, during the postindependence period, was steadily molding India into a uniform "nation-state" along Western lines. Buttressed by the resources of modern technology and corporate business, this nation-state—in Kothari's view—was reerecting or deepening the structure of social inequality that the struggle against colonialism had aimed to erase. The situation was further aggravated by the progressive militarization of the state promoted in the name of "national security." These and related factors conspired to produce a sociopolitical crisis which, according to Kothari, was changing or perverting the character of the state: namely, from "being an instrument of liberation of the masses to being a source of so much oppression for them."[14] The critique of state-centered accumulation of power was extended into the global arena in the second book, *Transformation and Survival*. Paralleling the growing stratification of domestic society, the operation of the international state system—in Kothari's account—promoted and reinforced a global structure of asymmetry between North and South, "developed" and "developing" societies, and center and periphery. As on the national level, this global asymmetry was compounded by the concentration of technological, economic, and military resources in the hands of hegemonic (developed) states or superpowers. In combination, these forces posed a threat to the natural environment, international peace, and ultimately the survival of humankind itself.

As an antidote to these dangers, the two cited volumes formulated an alternative vision of human existence and sociopolitical life that was not beholden to any of the reigning ideologies of the time. In fact, as Kothari insisted, it was necessary to move beyond both the liberal-capitalist and the orthodox Marxist paradigms, since both derived from the same Cartesian worldview: they were both "offshoots of the some philosophic pedigree of the Enlightenment and nineteenth-century (mechanistic) humanism" with their unlimited faith in progress fueled by technological mastery over nature. In lieu of this "modernist" and positivist pedigree, the books invoked the legacy of the Mahatma Gandhi whose lifework had challenged Western imperialism while at the same time enlisting popular grassroots beliefs and traditions for democratic purposes. In both his writings and his actions, Gandhi had thus honored "the moral imperative of treating [ordinary] people as a source in the recovery of a humane order." In addition to Gandhian teachings, the texts also drew inspiration from various left-leaning modes of political radicalism wedded to the promotion of human freedom and social justice. As used by Kothari, "freedom" was neither a synonym for the pursuit of libertarian self-interest nor for a retreat into public abstinence, but rather denoted the capacity (or capability) for public participation and the promotion of social well-being. To this extent, the notion of "human rights" signaled not only private entitlements or privileges as rather basic constituents of a good and "humane" social order.[15]

Kothari's *Rethinking Development* sought to expose both the pitfalls and the muddleheadedness of much of the dominant literature and planning in this field. Both in mainstream writings and mainline policy making, he noted, "development" has tended to be equated with unfettered economic and industrial expansion propelled by advances in modern science and technology. As was to be expected, this approach has engendered not only a deadly arms race and a wasteful, consumption-driven economy, but also a pernicious class structure on both the national and the global levels. As a consequence, democracy was under siege both at home and in the world at large. For Kothari, the trouble with the dominant approach was that it was not only difficult to implement but inherently flawed and misguided. Echoing again Horkheimer, his text located the root problem of the "developmental" ideology in its attachment to a dominant worldview or philosophical doctrine which, although originating in Europe, was now encircling the globe: the "doctrine of modernity" according to which "the end of life is narrowly defined as to be within the grasp of all—progress based on economic prosperity." Fueled by the Enlightenment teachings, this doctrine presented social advancement entirely as a matter of social engineering, backed up by "science-based technology"; all that human beings and societies had to do according to this model was to "discard tradition and superstition and become rational and 'modern.'" In language reminiscent (but also sharpening the edge) of the "dialectic of enlightenment" articulated by Horkheimer and Theodor Adorno, *Rethinking Development* asked these questions:

> Isn't the theory of progress, as developed in the West, based on an anthropocentric view of nature and a positivist conception of knowledge and science, which are responsible for a model of development spelling domination and exploitation? And if these be the essence of Occidental culture and its contribution to human thought and values, shouldn't we discard large parts of it and look for alternative modes of thought and values embedded in some other cultures?[16]

Growing Amnesia was published four years later, in the wake of the dismantling of the Soviet Union and the vanishing of the so-called nonalignment policy (sponsored by India and other "developing" countries). Although widely hailed in the West as the dawn of a new "world order," the emerging global situation raised serious worries and apprehensions for Kothari. In his view, the turn of events signaled basically the triumph of corporate capitalism, a triumph that augured ill for the cause of social justice and participatory or grassroots democracy. Given the concentration of power and wealth in developed countries and multinational conglomerates, the existing gulf between North and South, center and periphery was prone to be further deepened, while the fate of underprivileged masses around the world was bound to be abandoned to apathy or else consigned to "growing amnesia." Above all, the priority granted to policies of "deregulation" and "liberalization" of the market was bought at a steep price: its overall effect was to "destabilize the democratic polity, put the masses under severe strain, turn against labor and further marginalize the poor." To be sure, the remedy for deregulation could not reside in a centralized state bureaucracy controlling and planning every facet of social life in a top-down fashion. In opposition to the dystopias of both the Leviathan-state and unchecked market forces, *Growing Amnesia* sponsored a social-democratic alternative where the apparatus of the modern state was retained but sharply refocused in the direction of democratic participation and self-rule. Embracing again aspects of the Gandhian legacy, the alternative placed a strong accent on political and economic decentralization as an antidote to technocratic or corporate elitism. Such a shift of accent, Kothari argued, was guided and inspired by a commitment to "take people seriously," by "respecting their thinking and wisdom" and by fostering institutions that would "respond to their needs." Only by following these guideposts was it possible to avoid both plutocracy and rampant consumerism and to establish an economic system that, in Gandhi's words, "not only produces for the mass of the people but in which the mass of the people are also the producers."[17]

Next to Kothari, the most prominent member of the Delhi Centre is Ashis Nandy, a senior fellow and sometime director of the institute. In its basic thrust, Nandy shares Kothari's political orientation: the commitment to democratic transformative change—but a change popularly or locally legitimated rather than imposed by hegemonic (colonial or neocolonial) forces. A main difference between the two thinkers has to do with disciplinary focus: whereas Kothari has tended to center stage issues of political economy and sociology, Nandy—a trained psychologist and psychoanalyst—has been more concerned with psychic or psycho-cultural sources of popular resistance as well as the inner traumas of colonial oppression. One of his early publications, *At the Edge of Psychology* (1980), traced the intersections linking politics, culture, and psychology, especially as experienced in non-Western societies. His next book, *The Intimate Enemy* (1983), probed these linkages more concretely by focusing on the introjection or internalization of the colonizer's worldview, which, among the colonized, can lead to self-hatred and "loss of self." Nandy's own alternative vision was outlined in *Traditions, Tyranny, and Utopia* (1987), especially in the chapter "Toward a Third World Utopia." The chapter deliberately took its stand at the grassroots level by viewing the world "from the bottom up." As Nandy emphasized, the notion "Third World" was not a timeless, metaphysical idea but rather a political and economic category "born of poverty, exploitation, indignity and self-contempt." Given this stark historical background, the formulation of an alternative future for non-Western societies had to start from the experience of "man-made suffering"—not for the sake of inducing self-pity, but in order to permit a therapeutic "working through" of the traumas of oppression. As helpmates in this process of coping and working through, the text invoked the healing powers latent in indigenous traditions, especially powers such as those tapped in the Gandhian struggle for independence. An additional helpmate was the relative distance of non-Western cultures from the modern Cartesian paradigm with its dualisms and dichotomies—between subject and object, humans and nature, and colonizers and colonized.[18]

In still more forceful terms, Nandy's alternative vision for the future was spelled out in his essay "Cultural Frames for Social Transformation: A Credo," published in the Centre's journal *Alternatives* (in 1987). The essay took its point of departure from the anticolonial struggle in Africa, especially from Amilcar Cabral's stress on popular or indigenous culture as a counterpoint to hegemonic oppression. In Nandy's view, this outlook could be extended to other colonial or postcolonial societies. Basically, the stress on indigenous legacies signaled a defiance of the modern (Western) idea of intellectual and scientific "expertise" uncontaminated by popular customs or beliefs; it gave voice to societies and peoples "which have been the victims of history and are now trying to rediscover their own visions of a desirable society." In our time of relentless globalization and Western-style standardization, this kind of self-assertion and defiance gained global significance. To this extent, the stress on "cultural frames of social transformation" constitutes in our time "a plea for a minimum cultural plurality in an increasingly uniformized world." One of the prominent features of global standardization was for Nandy the imposition of the model of the "nation-state" and Western-style nationalism in all parts of the world, including the Indian subcontinent. This topic was pursued further in his subsequent study, *The Illegitimacy of Nationalism* (1994), which launched a blistering attack on the rise of centralization and nationalist standardization, which have become dominant traits of postindependence India. In Nandy's portrayal, nationalism and nation-state structures are basically Western imports foisted indiscriminately on non-Western societies and cultures. Indigenous cultural resources are again marshaled as antidotes to this imposition. Following the lead of Gandhi and Rabindranath Tagore, Nandy stressed the highly ambivalent role of nation-states as agents of both liberation and oppression; as an alternative he postulated a global perspective rooted in "the tolerance encoded in various traditional ways of life in a highly diverse, plural society."[19]

In his critique of nationalism and the nation-state, Nandy comes close to the position of another major intellectual school in postindependence India: the so-called Subaltern Studies project launched by the historian Ranajit Guha around 1982. By comparison with the Delhi Centre, the Subaltern Studies movement (in its early phase) was more directly inspired by the teaching of Antonio Gramsci and humanist Marxism. For members of the movement, the gaining of independence and the erection of the Indian nation-state were only very superficial and ambivalent accomplishments, involving basically the transfer of power from Britain to postcolonial bourgeois and capitalist elites. A major articulation of this outlook was provided by Partha Chatterjee, a prominent social scientist working and teaching in Calcutta. In his *Nationalist Thought and the Colonial World* (1986), Chatterjee denounced nationalist independence as a borrowed ideology and purely "derivative discourse" concealing and legitimating a mere shift in the agents of domination. His subsequent book, *The Nation and Its Fragments* (1993), offered a more nuanced and differentiated assessment, attentive to recent post-Marxist and poststructuralist tendencies. In this respect, Chatterjee's work is representative of a broader intellectual realignment characterizing the Subaltern Studies movement as a whole. In writing a preface to a volume seeking to provide an overview of the movement, Edward Said perceptively registered a certain shift away from the school's earlier Marxist and Gramscian moorings. As he observed: "None of the Subaltern Scholars is anything less than a critical student of Karl Marx"; moreover, today "the influence of structuralist and poststructuralist thinkers like Derrida, Foucault, Roland Barthes, and Louis Althusser is evident, along with the influence of British and American thinkers, like E. P. Thompson, Eric Hobsbawm, and others."[20]

Apart from multimember institutes and research agendas, India is, of course, replete with talented and innovative individual thinkers. For present purposes (given limitations of space), I want to single out three prominent recent philosophers: Daya Krishna, Sundara Rajan, and J. L. Mehta. Trained both in India and the West, Daya Krishna has been keenly attentive to, and critical of, dominant paradigms promulgated by Western social scientists during the Cold War era. Foremost among these were the formulas of "development" and "modernization" postulating the progressive assimilation of non-Western societies to Western yardsticks. For Krishna, these formulas were both theoretically confused and sociopolitically obnoxious. As he queried in his book *Political Development* (1979), how could one speak of linear development in the case of cultural frameworks, more specifically when comparing artworks of modernity with those of Greek antiquity or else with the masterpieces of India and China? Sociopolitically, he added, the relevant distinction should not be between "developed" and "undeveloped," but between "good" and "bad" or legitimate and illegitimate political regimes. His compatriot Sundara Rajan has been similarly critical of linear or one-dimensional schemes of social advancement, relying for his purposes on a combination of social phenomenology and Frankfurt School critical theory. As he wrote in his book *Innovative Competence and Social Change* (1986): "If the alignment of [Frankfurt-style] communicative competence and [phenomenological] social theory could be defended, then I suggest we have a possibility of carrying over a 'transcendental' point of view into the domain of social theory." In Rajan's later writings, the influence of Continental hermeneutics—especially Paul Riceour's version—became steadily more decisive, leading him to differentiate between contextual "signification" and a more de-contextualized critical-emancipatory "symbolization." In J. L. Mehta's case, finally, the most striking features of his work are the resonances he developed between Indian classical thought and aspects of Heideggerian ontology and Gadamerian hermeneutics.[21]

Turning to East Asia, one finds again a plethora of innovative and critical perspectives, developed by both Buddhist and Confucian intellectuals and scholars. In the Buddhist camp, one must mention first of all the renowned Kyoto School of philosophy in Japan, inaugurated by Kitaro Nishida and further developed by such thinkers as Keiji Nishitani, Hajime Tanabe, Hisamatsu Shin'ichi, and Masao Abe. In the case of all these thinkers the resonances with Continental thought are pronounced: while Nishida's work makes frequent appeal to Kierkegaard, Bergson, and Husserl, the writings of Nishitani and others reveal a more distinct Heideggerian slant. Given the heavy emphasis of the entire school on such key Zen notions of "nothingness" and "emptiness" (*sunyata*), one may wonder about the practical implications of their perspective. However, as soon as the affinity of "*sunyata*" with Heidegger's "nihilating nothingness" is taken into account, the practical and critical impulses spring instantly into view. For clearly, from the angle of nihilation, Buddhist thought can have no truck with totalizing modes of domination (with Derrida's "technical-economic-military positivism"). The only proper and legitimate form of action or agency, under Zen Buddhist auspices, is a nonpossessive and nondomineering kind of action—traditionally called "*wu-wei*" (again akin to Heidegger's "letting be").[22] Outside the confines of Kyoto, more resolutely praxis-oriented forms of Buddhist thought have emerged in recent decades in many parts of Asia and South Asia. Sometimes labeled "Buddhist liberation movement" or movement of "engaged Buddhism," this outlook—often aiming at radical social transformation—is represented by such figures as Thich Nhat Hanh (from Vietnam), the Dalai Lama (from Tibet), Sulak Sivaraksa (Thailand), A. T. Ariyaratne (Sri Lanka), and the late Dr. Ambedkar (India).[23] Despite limitations imposed by the regime in mainland China, Confucianism has also experienced a remarkable revival in East and Southeast Asia, often with a critical edge against centralizing or totalizing types of government.[24]

Contrary to simplistic assumptions much in vogue in the West, Islamic societies today are not uniformly dominated by dogmatic-clerical or "fundamentalist" doctrines, but display a rich welter of intellectual orientations—some of them with clearly practical-critical overtones. In Southeast Asia, the prototype of a critical Muslim intellectual is Chandra Muzaffer, head of an NGO called "Just World Trust," whose publications and public statements have been exemplary in denouncing both Western aggressive or imperialist policies and unjust or corrupt practices in the Islamic world.[25] Some of the liveliest intellectual debates in that part of the world are carried on today in Iran, with "reformers" and "conservatives" engaging each other in sustained exchanges on philosophical and political issues—often with a high degree of erudition and sophistication. As in India and East Asia, European resonances can readily be detected in these exchanges, particularly in the arguments of reformers whose writings frequently appeal to Continental perspectives, ranging from the Vienna School to Husserlian phenomenology, Heideggerian ontology, Gadamerian hermeneutics, and French-style postmodernism.[26] The influence of phenomenology and hermeneutics can also be found in the works of other Muslims thinkers, such as the Egyptian philosopher Hassan Hanafi, while aspects of Frankfurt School critical theory surface in the publications of the Moroccan Mohammed al-Jabiri.[27] Limitations of space prevent here a discussion of intellectual debates in Africa and Latin America—except to say that, in the one case, the legacies of Frantz Fanon and Aime Césaire continue to provide powerful support to critical praxis while, in the other case, the writings of Paulo Freire, Enrique Dussel, and others testify to their unflagging commitment to a "pedagogy of the oppressed."[28]

TOWARD A GLOBAL PUBLIC SPHERE

The preceding discussion was meant to provide a glimpse into arenas of critical theorizing in many parts of the world and thus to counteract parochial assumptions of a European (or Western) monopoly in the domain of critical philosophy and social thought. As has been shown, networks of critical intellectual life are present around the globe, stretching from East and South Asia to the Middle East, Africa, and South America; as has also been indicated, many of these networks stand in close and reciprocal inter-actions with schools or perspectives originating on the Continent. In our age of globalization, these interactions are bound to multiply and to deepen, leading to the emergence of a global community of critically engaged intel-lectuals—an updated and cosmopolitan version of the traditional "republic of letters." This development is crucially important in our time of immense superpower predominance, a domination which—following the model of earlier imperial systems—is hostile to the cultivation of critical scrutiny and contestation. To speak with Jacques Derrida, it is imperative in our time to defend the "right to philosophy," that is, the right to critical theorizing among ordinary people around the world, as an antidote and response to the dictates of a coercive "technical-economic-military positivism." In Der-rida's sense, this defense is necessary in order to preserve the open spaces needed for unregimented and "unrestricted" inquiry and questioning—open spaces which, in turn, serve as heralds or anticipations of a "democracy to come." To express the point in somewhat different language: the emerging global networks of critical thinking can be seen as way stations to the for-mation of a global public sphere—a sphere indispensable for anything like a democratically constituted cosmopolis.

In his plea for a "critical theory with a cosmopolitan intent," Ulrich Beck mentions a number of challenges or tasks that must be tackled by the emerg-ing networks of critical global theorizing. Foremost among these tasks is the need to break through and dismantle the ideological tactics and obfuscations employed by dominant hegemonic or nationalist powers, above all "the forms and strategies used to render cosmopolitan realities [or possibilities] invisi-ble." These strategies are particularly evident whenever existing global insti-tutions or norms are bypassed or erased in the name of the protection of "na-tional security" interests. Prominent examples that come to mind are the evisceration of provisions of the United Nations Charter, the shuttling of the Geneva Conventions, and the erosion of codes of military conduct. Next to the need to contest such strategies, Beck stresses the role of innovative social and political imagination, that is, the endeavor to make theoretical room for open spaces going beyond the confines of national sovereignties (but without merely surrendering to a global superpower). In his words, what is called for is a "reimagination of the political" that would explore and experiment with "the difference between the national viewpoint of political actors and the cosmopolitan perspective" becoming available today. Specifically reserved for critical intellectuals everywhere is the additional task of rethinking and re-formulating prevailing conceptual categories—especially categories used in social and political analysis—in favor of new and more "hospitable" theoretical frames of reference. As Beck summarizes his argument, the main focus in contemporary debates revolves around "gaining a new cosmopolitan perspective on the global power field, pushing new actors and actor networks, power potentials, strategies, and forms of organization of 'debounded' politics into the field of vision."[29]

To return to some points made at the beginning of this essay: critical theory situates itself in the prevailing agonies and dilemmas of the age and is willing to take a practical and normative stand in opposition to injustice, cruelty, and oppression. This does not mean that critical theory does not think or theorize—which would render it blind or myopic; but it does allow its thinking to be informed and nurtured by practical experience. In doing so, critical theorizing stands opposed to what Max Horkheimer called "traditional theory" and what I have termed a purely spectatorial stance—the assumption that human beings can be mere spectators or onlookers in a world torn apart by so much turmoil, misery, and suffering (and today the possibility of a nuclear holocaust). As indicated before, this spectatorial stance was in large measure promoted by the modern Cartesian worldview and its offshoots (as well as by certain modes of traditional metaphysics). What is required in our time is perhaps not a complete dismantling of this worldview but its resolute recasting and reformulation—in such a manner that spectators can return as participants in their experienced life-world. The old dispute between theory and praxis is thus not resolved in favor of a blind activism, but in favor of a more thoughtful and responsible praxis. Given the retreat of Cartesian egocentrism, this praxis is destined to be non-domineering, enabling, and liberating—without insisting at any point on its own meritorious agency or achievements. To recall a passage penned by Horkheimer toward the conclusion of his essay: "Critical theory has no specific influence on its side, except concern for the abolition of social injustice. This negative formulation . . . is the materialist content of the idealist concept of reason."

NOTES

1. Beck, "Toward a New Critical Theory with a Cosmopolitan Intent," pp. 453–468.

2. Max Horkheimer, "Traditional and Critical Theory," in Horkheimer, *Critical Theory: Selected Essays*, trans. Matthew J. O'Connell and others (New York: Herder & Herder, 1972), pp. 188-189. Compare also Henri Poincaré, *Science and Hypothesis*, trans. William J. Greenstrect (London: Walter Scott, 1905), p. 105.

3. Horkheimer, "Traditional and Critical Theory," pp. 189-190, 196-197 (corrected for gender bias). The essay includes in the category of traditional or specta-

torial theorizing also the "neo-Kantianism of the Marburg School" with its emphasis on universal categories and the pure *"logos"* of the world-mind (p. 198). As Horkheimer acknowledges (p. 204), Hegelian philosophy tried to overcome the Kantian antimonies (of noumena/phenomena, of activity/passivity) by "sublating" them on the level of objective and absolute spirit. However, this solution remained "a purely private assertion, a personal peace treaty between the philosopher and an inhuman world."

4. Horkheimer, "Traditional and Critical Theory," pp. 208, 227-229, 231.

5. Horkheimer, "Traditional and Critical Theory," pp. 227, 241-242.

6. Compare in this context Edmund Husserl, *Cartesian Meditations: An Introduction to Phenomenology*, trans. Dorion Cairns (The Hague: Martinus Nijhoff, 1973); and *The Crisis of the European Sciences and Transcendental Phenomenology: An Introduction to Phenomenological Philosophy*.

7. See Martin Heidegger, *The Question Concerning Technology and Other Essays*; also see Hatab, *Ethics and Finitude*, pp. 63, 72, 102. As Hatab adds (p. 109): "In a way we can understand Heidegger's ontology as a radicalization of Aristotelian teleology that inscribes creative openness into temporal development." Compare also Michael E. Zimmerman, *Heidegger's Confrontation with Modernity: Technology, Politics, Art* (Bloomington, IN: Indiana University Press, 1990).

8. See the essays "What is Practice?" and "Hermeneutics as Practical Philosophy," in Hans-Georg Gadamer, *Reason in the Age of Science*, trans. Frederick G. Lawrence (Cambridge, MA: MIT Press, 1981), pp. 70-71, 77, 111. Compare also Charles Taylor, "Social Theory as Practice," in *Philosophy and the Human Sciences: Philosophical Papers 2* (Cambridge, UK: Cambridge University Press, 1985), pp. 91-115.

9. See Jean-Paul Sartre, *Search for a Method*, trans. Hazel E. Barnes (New York: Alfred Knopf, 1963), pp. 22, 26-28. *Search* served as prefatory essay to Sartre's ambitious *Critique of Dialectical Reason* (1960).

10. See Merleau-Ponty, *Humanism and Terror: An Essay on the Communist Problem*, pp. xiv, xxiv; *In Praise of Philosophy* (*Éloge de la Philosophie*), pp. 60-61, 63.

11. See Derrida, *The Other Heading: Reflections on Today's Europe*, pp. 77, 79; also "The Right to Philosophy from the Cosmopolitical Point of View," in *Ethics, Institutions, and the Right to Philosophy*, trans. and ed. Peter P. Trifonas (Lanham, MD: Rowman & Littlefield, 2002), p. 15.

12. See Derrida, *On Cosmopolitanism and Forgiveness*, trans. Mark Dooley and Michael Hughes (London and New York: Routledge, 2001). The text *On Cosmopolitanism* is based on an address by Derrida to the International Parliament of Writers in Strasbourg in 1966, titled *"Cosmopolites de tous les pays, encore un effort!"*

13. A brief introduction to the perspective and work of the Centre is provided by Kothari in "Towards an Alternative Process of Knowledge," in his *Rethinking Development: In Search for Humane Alternatives* (New York: New Horizons Press, 1989), pp. 23-43. For a more detailed discussion of Kothari and the Centre see my "Global Development? Alternative Voices from Delhi," in *Alternative Visions: Paths in the Global Village*, pp. 219-240.

14. See Rajni Kothari, _State against Democracy: In Search of Humane Governance_ (Delhi: Ajanta, 1988), p. 60. As one should note, Kothari did not entirely condemn the modern state. In a progressive democratic vein, he endorsed the state provided it served as an agency of democratization and a guardian of the common people.

15. See Kothari, _State against Democracy_, pp. 2-3, 151; also _Transformation and Survival: In Search of a Humane World Order_ (Delhi: Ajanta, 1988), pp. 6, 170-171.

16. Kothari, _Rethinking Development_, pp. 3-5, 48-49, 51. Among the alternative modes of thought, Kothari included cultural and religious traditions of non-Western societies. In his words (p. 50): "The religions and civilizations of India, of the Islamic world, of the complex of humanist thought that has informed China, and of Buddhism provide major streams of thought that could substantially contribute to the present search for alternatives." As one should note, however, the text in no way supported a simple anti-Western or antimodern stance, but rather conceded (p. 52) that modernity is "part of us all" just as "the West is part of us all."

17. Kothari, _Growing Amnesia: An Essay on Poverty and the Human Condition_ (New Delhi: Viking, 1993), pp. 8-9, 123, 134, 149-151.

18. Ashis Nandy, _Traditions, Tyranny and Utopias: Essays in the Politics of Awareness_ (Delhi: Oxford University Press, 1987), pp. 21, 31-35. See also Nandy, _At the Edge of Psychology: Essays in Politics and Culture_ (Delhi: Oxford University Press, 1980), and _The Intimate Enemy: Loss and Recovery of Self under Colonialism_ (Delhi: Oxford University Press, 1983).

19. Nandy, _The Illegitimacy of Nationalism: Rabindranath Tagore and the Politics of Self_ (Delhi: Oxford University Press, 1994), pp. x-xi. See also "Cultural Frames for Social Transformation: A Credo," _Alternatives_ 12 (1987): pp. 113-116.

20. See Edward W. Said, "Foreword," in _Selected Subaltern Studies,_ ed. Ranajit Guha and Gayatri Chakravorty Spivak (New York: Oxford University Press, 1988), p. x. Compare also Partha Chatterjee, _Nationalist Thought and the Colonial World: A Derivative Discourse_ (Tokyo: Zed Books, 1986), and _The Nation and Its Fragments: Colonial and Postcolonial Histories_ (Princeton, NJ: Princeton University Press, 1993).

21. Compare the above Daya Krishna, _Political Development: A Critical Perspective_ (Delhi: Oxford University Press, 1979), pp. 187, 190, 201, and his _Considerations toward a Theory of Social Change_ (Bombay: Manaktalas, 1965); R. Sundara Rajan, _Innovative Competence and Social Change_ (Ganeshkind: Poona University Press, 1986), pp. 87-89; also his _Toward a Critique of Cultural Reason_ (Delhi: Oxford University Press, 1987) and _The Primacy of the Political_ (Delhi: Oxford University Press, 1991); J. L. Mehta, _Martin Heidegger: The Way and the Vision_ (Honolulu: University Press of Hawaii, 1976); also his _India and the West: The Problem of Understanding_ (Chico, CA: Scholars Press, 1985), and _Philosophy and Religion: Essays in Interpretation_ (New Delhi: Manoharlal Publ., 1990). For a fuller development of these thinkers' views see the chapters "Heidegger, Bhaki, and Vedanta" and "Modernization and Postmodernization" in my _Beyond Orientalism_, pp. 89-114, 149-174. Apart from these philosophers there are several social and political theorists who, in their own ways, have articulated a critical Indian perspective. Among them I should mention Thomas Pantham (University of Bar-

oda); Vrajendra Raj Mehta (former vice-chancellor of Delhi University); Rajeev Bhargava (Delhi University); Ananta K. Giri (Center for Developing Societies, Chennai), and the prominent expatriate political theorist Bhikhu Parekh (now Lord Parekh), a leading student of Gandhi's thought.

22. For some writings of Kyoto School thinkers, see Kitaro Nishida, *Intelligibility and the Philosophy of Nothingness: Three Philosophical Essays*, trans. Robert Schinzinger (Honolulu: East-West Center Press, 1958); Keiji Nishitani, *Religion and Nothingness*, trans. Jan Van Bragt (Berkeley: University of California Press, 1982); Hajime Tanabe, *Philosophy as Metanoetics*, trans. Takouchi Yoshinori et al. (Berkeley: University of California Press, 1987); Hisamatsu Shin'ichi, *Zen and the Fine Arts* (Tokyo: Kodansha International, 1971); and Masao Abe, *Zen and Western Thought*, ed. William R. LaFleur (Honolulu: University of Hawaii Press, 1985). Compare also my *"Sunyata* East and West: Emptiness and Global Democracy," in my *Beyond Orientalism*, pp. 175-199; also "Nothingness and *Sunyata*: A Comparison of Heidegger and Nishitani," *Philosophy East and West* 42 (1992): pp. 37-48.

23. Compare, e.g., Thich Nhat Hanh, *Vietnam: Lotus in a Sea of Fire*, with a foreword by Thomas Merton (New York: Hill and Wang, 1967); Sulak Sivaraksa, *A Buddhist Vision for Renewing Society* (Bangkok: Thai Interreligious Commission for Development, 1994); B. R. Ambedkar, *The Buddha and His Dharma*, 3rd ed. (Bombay: Siddarth Publications, 1984). See also Christopher S. Queen and Sallie B. King, eds., *Engaged Buddhism: Buddhist Liberation Movements in Asia* (Albany, NY: State University of New York Press, 1996).

24. Compare, e.g., Tu Wei-Ming, *Confucian Thought: Selfhood as Creative Transformation* (Albany, NY: State University of New York Press, 1985); Daniel Bell and Chaibong Hahm, eds., *Confucianism for the Modern World* (Cambridge, UK: Cambridge University Press, 2003); also my "Humanity and Humanization: Comments on Confucianism," in *Alternatives Visions*, pp. 123-144.

25. See, e.g., Chandra Muzaffer, *Rights, Religion and Reform* (London and New York: Routledge Curzon, 2002); *Human Rights and the New World Order* (Penang, Malaysia: Just World Trust, 1993).

26. On intellectual debates in Iran see, e.g., Mehrzad Boroujerdi, *Iranian Intellectuals and the West* (Syracuse, NY: Syracuse University Press, 1996); Forough Jahanbaksh, *Islam, Democracy, and Religious Modernism in Iran, 1953-2000* (Boston: Brill, 2001); Ali Mirsepassi, *Intellectual Discourse and the Politics of Modernization: Negotiating Modernity in Iran* (Cambridge, UK: Cambridge University Press, 2000); Ramin Jahanbegloo, ed., *Iran: Between Tradition and Modernity* (Lanham, MD: Lexington Books, 2004). Compare also the section "Toward an Islamic Modernity?" and the chapter "Islam and Democracy: Reflections on Abdolkarim Soroush" in my *Dialogue Among Civilizations: Some Exemplary Voices*, pp. 100-104, 167-184.

27. See, e.g., Hassan Hanafi, *Les méthodes d'exégèse* (Cairo: Conseil des Arts, 1965), and Muhammed Abed al-Jabiri, *Arab-Islamic Philosophy: A Contemporary Critique*, trans. Aziz Abassi (Austin: University of Texas Press, 1999).

28. See, e.g., Paulo Freire, *Pedagogy of the Oppressed* (New York: Continuum, 1982); Dussel, *The Invention of the Americas*, Ofelia Schutte; *Cultural Identity and*

Social Liberation in Latin American Thought (Albany, NY: State University of New York Press, 1993); Frantz Fanon, *The Wretched of the Earth* (New York: Grove Press, 1968); Aimé Césaire, *Return to My Native Land*, trans. Emile Snyders (Paris: Présence Africaine, 1968); Paulin J. Hountondji, *African Philosophy: Myth & Reality*, 2nd ed. (Bloomington, IN: Indiana University Press, 1996); D. A. Masolo, *African Philosophy in Search of Identity* (Bloomington, IN: Indiana University Press, 1994).

29. Beck, "Toward a New Critical Theory with a Cosmopolitan Intent," p. 467.

Chapter Seven

Social Identity and Creative Praxis: Hommage à Merleau-Ponty

Despite historical fluctuations, human identity—the answer to the question "Who am I?" or "Who are we?"—has never been very stable. As we know, at the beginning of the Christian era, St. Augustine voiced existential anguish by stating "I have become a question to myself (*questio mihi factus sum*)"—an anguish triggered by his exposure to the multiple perspectives of the Hellenistic period, including Stoicism, Platonism, and many others. However, long before Augustine, the same question had been inscribed on the birth certificate of Western philosophy, in the form of Socratic questioning and Platonic "*thaumazein*" (wondering). Still, during earlier years, existential anguish was largely limited to a few rare minds, while the great majority of peoples tended to live their lives embedded in relatively stable social customs and traditions insuring a sense of personal and cultural identity. This situation began to change radically with the onset of Western modernity, highlighted by the Protestant Reformation and European Enlightenment. In their combined operation, the Protestant focus on "inwardness" and the Cartesian method of doubt called into question existing social conventions seen as alien or recalcitrant to a properly authentic or examined life. In practical political terms, these trends reached their apogee in the series of modern revolutions, especially the French Revolution, which sought to draw a decisive boundary between modern human autonomy or self-determination and the presumed quietism or conventionalism of the past.

From this time forward, one can detect a persistent trajectory of Western "modernization," a trajectory leading from political to social and economic (capitalist) revolutions in the direction of a future where, in Marx's words, "everything solid [would] melt into air." As it happens, however, this trajectory was for a long time muffled or circumscribed, at least in the context of modern Western societies. One of the retarding factors was nationalism, a feature—linked with the system of European nation-states—which was not so much sidelined as rather intensified by the aftermath of the French Revolution. Another factor was the rise of encompassing ideologies (sometimes styled "grand metanarratives") which assigned to members or subscribers a relatively stable social role or identity. A further element was the transformation of the *cogito*, the carrier of Cartesian doubt, into a kind of Archimedian point (called "subjectivity"), which served to provide metaphysical anchorage. Overshadowing all these factors was the erection of Europe or the West itself into a privileged cultural-political identity or benchmark. Under the auspices of what has come to be known as "Eurocentrism," the modern West ascribed to itself a universal political and cultural task carried forward by the instruments of imperialism and colonialism. The closely affiliated strategy of "Orientalism" assigned to Western academics and intellectuals the privilege of analyzing, categorizing, and "knowing" the "Orient," without any need for reciprocity or reciprocal learning. Through these and other devices the West established itself as the promontory or advanced "heading" of the world, as the mature headmaster with respect to all the underdeveloped or developing societies whose customs and traditional identities needed to be disrupted, transformed, or erased, for the sake of their own advancement.[1]

In the meantime, the stakes of advancement have been further raised by the relentless process of globalization, which today holds the entire world in its grip. Although worldwide in its effects, the process does not erase the distinction between development and underdevelopment, a distinction that now surfaces as the difference between globalizing forces—that is, forces carrying forward a universal global agenda—and populations who are being globalized or developed. In this encounter between globalizers and globalized (corresponding largely to the divide between North and South), human identity and "identity politics" clearly play a crucial role. The basic question here is this: whose and what kind of identity should be cultivated by whom? The question, in my view, cannot be avoided by a leap into a universal sameness or "nonidentity"—which usually only serves as a camouflage for hegemonic privilege. In order to examine these issues I shall proceed in three steps. The opening section explores (once again) the conundrum of universalism and particularism, more specifically the collusion between "essential" universal sameness and "essential" difference or particularity. Next, attention is shifted to initiatives that, in partial response to competing essentialisms, make identity the outgrowth of contingent construction or arbitrary fabrication. Deviating from radical constructivism, the conclusion presents identity as the work of an ever-renewed creative praxis, a praxis mediating between convention and invention and between past sedimentations and imagined possible futures (as depicted in exemplary fashion by Maurice Merleau-Ponty).

UNIVERSALISM AND PARTICULARISM

Before proceeding further, it may be useful to ponder briefly the meaning of "identity"—which, in recent times, has been the topic of much scholarly discussion. Clearly, human identity implies a certain distinctness of character, that is, a specifiable difference of persons or groups from other persons or groups (and also from a universal sameness devoid of distinct features). In addition, difference seems to include the prospect of reidentification, that is, the possibility of holding distinct features steady over a period of time. Limiting herself to the individual level, Amélie Rorty in her book *The Identities of Persons* defines the central issue as follows: "What sorts of characteristics identify a person as essentially the person she is, such that if those characteristics were changed, she would be a significantly different person, though she might still be differentiated and reidentified as the same?"[2] One may note here the emphasis on an "essential" distinctness, on a difference that is not purely accidental, contingent, or ephemeral. In introducing his book *Multiculturalism, Liberalism and Democracy*, Indian political theorist Rajeev Bhargava strikes a similar note when he writes:

> It is a commonplace in logic that the concept of identity has to do with sameness. Equally trivial is the observation that anything whatsoever is the same with itself at any given time. . . . If an object is to retain identity, it must remain same with itself over time. A thing with a plausible sense of identity must endure. . . . To have an identity, a thing must have features that are both relevant and enduring. . . . If this is true of the identity of all objects, it must equally be true for the identity of human persons. To remain constant over time with herself or himself or with others, to possess or share identity, a person must be identical with some of her/his enduring and relevant attributes.[3]

Enduring and relevant attributes might also be called basic or "essential" or—what Bhargava himself calls—"critically defining" attributes. In order to distinguish the latter from merely contingent or accidental features, Bhargava speaks of "*identity-constituting* beliefs and desires," that is, distinctive values which furnish "the criterion of relevance constitutive of identity."[4] Now, it is equally a commonplace in logic that "identity-constituting" features or markers of difference cannot be provided by the particular thing, person, or group of persons in question, but only by a broader framework of significance which precisely furnishes the "criteria of relevance" for the differentiation. It is this insight which, throughout the centuries of metaphysics, has prompted the recourse to a transparticular or "universal" perspective which presumably is able to assign to each particular identity its place and role. It is here that we encounter the realm of perennial ideas and values and, in modern Western philosophy, the invocation of transcendental consciousness or a transcendental-spectatorial "subjectivity" capable of surveying, and adjudicating between, all mundane phenomena and particular identities. The same invocation surfaces also in other cultural contexts and other philosophical vocabularies; thus, variants can be found in the Indian Vedantic distinction between *"brahman"* and *"maya"* (the world of illusory phenomena) and in a certain (mis)interpretation of the so-called ontic-ontological difference between "Being" and "beings" where the former would function as a transcendental metaconcept embracing, and subordinating to itself, all particular "beings" or phenomena in a gesture of metaphysical imperialism.[5]

Despite the need for broad frames of significance, the transcendental construal of such frameworks is fraught with insoluble problems. On a concrete level, the motivation for such construal is often political: the hoped-for emancipation or liberation from particular contexts or identities which have become stifling or oppressive for some people or groups. It is important, however, to distinguish between political and metaphysical emancipation; while the former may often be plausible and desirable, the latter is dubious and questionable on numerous grounds.[6] If, metaphysically construed, emancipation means the liberation from all contexts or particularities, then the path leads into an empty space or else into a space of purely formal limit-concepts devoid of (general or particular) semantic significance. The term "universalism"—often used as a synonym for a transcendental-spectatorial stance—at this point becomes a pure mantra or shibboleth incapable of furnishing the "criteria of relevance" required for marking, and adjudicating between, concrete differences. On the other hand, as soon as the transcendental-universal marker is filled out with some distinctive character, it becomes itself a distinctive particularity—albeit a particularity which assigns to itself a superior or privileged status vis-à-vis all others. What surfaces here again is the contagion or subterranean complicity between universalism and imperialism.

In many ways, this complicity is illustrated in the French Revolution and its aftermath. In its deeper aspirations, that revolution certainly was motivated by universal guideposts: the principles of republicanism and the basic liberty and equality of human beings. In their concrete application, however, these principles were disseminated by Napoleon and his armies as the executive agents of the French nation and its *"mission civilisatrice."* This point is ably presented by Immanuel Wallerstein, a writer hardly suspect of pampering invidious particularities. Napoleon's empire, Wallerstein notes pointedly in his book *Geopolitics and Geoculture*, "expressed in concrete practice all the ambiguity of a universalizing idea with which we are so conversant today." For, on the one hand, the French Revolution and Napoleon's armies "were seen not only by the French themselves but by other Europeans as the carrier of a universal idea, precisely that of civilization, and were welcomed as such."

But, on the other hand, "many of the same welcoming Europeans very soon reacted as local 'nationalists' against French 'imperialism.'" From this encounter, Wallerstein draws a general lesson to which it will be important to return at a later point. In an international situation of structural inequality—between the rich and the poor, the strong and the weak, the developed and the undeveloped—universalism is bound to be ambiguously received by subaltern people who may welcome its emancipatory potential but resist its hegemonic practices. As he adds:

> Universalism is a "gift" of the powerful to the weak, which confronts the latter with a double bind: to refuse the gift is to lose; to accept the gift is to lose. The only plausible reaction of the weak is neither to refuse nor to accept, or both to refuse and to accept—in short, the path of the seemingly irrational zigzags (both cultural and political) of the weak that has characterized most of nineteenth and especially twentieth-century history.[7]

As Wallerstein would no doubt agree, the dilemma is not restricted to the last two centuries. It surfaced already at the very beginning of Western modernity: at the time of the discovery and conquest of the Americas by the Europeans. As presented by Enrique Dussel, in his iconoclastic book *The Invention of the Americas*, the conquest (*conquista*) was not only a marginal or peripheral occurrence, but a constitutive event in the emergence of Western modernity: a pivot in the formation of European self-consciousness, of the European self-construal as an advanced and superior civilization in comparison with the indigenous peoples (especially the Aztecs). In Dussel's words, the discovery and conquest of the Americas encouraged the profiling of a distinct European "subjectivity," the assertion of its intrinsic Greco-Roman and Cartesian rationality as contrasted with the rest of the world. With particular vehemence, this self-construal surfaced "in the person of Hernán Cortés presiding over the conquest of Mexico, the first place where this [Western] ego effects its prototypical development by setting itself up as lord-of-the-world and will-to-power." Dussel also refers to the imperial apologist of the conquest, Ginés de Sepúlveda, who in deft fashion employed the entire gamut of arguments used in later colonial ventures. Among the reasons justifying conquest, Sepúlveda cited prominently the absence, among the Indians, of proper notions of individual liberty, private property, and moral education. Recapitulating Sepúlveda's argumentative strategy, Dussel offers this brief synopsis: first, "Europe is more developed; its civilization is superior to others (major premise of all *Eurocentrism*)"; second, "a culture's abandonment of its barbarity and underdevelopment through a civilizing process implies, as a conclusion, progress, development, well-being and *emancipation* for that culture"; third, as a corollary, "one defends Europe's domination over other cultures as a *necessary*, pedagogic violence (just war) which produces civilization and modernization."[8]

In ominous fashion, the inaugural event discussed by Dussel has cast its shadow over subsequent historical developments. In our own time, the dilemma of universalism and particularism reappears as the conflict between globalizers and globalized, between North and South, or—in Samuel Huntington's phrase—between "the West and the Rest."[9] Recent acts of violence have further aggravated the dilemma. In the wake of September 11, policy makers in the West (particularly in the United States) have begun to define their task as the defense of Western civilization, and indeed of "universal" civilization. To an extent, this self-designation acquires some plausibility and legitimacy by virtue of the particularly horrible and offensive nature of terrorist acts (which presumably should be abhorred by all civilizations or cultures). Yet, in my view, care should be taken lest the "war on terrorism" does not inadvertently slide into forms of *conquista*, Eurocentrism, or *mission civilisatrice* in Napoleonic style. If antiterrorism were perverted in this direction, subaltern peoples would inevitably be forced into the kind of double bind described by Wallerstein. In still more forceful terms, the double bind has been pinpointed by Abdallah Laroui. Under conditions of structural global asymmetries, he writes, "the Third World will always have the reaction that Europe had to Napoleon, the Napoleon of universalization by force of arms, for this abstract universalization by imperialism is a disguised murder."[10]

CONTINGENCY AND IDENTITY CONSTRUCTION

Although provocatively couched, Laroui's warning cannot lightly be brushed aside. Under the aegis of military, technological, and economic agendas, large masses of peoples are relentlessly streamlined today into a hegemonic world order—an induction often accompanied by overt or covert modes of violence. On the part of the globalizers, the process tends to be justified as the birth pangs of a nascent rational humanity and as the liberation of "backward" peoples from oppressive traditions—an argument perceived by the latter as a Napoleonic gesture. As it happens, the conundrum of competing identities—especially of "essentialized" global and particular identities—has not escaped the attention of thoughtful contemporary observers and theorists. In his important book *Identity/Difference*, William Connolly detects in the very conception of identity an intrinsic paradox. As he writes: "Without a set of standards of identity and responsibility, there is no possibility of ethical [or political] discrimination; but the application of any such set of historical constructions also does violence to those to whom it is applied." Although standards or criteria of identification are "indispensable" in social life, one has to guard against treating them as either "disposable fictions" or as "natural [i.e., essential] kinds." The main danger here is that people insist upon treating prevailing criteria as if they were absolutely or "intrinsically true," as if the correlation "between the imperatives of social life and the terms of identity/responsibility corresponded to an intrinsic design of human being itself."[11]

Sometimes, to avoid the danger of oppressive fixation, writers take recourse to a strategy of radical reversal or subversion: that is, to a conception of human beings as utterly malleable, and of identity as the result of arbitrary and ephemeral construction (something Connolly carefully avoids). Despite his own different (more dialogical) inclinations, Rajeev Bhargava occasionally gives credence to this model of radical construction—as when he writes that "the identity of a person is largely a matter of social construction," adding that this holds true for the "manufacturing" of both personal and social identity.[12] In recent decades, this constructive or manufacturing model has received a powerful boost from certain strands of postmodernism and deconstructivism: namely, versions which, center staging the role of negation or negativity, construe all determinate phenomena as derivative adjuncts of a basic absence or lack (of identity). Most prominently, this deconstructive/constructivist approach has been formulated by the Argentian-British political theorist Ernesto Laclau. In his book *The Making of Political Identities*, Laclau presents the issue of identity precisely under the rubric of a "gap" or caesura between a deconstructive absence and a constituted or constructed presence, between an indeterminate nothingness (also styled as "freedom") and a world of determinate beings or contents. As he writes pointedly, his argument means to lead to "the very center" of the problem of identity and identification: namely, to the realization that the source of the latter is a kind of empty agency (or nonidentity) or "the subject of a lack."[13]

In developing his argument, Laclau resorts to a radical notion of freedom as negativity (familiar to some extent from Jean-Paul Sartre). Freedom in this perspective is treated as "self-determination" or as the realization of a constitutive "subjectivity"—but precisely of an empty subjectivity devoid of identifying markers. In his words: if the condition of freedom is self-determination, and if "no determinate content follows *a priori*" from this freedom, then two necessary conclusions follow: first, "that the condition of freedom is indeterminacy"; and second, "that all determinate content is objective rather than subjective," heteronomous rather than autonomous. Proceeding along this road, Laclau lodges strong reservations against Hegelian-style mediations in favor of a stark dichotomy or antimony between absence and presence, freedom and determinate content. "Determination," he states, "can only be the result of the 'alienation' of subjectivity [or freedom], of its becoming the opposite of itself." While, in Hegelian thought, indeterminate negativity tends to be "sublated" in a dialectical movement, deconstruction postulates a more radical "gap" or hiatus: namely, an unmediated "passage from the indeterminate to determination as such—a certain indifference or distance of the indeterminate vis-à-vis the forms of determination that supersede it." Seen from this deconstructive/constructivist perspective, the relation between indeterminacy and determination is actually a nonrelation or better a conflictual relation; in any case, "there will never be real supersession, nor peace, between the two." The simple reason for this is that freedom "will only acquire a content by alienating itself in an objectivity which is its opposite"—which is precisely "what is involved in the notion of *identification*." Against this background it becomes clear why deconstructive identity is always inherently unstable and predicated on a constitutive "gap"—a gap that needs to be "minded" or respected.[14]

In Laclau's presentation, this gap does not vanish or disappear in the process of identification; rather, freedom or indeterminacy continues to haunt every determinate content rendering the latter vulnerable and subject to contestation or subversion. "An active identification," he states (again in a Sartrean vein), "is not a purely submissive act on the part of the subject, who would passively incorporate all the determinations of the object. The act of identification, on the contrary, destabilizes the identity of the object." Given the persistent undercurrent of freedom and negativity, every act of identification necessarily constitutes the object or content of identity "as a *split* object." It is precisely at this point that the constructivist dimension of the deconstructive approach comes to the fore: the aspect that every identification is basically an arbitrary or willful construction in the sense that no determination can logically or rationally be derived from a constitutive indeterminacy or freedom. To quote Laclau again: Any act of identification involves an effort to "'fill' an originary lack"—where the content of the "filling" remains basically contingent and "external" to the constitutive emptiness. This means that, given the premise of an "originary and *ineradicable* lack," any identification will have to represent also the gap or the "lack itself," that is, its contingent and arbitrary character. Differently and more elaborately phrased: "The filling function requires an empty place, and the latter is, to some extent, indifferent to the content of the filling, though this filling function has to be incarnated in *some* concrete contents, whatever these contents may be." This means, in turn, that between the "filling function" (or the construction of identity) and "the concrete content that actualizes it," there remains necessarily a "constitutive incommensurability" revealing the "radical character of the opposition between 'organization' [social identity] and nothingness." Given the contingent and arbitrary character of construction, any concrete determination involves the exercise of power that decides or cuts the Gordian knot between competing possible contents. From this it follows that, in Laclau's words, "power is the *source* of the social" and "the absolute origin of whatever order there is in society."[15]

As one should note, "power" for Laclau is not a metaphysical category or the attribute of an "essential" quality but rather the outcome of an act of will—which is always contestable by other wills even when the latter are (temporarily) subdued. As he observes, a main condition for a relation of power to exist is that "there has to be a conflict of wills in which one of them would prevail." (One may note here, in parenthesis, that social or intersubjective relations in Sartre's early philosophy were also marked by radical conflict.) In a quasi-Hobbesian vein, Laclau adds that power and legitimacy are always at odds because, given its contingent source, power can never be rationally or ethically justified; the only way for the powerful to forfeit their power is if they are no longer able to insure public order. In a more recent writing, Laclau has further accentuated the aporetic and conflictual character of identity, while moving the discussion more resolutely onto the political terrain. As he states there, politics is crucial because it provides society with the kind of determinations required for identifiable policies and agendas; at the same time, it is aporetic because it can never provide the "correct" determination. In his words, one has to admit "an expansion of the political at the expense of the social," while simultaneously recognizing politics as a merely "*contingent* production of the social link." Differently and more forcefully put: that which makes politics possible and necessary—"the contingency of the acts of institution"—is also what makes it impossible or aporetic because "ultimately no constituting act is fully achievable" (by providing full legitimacy). At this point the connection between deconstruction and constructivism comes fully into view. Employing the notions of "undecidability" and "decision" for the earlier terms "indeterminacy" and "determination," Laclau describes his perspective as involving two basic moves: namely, first, "a widening of the field of structural undecidability"; and second, "a clearing of the field for a theory of decision as taken in an undecidable terrain."[16]

The aporetic tension between these two moves has crucial implications for identity formation or identification. "If there is need for identification," Laclau says, "it is because there is no identity in the first place," but rather an undecidable terrain of possibilities. To pinpoint further the complexity of the tension, he introduces the important term "hegemony" denoting the purely contingent character of political determination or identification. In a political context, he notes, the indeterminacy (or "absent fullness") of the social terrain "has to be represented/misrepresented by one of its particular contents (a political force, a class, a group). This relation by which a particular element assumes the impossible task of a universal [fully legitimate] representation, is what I call a *hegemonic* relation." This relation reveals again the constitutive "gap" operating in social and political life: the gap between indeterminacy and determination, between undecidability and decision—the two terms which together "make possible *a political* society." As Laclau elaborates, "decision" in this context is always contingent, rationally ungrounded, and hegemonically constructed—in the sense that it is both "self-grounded" and "exclusionary" (by obstructing alternative agendas). Being radically ungrounded or self-grounded and, at the same time, aspiring to a fully comprehensive determination, political decision in a way resembles the power of God who is likewise self-grounded and at the same time fully determining. (At this point, another parallel surfaces, with Sartre who had defined human longing for complete identity as an imitation of God and hence as a "useless passion.") "To take a decision," Laclau writes, "is like impersonating God. It is like asserting that one does not have the means of being God, and one has, however, to proceed as if one were Him." Coming out of nowhere or undecidability, political decision—although perhaps externally constrained—follows no intrinsic criteria and hence reflects pure will: "The madness of the decision is the blind spot in the [social] structure in which something totally heterogeneous with it . . . has, however, to supplement it."[17]

In center-staging the role of an undetermined, nearly capricious decision, Laclau in some respects follows the lead of Jacques Derrida who, on various occasions, had celebrated the function of extra-rational interventions, aligning himself on this point with Kierkegaard's "leap." As he wrote in a famous essay called "Force of Law" and subtitled "The 'Mystical Foundation of Authority'": "The moment of *decision, as such*, always remains a finite moment of urgency and precipitation, since it must not be the consequence or the effect of this theoretical or historical moment, of this [rational] reflection or deliberation, since it always marks the interruption of the . . . deliberation that precedes it, that must precede it. The instance of the decision is a madness, says Kierkegaard." In the same context, Derrida also described decision making—the move from radical undecidability to decision—as a mode of "irruptive violence," because it cannot help but disrupt or dislodge prevailing arrangements and habitual identities.[18] In a more recent text, responding in part to Laclau's arguments, Derrida has sought to clarify the extent of both his agreement and his disagreement with the former's position. The concurrence or agreement has to do mainly with the juxtaposition of undecidability and decision, of indeterminacy and determination. "I am in complete agreement," he observers, "with everything that Ernesto Laclau has said on the question of hegemony and power, and I also agree that [in the formation of hegemony] . . . force and violence are present." To be sure, the force of hegemonic determination is silhouetted here against the backdrop of a pervasive indeterminacy that can be described, in a sense, as a mode of nonviolence. Using slightly different vocabulary, Derrida depicts the tension between indecision and decision as the contest between stability and instability, between order and chaos, stating:

> Once it is granted that violence is *in fact* irreducible, it becomes necessary—and this is the moment of politics—to have rules, conventions and stabilizations of power. All that a deconstructive point of view tries to show is that, since conventions, institutions and consensus are stabilizations, . . . this means that they are stabilizations of something essentially unstable and chaotic. Thus, it becomes necessary to stabilize precisely because stability is not natural [but constructed]; . . . it is because there is chaos that there is need for stability. . . . If there were continual stability, there would be no need for politics, and it is to the extent that stability is not natural, essential or substantial, that politics exists.[19]

The disagreement between the two thinkers revolves basically around the role of the "subject" or agent of decision—a role that Laclau considers crucial for the constructivist dimension of politics, while Derrida prefers to relegate it to a derivative outcome of decision making. "The question here is," he writes, "whether it is through the decision that one becomes a subject who decides something." In a bold formulation (harking back in some ways to Sartre's famous *The Transcendence of the Ego*), he adds: "I would say that once one poses the question in that form and one imagines that the who and the what of the subject can be determined in advance, then there is no decision." Differently put: "The decision (if there is such a thing) must bracket if not render impossible in advance the who and the what." What Derrida aims to accomplish with this move is to forestall the possibility that decision making could be derived from, or guided by, any preexisting content, including the structure of a subject. In this manner, he underscores the arbitrary contingency and indeterminacy of the decision—its character as a pure irruption or disruption—more resolutely even than Laclau admits: "If there is a decision, it presupposes that the subject of the decision does not yet exist and neither does the object." What emerges here is a radical or absolute form of constructivism, a kind of pure *creatio ex nihilo* of all identities and determinate beings whose stability is permanently threatened or undercut by nothingness: "When I decide I invent the subject," that is, "I invent the who, and I decide who decides what." Despite the recognized need for, and even indispensable function of identification (which is the outcome of decision or construction), its status resembles Penelope's labor: countermanding the need, there is also "a process of disidentification, because if the decision is identification, then the decision also destroys itself."[20]

DIALOGUE AND CREATIVE PRAXIS

As an antidote to fixed or essentialized identities, constructivism clearly has a liberating élan, opening the social field for many innovative initiatives. As the preceding discussion aimed to show, constructivism relies on a series of basic paradoxes or antinomies—especially the antinomies of absence and presence, negativity and positivity—although these aspects are rarely fully foregrounded or embraced by its defenders. In the above presentation, Laclau's and Derrida's arguments were singled out precisely because of their radicalism, internal consistency, and unwillingness to evade theoretical implications. Although broadly sympathetic to their outlook, many other writers espouse more moderate or toned-down versions of their approach—testifying to the fact that constructivism has emerged as a dominant paradigm in contemporary social theory (functioning sometimes almost like a mantra). Little purpose would be served in sampling or offering a survey of relevant literature, especially since such a survey would hardly yield more than variations on a basic theme.[21] All that needs to be stated here is that popularity of a paradigm does not shield it against critical reservations and scrutiny.

Irrespective of its liberating potential, constructivism (in my view) suffers from a series of important drawbacks. For one thing, the model relies necessarily on a constructing agent or "subject"—regardless of whether the latter is viewed as a precondition or as a by-product (or emergent property) of decison making. To this extent, the model runs counter to the "linguistic turn" in recent philosophy and, perhaps more relevantly, to the vaunted "decentering of the subject" from which much of postmodernism and post-structuralism took their departure. With this reliance on the subject, and its rejection of all forms of mediation, the paradigm also reinstates prominently the dualism between subject and object, pure act and content of decision—together with the other antinomies (previously mentioned) between negativity and positivity, immanence and transcendence. As a corollary of this reinstatement, conflict surfaces as a hallmark of the model on several levels: conflict between undecidability and decision, and between different decision-making agendas—a collision which is never far removed from violence and which ironically replicates the clash of "essential" identities (meant to be exorcised).[22] The major drawback of constructivism, however, resides in the idea of "construction" itself, which usually operates as a synonym for manufacturing or social engineering. With this idea, the paradigm confirms or "buys into" the basic modern trajectory, inaugurated by Francis Bacon and Thomas Hobbes, which center-stages and celebrates the virtues of fabrication and instrumental design—a trajectory buttressing the primacy of technology and technical mastery (coupled with economic productivity) in the modern world. What urgently needs to be remembered in this context is the distinction between "*techne*" and "*praxis*," between monological-instrumental designs and modes of social activity that, though creatively innovative, remain attentive and responsive to interactive contexts (thus shunning *creatio ex nihilo*).[23]

The limitations of constructivism are recognized even by writers otherwise friendly to postmodern sensibilities. In his (previously mentioned) book *Identity/Difference*, Connolly acknowledges their intimate correlation, stating: "An identity is established in relation to a series of differences that have become socially recognized. These differences are essential to its being; if they did not exist as differences, it would not exist in its distinctness and solidity." From this premise, Connolly draws the moral and political conclusion that—construed as "both historically contingent and inherently relational"— a lived or concrete identity opens up the possibility for agendas that exceed "the models of conquest, conversion, [homogenized] community, and [paternalistic] tolerance."[24] More explicitly, Bhargava criticizes the notion of a unilateral or monological constructivism. Although it may be true, he notes, that cultural identities are not "natural and transparent" in an essentialist manner, it does not follow by any means "that the politics of cultural difference rests on a total hoax" or that the identity/difference couplet is entirely "invented" or manufactured. What militates against the latter assumption is the relational character of identity formation: the fact that social identities are formed to a significant extent in response to social contexts, especially the contexts of language, culture, and historical experiences and memories. "The identity of persons," he affirms, "is constituted in large measure by the language and vocabulary used by them" and prevailing cultural beliefs and narratives. Language and cultural beliefs, however, are not merely mental phenomena but inscribed in practical ways of life or modes of conduct. With this insight, Bhargava is led to underscore the formative role of "social practice" or praxis—which he describes as a set of "actions of several [interacting] individuals" whose self-descriptions are "social" and hence not purely unilateral.[25]

In the context of contemporary philosophy and political theory, the interactive and multilateral formation of identity is underscored especially in the work of Charles Taylor. As he observes in his seminal essay "The Politics of Recognition," the sense of human personhood or identity is lost sight of if it is construed monologically. "The crucial feature of human life," he insists, "is its fundamentally *dialogical* character. We become full human agents, capable of understanding ourselves and hence of defining our identity, through our acquisition of rich human languages of expression." By emphasizing the role of language, Taylor does not mean to focus narrowly on spoken words but to bring into view broader cultural practices and symbolic acts—including "the 'languages' of art, of gesture, of love, and the like." The main point here is that identity formation always involves a form of interactive responsiveness, whereas unilateralism shortchanges or excludes the role of others—especially "significant others"—in our lives. Above all, the latter forgets "how our understanding of the good things in life can be transformed by our enjoying them in common with people we love." For Taylor, dialogical interaction does not always entail common enjoyment or agreement, but may also involve mutual contestation and even struggle—just as long as contestation does not preclude further interaction (through a retreat into monologue, parochial separation or "communalism"). Like other modern and so-called liberal thinkers, Taylor values the importance of individual freedom: of the individual's ("inward") contribution to identity formation, and hence his/her ability to challenge social conventions which may have become obsolete or oppressive. It is precisely this modern freedom that lends crucial weight to interactive "recognition," to the task of continuously redefining and renegotiating social and political relationships. In his words, far from undercutting the need for dialogue, the emergence of "an ideal of inwardly generated identity" provides impetus for the "politics of recognition."[26]

Given the extent to which constructivism relies (mostly covertly) on Sartrean teachings, it may not be inappropriate to turn here to one of Sartre's closest philosophical allies and most perspective critics: Maurice Merleau-Ponty. In several of his writings, Merleau-Ponty objected to Sartre's purely conflictual or anti-nomial conception of intersubjective relations and to his unilateral construal of self and other-identity. In a more positive vein, an alternative conception of human relations surfaced in some of his later works, especially in his (posthumously assembled) *The Prose of the World*. There, in a chapter on "Dialogue and the Perception of the Other," Merleau-Ponty asks the basic question: how can the self relate to an "other" or others without appropriating them or else surrendering to them as their victim? What is needed, in his view, is an approach that bypasses both the clash of rigid (essentialized) identities and their submergence in a superior synthesis, in favor of a more complex collusion or intertwining. "Myself and the other," he states, "are like two *nearly* concentric circles which can be distinguished only by a slight and mysterious slippage." The formulation brings into view a mode of human relationship that remains inconceivable as long as self presumes to construct *ex nihilo* and confronts the other "like a sheer cliff." What is presupposed here is the abandonment of solipsism: the aspect that identities (of self and other) are no longer unilaterally constructed or manufactured, but are seen as emerging in an open space or a shared "world"—although this world may be inhabited in very different ways. It is by virtue of this shared "being-in-the world" that self-other perception and understanding are possible. In his words:

As long as it adheres to my body like the tunic of Nessus, the world exists not only for me but for everyone in it who makes gestures toward it. There is a universality of feeling—and it is upon this that our identification rests, the generalization of my body, the perception of the other.[27]

As one should note, the intertwining sketched here is not quite the same as mutual "recognition"—as long as that term is interpreted in a purely cognitive or cerebral sense. In Merleau-Ponty's treatment, human relationship proceeds not only by rational argumentation, but involves a deeper existential engagement, an engagement of "being" operating on the levels of thought, utterances, feelings, and corporeal experience. Such engagement occurs always in concretely situated contexts that, in turn, include cultural frames of meaning, historical narratives, and sociopolitical arrangements. World-contexts, moreover, are not merely static fixtures or externally imposed structures but malleable forms of social life nurtured and continuously reshaped by practical participation and creative modes of social praxis; it is in this sense that Merleau-Ponty notes that "communities of being" are transformed and reconceptualized as "communities of doing."[28] In many instances, prevailing cultural and sociopolitical contexts are marked by profound agonies and fissures, by festering traumas in the social body deriving from perceived injuries and injustices in the past. To this extent, historical narratives are not only celebrations of shared meanings and achievements, but also the record of social wounds inflicted by various forms of oppression, exclusion, and nonrecognition. It is precisely at this point that memory-work has to come into play—not for the sake of solidifying and perpetuating resentments or hostilities, but with the aim of social healing or therapy through the imaginative-creative refashioning of social relationships. Bhargava is right on target when he insists (in a Freudian manner) that history cannot be exorcised but needs to be "worked through." Without a proper engagement with the past and an institutionalized remembering, he writes, "societies are condemned to repeat, reenact, and relive the horror" of past injuries. Only a willingness to deal concretely and creatively with history and its contemporary repercussions can prepare the groundwork for "a livable common future"—and this has to happen not only through rational discussion but also "at the level of emotions," that is, the level of human sufferings and aspirations.[29]

By way of conclusion, let me briefly summarize some of the points of the preceding presentation. Taking my departure from the present world situation, I tried to show initially how the process of globalization fosters (or can foster) a propensity for fixed or "essentialized" identities: for a "clash of civilizations" pitting against each other globalizers and globalized, the North and the South, or "the West versus the Rest." In this confrontation, the idea of "universalism" often serves as a camouflage for particular hegemonic ambitions—ambitions that tend to be resisted on the part of nonhegemonic societies or cultures through a retreat into nostalgic (and essentialized) forms of parochialism, communalism, or ethnocentrism. One exit route from this (potentially violent) clash of identities—a route favored by some postmodern thinkers—is the strategy of constructivism, a strategy which negates or "deconstructs" all existing identities in favor of contingent fabrication. In its most radical formulation, the model relies on a "nihilating" indeterminacy or undecidability supplemented by a determining "decision" which proceeds without grounds (or *ex nihilo*). While appreciating the liberating élan of this strategy, I have also pointed out some of its shortcomings: its subservience to the modern (Western) infatuation with technical production; its propensity toward conflict (possibly violence); and, above all, its neglect of social praxis. It was chiefly the latter deficiency which led me to the consideration of an alternative approach to identity formation: an approach which center stages dialogue and concrete social and existential interaction. The advantage of this approach, in my view, is that it avoids the danger of essentialism or identity fixation, while simultaneously escaping the pitfalls of unilateralism and unmitigated willfulness. Dialogical engagement also has a moral and ethical-political advantage. Partners to the engagement do not seek to manipulate, assimilate, or appropriate each other, thus treating each other (at least potentially) as "ends" rather than means. On an ethical-political plane, interactive engagement reduces the chances of collision or violent conflict, thus enhancing the prospect of social peace or (what Bhargava calls) "a livable common future." In an age like ours—marked by brutality and seemingly endless bloodshed—this prospect must surely be welcome.

NOTES

1. See Derrida, *The Other Heading: Reflections on Today's Europe*, and Edward W. Said, *Orientalism* (New York: Vintage Books, 1979).
2. Amélie Rorty, *The Identities of Persons* (Berkeley: University of California Press, 1976), p. 2.
3. Rajeev Bhargava, "Introducing Multiculturalism," in *Multiculturalism, Liberalism and Democracy,* ed. R. Bhargava, A. K. Bagchi, and R. Sudarshan (New Delhi: Oxford University Press, 1999), pp. 4-5.
4. Bhargava, "Introducing Multiculturalism," p. 7.
5. The notion of the "ontic-ontological difference" is associated with the philosophy of Martin Heidegger. In the opening pages of *Being and Time*, Heidegger

resolutely rejects the construal of "Being" as a transcendental meta-concept. See *Being and Time*, pp. 2-7. On Vedantic philosophy see, e.g., Eliot Deutsch, *Advaita Vedanta: A Philosophical Reconstruction* (Honolulu: University of Hawaii Press, 1973).

6. On this distinction see the comments of Chantal Mouffe in "Radical Democracy: Modern or Postmodern?" in her *The Return of the Political* (London: Verso, 1993), pp. 9-22.

7. Immanuel Wallerstein, *Geopolitics and Geoculture: Essays on the Changing World-System* (Cambridge: Cambridge University Press, 1991), pp. 216-217.

8. Dussel, *The Invention of the Americas*, pp. 26, 65-66.

9. Samuel Huntington, "The Clash of Civilizations?" in *Foreign Affairs* 72 (1993): pp. 22-49.

10. Abdallah Laroui, "L'intellectuel du Tiers Monde et Marx, ou encore une fois le problème du retard historique," in International Social Science Council (UNESCO), *Marx and Contemporary Scientific Thought* (The Hague: Mouton, 1969), p. 281.

11. William E. Connolly, *Identity/Difference: Democratic Negotiations of Political Paradox* (Ithaca, NY: Cornell University Press, 1991), p. 12.

12. Bhargava, "Introducing Multiculturalism," p. 9.

13. Ernesto Laclau and Lilian Zac, "Minding the Gap: The Subject of Politics," in *The Making of Political Identities,* ed. Laclau (London: Verso, 1994), p. 12.

14. Laclau and Zac, "Minding the Gap," pp. 12-13. The chief work of Jean-Paul Sartre relevant in this context is his *Being and Nothingness: An Essay on Phenomenological Ontology*, trans. Hazel E. Barnes (New York: Philosophical Library, 1956).

15. Laclau and Zac, "Minding the Gap," pp. 14-17.

16. Laclau and Zac, "Minding the Gap," pp. 18-22; Laclau, "Deconstruction, Pragmatism, Hegemony," in *Deconstruction and Pragmatism, ed.* Chantal Mouffe (London and New York: Routledge, 1996), p. 48.

17. Laclau, "Deconstruction, Pragmatism, Hegemony," pp. 55-56, 59-60. Noting the presence of external constraints, Laclau moderates these bold statements somewhat by adding (pp. 57-58): "I did not mean there is a radical absence of rules and that all decision is entirely free. . . . The madness of the decision is, if you want, as all madness, a regulated one. . . . The highest forms of rationality that society can reach is that of a regulated madness." On the notion of "hegemony" see also Laclau and Chantal Mouffe, *Hegemony and Socialist Strategy: Towards a Radical Democratic Politics* (London: Verso, 1985).

18. Jacques Derrida, "Force of Law: The 'Mystical Foundation of Authority,'" in *Deconstruction and the Possibility of Justice*, ed. Drucilla Cornell, Michel Rosenfeld, and David G. Carlson (New York and London: Routledge, 1992), pp. 26-27. For a very different treatment of violence, see his "Violence and Metaphysics: An Essay on the Thought of Emmanuel Levinas," in *Writing and Difference*, trans. Alan Bass (Chicago: University of Chicago Press, 1978), pp. 79-153.

19. Derrida, "Remarks on Deconstruction and Pragmatism," in *Deconstruction and Pragmatism*, pp. 83-84.

20. Derrida, "Remarks on Deconstruction and Pragmatism," p. 84. Compare in this context Sartre, *The Transcendence of the Ego*, trans. F. Williams and R. Kirkpatrick (New York: Noonday Press, 1957).

21. For some literature in this genre compare, e.g., Ted Hopf, *Social Construction of International Politics: Identities and Foreign Policies* (Ithaca, NY: Cornell University Press, 2002); Jo Labanyi, ed., *Constructing Identity in Contemporary Spain* (Oxford: Oxford University Press, 2002); Ruth Wodak et al., eds., *The Discursive Construction of National Identity* (Edinburgh: Edinburgh University Press, 1999); Allen J. Frantzen and John D. Niles, eds., *Anglo-Saxonism and the Construction of Social Identity* (Gainesville: University Press of Florida, 1997); Rashif Kalidi, *Palestinian Identity: The Construction of Modern National Consciousness* (New York: Columbia University Press, 1997); Kristi S. Long and Matthew Nadelhaft, eds., *America under Construction: Boundaries and Identities of Popular Culture* (New York: Garland, 1997).

22. It is against this background that one can understand the attractiveness of Carl Schmitt's thought for many postmodern constructivists, especially his definition of politics as the "friend-enemy" collision. See, e.g., Chantal Mouffe, ed., *The Challenge of Carl Schmitt* (London: Verso, 1999); also her "Pluralism and Modern Democracy: The Challenge of Carl Schmitt," in Mouffe, *The Return of the Political*, pp. 117-134.

23. For this distinction see, e.g., Heidegger, *The Question Concerning Technology and Other Essays*; Hans-Georg Gadamer, "What is Praxis? The Conditions of Social Reason," in his *Reason in the Age of Science*; and Hannah Arendt, *The Human Condition: A Study of the Central Dilemmas Facing Modern Man* (Chicago: University of Chicago Press, 1958), especially pp. 9-18.

24. Connolly, *Identity/Difference*, pp. 48, 64.

25. Bhargava, "Introducing Multiculturalism," pp. 7, 9, 32. In this context, he also points to "a revival of interest in hermeneutics and a vigorous impetus from anthropological studies which challenged the view that knowledge of cultures can be obtained by observing [or constructing] them from the outside" (p. 14).

26. Charles Taylor, "The Politics of Recognition," in *Multiculturalism and "The Politics of Recognition,"* ed. Amy Gutmann (Princeton: Princeton University Press, 1994), pp. 32-34. For similar comments compare also his "A Tension in Modern Democracy," in *Democracy and Vision: Sheldon Wolin and the Vicissitudes of the Political*, ed. Aryeh Botwinick and William E. Connolly (Princeton: Princeton University Press, 2001), pp. 79-95. Taylor in this context also invokes for support "Gadamerian hermeneutics" (p. 91).

27. Merleau-Ponty, "Dialogue and the Perception of the Other," in *The Prose of the World*, pp. 134, 137. For a further deepening of this line of thought see Merleau-Ponty, *The Visible and the Invisible*.

28. Merleau-Ponty, "Dialogue and the Perception of the Other," in *The Prose of the World*, p. 140. Compare also these comments in *The Visible and the Invisible* (pp. 159–160): "We do not have to choose between a philosophy that installs itself in the world or in the other and a philosophy that installs itself 'in us': . . . these alternatives are not imperative, since perhaps the self and the nonself are like the observe and the reverse and since perhaps our own experience *is* this turning round

that installs us far indeed from 'ourselves,' in the other, in the things. Like the natural man, we situate ourselves in ourselves *and* in the things, in ourselves *and* in the other, at the point where, by a sort of *chiasm*, we become the others and we become the world." In the attached "Working Notes" we read (p. 263): "In reality there is neither me nor the other as positive, posited subjectivities. There are two caverns, two opennesses, two stages where something will take place—and which both belong to the same world, to the stage of Being." What needs to be noted is that, seem from this angle, action or praxis is not a unilateral "decision" or "project," but just as much a passion or passivity (pp. 139, 221).

   29. Bhargava, "Introducing Multiculturalism," pp. 52, 54-55. Compare also Sheldon Wolin, "Injustice and Collective Memory," in his *The Presence of the Past* (Baltimore: Johns Hopkins University Press, 1989), pp. 32-40; and my "Memory and Social Imagination: Latin American Reflections," in *Dialogue Among Civilizations: Some Exemplary Voices*, pp. 105-118.

Chapter Eight

Nature and Artifact: Gadamer on Human Health

In many ways, modernity in the West constitutes a conspiracy against nature in favor of artifact or deliberate construction. In virtually all domains of human endeavor—from philosophy and science to industry and forms of modern art—we find a celebration of construction or production coupled with a near-contempt for "nature's ways." Even intellectual tendencies critical of aspects of Western modernity readily pay homage to the modern ethos by employing self-chosen labels like "constructivism," "reconstruction," and "deconstruction." No doubt, this modern ethos also carries ennobling features: ultimately, the zeal for construction testifies to human creativity and inventiveness, to the strong Promethean streak operative in humankind. Yet, relentlessly pursued, Prometheanism carries a heavy price: that of potential self-destruction. Although deliberately seeking to expand the range of human possibilities (perhaps infinitely), construction runs headlong into the vortex of finitude, thus endangering the very source of possibilities (or its own "condition of possibility"). In large measure, this danger has to do with modernity's liaison with mastery and forceful, even violent intervention: virtually all forms of modern construction forcefully disrupt or redirect natural processes whose regenerative powers are hardly unlimited. The destructive potential of constructivism is vividly evident in the arsenal of nuclear weapons threatening global survival; it is also manifest in the steadily intensifying ecological crisis, which erodes the moorings of human habitation (*oikos*) on earth.

The dilemmas of construction are also reflected in the field of human illness and health, that is, in the domain of medical treatment and its limits. Here again, Prometheanism has yielded impressive triumphs. Undeniably, the advances of medical science have been able to combat and even eradicate major illnesses that had plagued humankind in the past; yet, its competence in attacking illness does not equally extend to fostering and sustaining human health and natural well-being. Although remarkably efficient in artificially prolonging the duration of life, medicine is not similarly able to produce natural longevity and with it the benefit of seasoning accruing to a richly textured old age. Among contemporary philosophers, no one has reflected more intensively on questions of illness and health than Hans-Georg Gadamer, the late "dean" of Continental philosophy whose entire lifework steered a subtle course between hermeneutical questioning and listening, between artful construction and "letting-be" (or between nature and art). Gadamer's reflections are all the more significant as his own life exemplifies concretely the point of his theoretical teaching. Born in 1900 and reaching the biblical age of 102, Gadamer was a witness of the turbulent course of an entire century—all the while maintaining a steady path throughout these turbulent events. Surely much can be learned from his example about steadiness and about aging as a mode of continued seasoning. Gadamer's reflections on these topics are contained mainly in a book first published in German in 1993 and subsequently translated into English under the title *The Enigma of Health* (in 1996). In the following I shall first of all review the main arguments regarding illness and health presented by Gadamer in that book. Next, I shall correlate and compare these arguments with prominent themes found in some of his other writings. By way of conclusion, I shall broaden the focus by inserting Gadamer's insights into the larger context of contemporary philosophical discussions and global political experiences.

THE ENIGMA OF HEALTH

Gadamer's *The Enigma of Health* carries the subtitle *The Art of Healing in a Scientific Age*. The subtitle is revealing as it points to one of the book's main concerns: the tension and even conflict between modern science, including medical science, and the practice of healing seen as the restoration and maintenance of health. From Gadamer's perspective—which he shares with such different thinkers as Heidegger and Habermas—modern science involves basically a process of distantiation from and objectification of the world geared toward the goal of human mastery or control over nature. As he writes, modern science denotes no longer "the totality of the knowledge of the world" which Greek philosophy had elaborated; rather, based on a unitary methodology as formulated by Descartes, modern science functions as a "tribunal of verification" before which nature's laws can be confirmed or refuted. Predicated on this methodology, modern science no longer blends with nature, but rather makes possible a "knowledge directed to the power of making, a knowing mastery of nature"—which is the essence of technology. As contrasted with the natural philosophy of antiquity, modern science in Gadamer's view is no longer concerned with nature seen as "a self-maintaining and self-restoring totality." Rather, wedded to strategic intervention and the Kantian motto of "forcing nature to yield its secrets," science bears the earmarks of "making and producing," and especially those of "projective construction." Modern science, we read,

> understands itself precisely as a kind of knowledge that is guided by the idea of transforming nature into a human world, indeed almost of eliminating the natural dimension by means of rationally controlled projective "construction." As science this knowledge allows us to calculate and to control natural processes to such an extent that it finally becomes capable of *replacing* the natural by the artificial.[1]

As presented by Gadamer, modern science not only stands in opposition to classical or premodern forms of knowledge, but also obscures or pushes aside the distinction between technical application of rules and ordinary life practice—or in Greek terms, the distinction between *techne* and *praxis*. For Gadamer as for the Greeks, practice is closely related not to "making" but to a person's being and sense of life. This relation, he writes, is reflected in the figurative German expression "*Was machst du denn?*"—that "does not ask, literally, what are you doing but, rather how *are* you?" As a student of Heidegger, Gadamer clearly perceives the connection between life practice and the phenomenological notions of "life-world" and "being-in-the-world" which are irreducible to objectification. Formulating the difference in terms of perspectives he notes that, alongside the scientific worldview, which treats the world "as an object to be dominated and as a mere field of resistance," there is another perspective irreducible to it. While the former sees every object as "something to be broken down and mastered," the alternative view relies on the "idea of the life-world, introduced into the philosophy of this century by Husserl." Despite our deep impregnation by scientific method, the life-world remains an arena of practical involvement and engagement and the task which falls on all human beings is to "find our own way" in that world and to "learn to accept our real limits." Finding one's way in the life-world requires not so much the technical application of rules as the exercise and cultivation of practical judgment—a faculty which today is greatly endangered. While the capacity for scientific and technical rationality is celebrated and continuously refined, the "autonomous formation of judgment and of action" is correspondingly neglected. This neglect, for Gadamer, has its basis in the character of modern civilization, an aspect which can be captured in the following broad maxim: "The more strongly the sphere of application becomes rationalized, the more does proper exercise of judgment along with practical experience in the proper sense tend to atrophy."[2]

Seen against this background modern medical science occupies a precarious and ambivalent position, being pulled simultaneously into the conflicting directions of growing rationalization and the tradition of prudential, personalized treatment. On the one hand, modern medicine shares with natural science the ambition to explain illness and health in purely physiological or neurophysiological terms. On the other hand, many doctors still maintain a "special relation" with their patients, a relationship conceived under the auspices of the "art of healing." In Gadamer's words, modern medicine finds itself in "an exceptional and problematic position" vis-à-vis other forms of knowledge or know-how. Although keenly aware of, and influenced by, advances in modern natural science (especially neurobiology), physicians still find it difficult, and even objectionable, simply to subsume their patients under general scientific schemata. Thus, in modern medical practice, the different concerns of prudential treatment and scientific intervention, of nature and artful technique, stand in "a particularly tense and antagonistic relationship." For Gadamer, the tension cannot be relieved by a simple dismissal of modern science; but it can certainly not be cured or remedied by a neglect of prudential judgment. Among the diverse modes of professional competence medicine represents a "peculiar unity of theoretical knowledge and practical know-how," a unity moreover which cannot simply be understood as the "application of science to the field of praxis." Given its blending of concerns, medicine constitutes "a peculiar kind of practical science for which modern thought no longer possesses an adequate concept."[3]

A main reason for the unique status of medicine is the peculiar character of human health—what Gadamer calls "the enigma of health." Although illness may be subject (within limits) to technical intervention and control, human health is something which happens or operates naturally or by itself. To this extent, health as such cannot fall under the aegis of construction or production. Gadamer's book is eloquent in castigating or challenging the notion that health can somehow be technically engineered or "made." As he notes, "the limits of what can be measured and, above all, of what can be effected through intervention reach deep into the realm of health care"; in fact, "health is not something that can simply be made or produced." Instead of being the result of manipulation or forceful intervention, our health is something that "each and everyone of us must take care of through the way in which we lead our lives." Far from being amenable to construction or the project of mastery, health in a way antedates and undergirds our deliberate projects and designs. Against this background, what medical practice can aim to accomplish is not so much the production as the recovery of health through the removal or containment of disease. In Gadamer's words, the special character of medical know-how resides in the fact that "it does not 'make' or 'produce' but cooperates in the recovery of the ill." The effort to "master" a disease thus means simply "to know its course and be able to control it—not to be master of 'nature' to such a degree that one could simply 'take away' the disease." The task of medical practice hence is not to force or control nature but to assist in the recovery of the patient—until the point is reached where natural health "kicks in" again, rendering medicine and the doctor's help superfluous. Underscoring the broader significance of this aspect the text states:

> The doctor's profession possesses in a certain sense a symbolic value. For the task which confronts the doctor is not one of "making" something but rather one of providing help, of enabling patients to recover their health and to return to their everyday lives. Doctors can never completely entertain the illusion that health is something they simply "make" or which they fully control. They know that it is not themselves or their abilities but rather nature that they help to victory.[4]

These comments underscore and confirm what Gadamer calls the "enigma" or the "hidden" and "mysterious" character of health. In contrast to symptoms of illness, health as such does not actually "present itself to us"; rather, it lies in the very nature of health that it conceals itself from notice and simply "sustains its own proper balance and proportion." Contrary to the modern fascination with measurement and self-inspection, health is not a condition that one "diagnoses in oneself." Rather, for Gadamer, it is a "natural" mode of human *Dasein*, a "condition of being involved, of being in the world, of being together with one's fellow human beings, of active and rewarding engagement in one's everyday tasks." Beyond such active involvement, the hidden or concealed character of health is manifest in such rhythmic processes of human existence as breathing, digesting, and sleeping—and particularly in the condition of deep sleep (which is "one of the greatest enigmas we experience in our lives"). Although not deliberate or constructed, these rhythmic processes are "what actually sustains us"; and yet they have little to do "with the consumption of tablets and the conscious attempt to exert an influence on them." The semiconscious or unconscious character of these processes testifies to the inherence of human evidence in "nature" at large—an inherence that can never be reduced to construction or production. Whenever we are in good health, Gadamer adds, we seem to be supported "by a deeper stratum of unconscious life, by a general sense of self-being," which as such remains shielded or hidden from view. Particularly the process of falling asleep and waking up illustrates the limits of purposive design, for we cannot "experience" our falling asleep. This alternation of waking and sleeping reminds Gadamer of some of the sayings of Heraclitus, particularly the fragment which states: "The harmony which remains hidden is mightier than the harmony which is revealed"—prompting him to describe health as "a miraculous example of such a strong but concealed harmony."[5]

Located at the margin of intentional design, human health participates in the general self-maintenance and self-balancing of nature at large, that is, in the "natural condition of equilibrium." In its self-balancing capacity nature discloses itself as something that "as it were holds to its own course and does so in and of itself." Although amenable to some corrective measures, this course itself is not the outcome of construction or production. In regard to human illness and health, the genuine work of medical practice can consist not in Promethean "making," but only in the attempt "to restore an equilibrium that has been disturbed." By contrast, those who strive to engineer this equilibrium find themselves "thrown back, as it were, by something that is somehow self-sufficient and complete." As one should note, equilibrium here does not merely refer to a physiological homeostasis, but rather to a much broader, and in fact cosmic, balance. Gadamer repeatedly refers to Plato's *Phaedrus* and its "holistic" understanding of human being and the world. As Socrates insists in that dialogue, it is impossible to heal the body without knowing something about the soul; and it is impossible to heal body and soul without knowing something about the "whole"—which Gadamer interprets as "the unity of being itself." "It is the 'whole,'" he comments, "in the sense of the movement of the stars above and the changes of weather below, the rise and fall of the oceans and the living nature of the woods and fields." The whole includes everything that "surrounds and encompasses the nature of human beings" and that "determines whether they find themselves in a condition of safe health or exposed to dangerous threat." In the *Phaedrus*, medicine is compared with the genuine art of rhetoric that allows "the right kinds of discourse to exercise an effect on the soul in the right way." Similarly, medical practice means the right kind of treatment considering "the entire life situation of the patient, and even of the physician." Differentiating holism from a mere conceptual synthesis and insisting on the full meaning of the Greek "*holon*" (as denoting both "whole" and sound or "hale"), Gadamer comments:

> The parallel between the art of rhetoric and the art of medicine is also valid to the extent that the constitution of the body passes over into the constitution of the human being as a whole. The position of the human individual within the totality of being is a balancing position not merely in the sense of stably maintained health but also in a much more comprehensive sense . . . [I]n the last analysis there is only one single great equilibrium which sustains human life and which, though it sometimes wavers and flickers, fundamentally shapes our very state of being.[6]

As these comments indicate, human wholeness involves not only the proper correlation of body and soul, but also a broader attunement to the natural and cultural context, including social and political dimensions. Far from centering on the condition of an isolated patient, good health involves a way of life consonant with both the natural and the social-political environment. Gadamer in this context invokes the testimony of another Platonic dialogue, *The Statesman*, where Socrates distinguishes between different kinds of standards or measurements. While one kind of measure (*metron*) is imposed on an object from without, another measure (*metrion*) resides and can be found within the object itself. Whereas the first kind—preferred by modern science—tries to apply a uniform (possibly quantitative) scale to all phenomena, the second type seeks to be attentive to the "wholeness of our being-in-the-world" and requires an alert prudential judgment: the judgment as to what is "fitting" or "appropriate" (*das Angemessene*) in a given context. As Gadamer emphasizes, the second type is not simply a negation of measure or akin to the "unmeasurable"—which would reduce it to an exercise of arbitrary whim; rather, what is "fitting" or "appropriate" has its own form of "rightness" and does not need to be defined merely by negation. For Plato, in any case, social and political life demanded not only general rules but also the cultivation of holistic judgment regarding goodness and evil, health and decay—which ultimately undergirds human well-being. Seen in this light, wholeness and health exceed the confines of modern science with its correlation of cause and effect, intervention and success. Rather, as Gadamer says, they point to

> that hidden harmony which we must seek to recover and in which we discover both the miracle of reconvalescence and the mystery of health. Such harmony can be understood as a form of protected composure, of *Geborgenheit*.[7]

ART AND NATURE'S WAY

Gadamer's *The Enigma of Health* is a collection of some of his later essays specifically dealing with issues of illness and health; but it is by no means idiosyncratic or discontinuous with the rest of his work. In fact, students of his philosophy will readily recognize in the book themes familiar from some of his other publications, including his magisterial *Truth and Method*. Prominent among these themes is the critique of the supremacy of scientific method; the vindication of prudential judgment; the recovery of the notion of "nature" and its correlation with artful (but nontechnical) practice; and the defense of the conception of natural "rightness" or "appropriateness" (in contrast to artificial measurement). Taken as a whole, *Truth and Method* aims to retrieve the truth-quality of ordinary life practice and experience, as opposed to the sway of modern methodology—an opposition that can readily be translated into the distinction between the practical "art of healing" and the scientific ambitions of modern medicine. As is well known, *Truth and Method* opens with a chapter devoted to a discussion of the "problem of method" and the special significance of the humanities (or the "humanist tradition") for a proper resolution of that problem. As Gadamer points out, the self-understanding of the human sciences, as they developed in the nineteenth century, was entirely "governed by the model of the natural sciences." The goal of practitioners at the time was not to reclaim the intrinsic quality of the humanities, but to affirm the inductive method of experimental science as "the only valid method as such." Here Gadamer voices his important caveats or reservations:

> Now the real issue posed by the human sciences is that one misjudges their nature when applying to them the yardstick of a progressive inquiry into law-governed behavior. The experience of the socio-historical world cannot be scientifically decoded through the inductive procedure of natural science. Whatever "science" may mean here . . . historical research does not endeavor to grasp the concrete phenomenon as an instance of a general rule; . . . its ideal is rather to understand the phenomenon itself in its unique and historical concreteness.[8]

In an attempt to pinpoint more clearly the nature of the humanities, Gadamer turns to insights of the older "humanist tradition," particularly to such traditional notions as *"Bildung"* (formation, culture), "common sense," and judgment. With regard to *Bildung*, the crucial point to remember is the distinction between mere career training and a genuine deepening of human insight, that is, the difference between *Ausbildung* and *Bildung*. While, in the former case, training is oriented toward extrinsic goals and pursued through application of general schemata, the second type involves an intrinsic seasoning and personal transformation. As Gadamer writes: "Like nature (in the Greek sense of *physis*), *Bildung* has no extrinsic goals." By contrast to the formation of native talents for purposes of business or career, in *Bildung* "that by which and through which one is formed becomes completely one's own" (beyond any instrumental function). The seasoning effected through *Bildung*, moreover, is not simply an individual or isolated affair but deeply saturated with social and political experience—an aspect captured in the traditional concept of "common sense" or *sensus communis*. In explicating this concept, *Truth and Method* initially relies on Giambattista Vico's retrieval of "topical" understanding against Cartesian methodology but quickly broadens and enriches Vico's approach through reliance on Aristotelian *phronesis* and prudential judgment. In the Aristotelian tradition, we read, *phronesis* or practical knowledge is an understanding "directed toward the concrete situation," seeking to grasp "the circumstances in their infinite variety"—though without neglecting a commonality of meaning. Judgment here does not merely denote the capacity to subsume a given case under general categories; but it *does* involve a shared "ethical motif" which later infuses the Roman-Stoic doctrine of the *sensus communis*. Accordingly, *phronesis* for Aristotle is an intellectual and practical "virtue" which can operate only within the holistic context of all ethical virtues. Far from being a synonym for mere cleverness or shrewdness, prudential judgment is located in a shared ethical matrix: it aims basically at "the discernment of the proper and improper, of the appropriate and inappropriate, and thus presupposes a moral attitude which it in turn informs."[9]

According to *Truth and Method*, the classical and humanistic tradition of judgment has largely atrophied in modern times. Under the influence of the Enlightenment—especially Kantian philosophy in Germany—judgment has tended to be reduced to the subsumption of cases under universal categories, while its linkage with ethics and common sense has been canceled or sidelined. A major effort of *Truth and Method* is devoted to the recovery of this linkage and hence to the reconnection of judgment with the discernment of the appropriate (*das Angemessene*) in concretely shared contexts. Repeatedly, the book refers to a mode of human conduct which can be judged to be "naturally right" or appropriate in an ethical relationship—although (and it is important to emphasize this point) natural rightness for Gadamer can never be erected into a dogmatic ideology, but can only serve as a critical antidote to legal positivism or the blind acceptance of established legal norms.[10] A similar aim inspires the book's endeavor to rescue the domain of art (*Kunst*) from modern subjectivism and private whim. Through a detailed critique of Kantian aesthetics—which anchored aesthetic judgment in "taste" (to the exclusion of common sense)—Gadamer seeks to reassert the inherent truth-quality of art, that is, its participation in a (non-private) disclosure of truth. As he indicates, art—in opposition to "making" or technical production—carries its measure of appropriateness within itself, in a manner that reveals the affinity or connectedness between art and nature (or between art and natural health). In his words, the playfulness of art is "also a natural process (*Naturvorgang*)." Precisely because and insofar as humans are part of nature, "the sense of artistic play is that of pure self-disclosure." Differently put: "By being without (extrinsic) aim or purpose, and by moving effortlessly in a constantly self-renewing play, nature can appear as a model for art."[11]

In slightly modified form, the same or similar themes can also be found in several of Gadamer's later writings. Thus, the topic of the relation between art and nature occupies a prominent place in a series of essays written during the decade following *Truth and Method* and collected in English under the title *The Relevance of the Beautiful*. One essay in that collection titled "The Speechless Image" (more literally, "The Growing Muteness of the Image") raises specifically the issue whether the classical idea of "mimesis," of the mimetic relation between nature and art, is still applicable to modern and contemporary art forms. As Gadamer readily concedes, recent art is no longer mimetic in the sense of revealing the inner nature or feelings of the artist (as during the Romantic period); nor it is mimetic in the sense of trying to imitate external nature (as in traditional landscape paintings). Yet, despite these changes, there is still a deeper correlation between the two domains in that both resist external utility and are governed by their own intrinsic standard or measure, a measure enabling them to "set up a world." Thus, the classical notion of mimesis acquires a new meaning in our time. While clearly sidestepping the connotations of copying or mimicking, art maintains a resemblance with nature: as in the latter, "there is something regular and binding about the self-contained nature that grows out from within." Mimesis also figures centrally in "Art and Imitation," another essay contained in the same collection. Going back to the Aristotelian meaning of the concept, Gadamer insists that it is a "far cry" from any simple naturalism and rather points to the disclosure of the being or "real essence" of things. As a mode of disclosure, mimesis reveals "the miracle of order that we call a *kosmos*"—a view which seems broad enough to encompass modern art. "If I had to propose a universal aesthetic category," Gadamer concludes, it would be "mimesis in its most original sense as the disclosure of order"; for the artwork provides a "perfect example of that universal trait of human existence—the never-ending process of building a world."[12]

The issue of the relation of art and nature has remained a leitmotif throughout Gadamer's later years. Almost three decades after the cited passages he wrote an essay titled "Word and Image" in which the notion of mimesis was further refined by being still more solidly anchored in both Greek and modern philosophy. Referring to Hegel's concept of the "absolute," Gadamer noted that the concept might properly be applied to the noninstrumental or nonutilitarian character of art, in contradistinction from modes of technical production. The "work" of the artwork clearly has a different status from an artificial product. To the extent that art "accomplishes" anything or lets anything happen, its work is reminiscent not of fabrication but rather of "nature which in springtime lets flowers blossom." In this manner art imitates nature in the Greek sense of *physis*, the latter term interpreted by means of Aristotelian *energeia* or "self-movement." As Gadamer stipulates at this point, "art consists in its movement or happening (*Vollzug*)"—which means that the nature of the artwork is "neither that of fabrication nor does it coincide with production or reproduction (on the part of the recipient)." As in the case of nature—and beyond any sense of mimicking—one can also detect in art or a given painting an intrinsic quality and even an "intrinsic dignity" (*eigene Hoheit*). Returning to Greek philosophy, Gadamer finds in Aristotle's *energeia* a deep insight into the character of living beings, an insight transgressing mathematical abstractions. While refusing to differentiate between artisans and artists, the Greeks did make a sharp distinction between *techne* and *physis*. The latter term designated the movement of living beings in all stages, from acorn or seedling to young sapling to ripe fruit: "In Aristotle's words, all this is a movement or happening 'from nature to nature.' But the same happening (*Vollzug*) is the mark of art, as distinguished from products of making."[13]

Roughly at the same time as these comments Gadamer wrote another essay, "From Word to Concept," which explicitly transferred the nature-art connection to the medical field, that is, to the domain of natural health and the art of healing. Appealing again to the testimony of Plato, and particularly his dialogue *The Statesman*, the essay reminds readers of different kinds of measuring or measurement: especially the distinction between the imposition of an external yardstick and the search for, or attunement to, an intrinsic measure. In the first case, Gadamer notes, the measure is applied in order to facilitate the mastery or control of phenomena; the guiding yardstick here is that of "quantity (in Greek *poson*)." By contrast, the other kind of measuring aims to find in phenomena the appropriate or "right measure" (*das Angemessene*). This kind of attunement is familiar to us from the harmonies of music, but also from the "harmonious well-being that we call health." In this case, we are in the domain of "quality (in Greek *poion*)." While human illness may call for medical "science" seen as a profession exerting control over disease (according to quantitative criteria), human health has a basically qualitative character. For, Gadamer writes, being well is obviously something that we "cannot observe and control in the same fashion." Rather, health is something "that we follow along in the same way as we follow a path or road" and where we gain the feeling that "now things are right." In this sense, health bears a resemblance to nature and to art (here the art of healing): "We must be content to break down the resistance of illness and to assist nature in regaining its own hidden movement. The latter, however, requires the *art* of the physician, the ability to find the right or appropriate mode of treatment."[14]

LETTING-BE AND HUMAN FREEDOM

Although innovative and richly suggestive, Gadamer's arguments are not entirely unique or outside the pale of twentieth-century philosophy. In many respects one notices the influence of his foremost teacher, Martin Heidegger, and the latter's departure from (or "*Destruktion*" of) modern subject-centered metaphysics. Thus when, interpreting Aristotle, Gadamer finds the core of *energeia* in self-movement or a noninstrumental "bringing-forth," one cannot help being reminded of Heidegger's "Letter on Humanism," and especially its lapidary opening sentences (too often neglected) which address the issue of noninstrumental action or praxis. As Heidegger writes there: "We are still far from pondering the essence of action decisively enough. We view action only as causing an effect"—which in turn is "valued according to its utility." But "the essence of action is accomplishment (*Vollbringen*)"—which means "to unfold something into the fullness of its essence, to lead it forth into this fullness." And only what really "is" (that is, being as such) can be noninstrumentally "accomplished" in this manner. Similarly, when Gadamer likens nature or natural health to a path or a road that we "follow along" patiently and uncoercively, one is again reminded of the "Letter on Humanism," this time its closing lines. Reflecting on postmetaphysical thinking (that is, a thinking beyond mastery and control), Heidegger states there that such thinking does not pursue an extrinsic goal or objective but rather "gathers language into simple saying," thereby allowing language "to be the language of being, as the clouds are the clouds of the sky." Such thinking, he adds, "lays inconspicuous furrows in language"—which are "still more inconspicuous than the furrows that the farmer, slow of step, draws through the field."[15]

Regarding the linkage of nature and art (*Kunst*), the influence of Heidegger's teachings can again be readily detected. More than a decade before the *Letter*, Heidegger had composed his famous monograph on "The Origin of the Work of Art." There, anticipating Gadamer's later comments, Heidegger had stressed the intrinsic self-movement of the artwork, its adherence to an internal measure and nonsubservience to externally imposed, instrumental goals. As he noted at the time: "Where does an artwork belong? The work belongs as such uniquely within the realm that is opened up by itself; for the work-being of art occurs essentially and only in such opening up (*Eröffnung*)." The "opening up" accomplished by art involved for Heidegger not the mere expression of the artist's intent nor a copying of external phenomena, but rather a genuine "setting up of a world," that is, a disclosure of the core or "truth" of beings—where "truth" has the sense of the Greek "*aletheia*" rendered as unconcealment. Taken in this sense, there is in art "a happening of truth (*Geschehnis der Wahrheit*) at work." As one should note, the opening up or unconcealment performed by art does not yield a pure "truth of reason" understood as a complete rational transparency. Rather, every act of concealing or revealing also implies a mode of concealing or sheltering. What is particularly sheltered or concealed in art is the "naturalness" of the artwork, its inherence in "nature"—the latter term taken in the Greek sense of *"physis."* In Heidegger's words: in art "tree and grass, eagle and bull, snake and cricket first enter into their dinstinctive shapes and thus come to appear as what they are"—a self-movement which the Greeks called *physis* and which his own monograph terms "the earth," commenting that earth here designates not a "mass of matter deposited somewhere" but rather that "whence opening up returns and shelters everything that arises." To this extent, the artwork in setting up a world also "sets forth the earth" by allowing or "letting the earth be earth." (One may also recall that, a few years after this monograph, Heidegger composed a long essay on the Aristotelian notion of *physis*, an essay which—rescuing the term from any kind of static essentialism—underscored the close linkage between *physis* as *energeia* and *aletheia* and thereby also the connection or "mimesis" between nature and art.)[16]

The affinities of Gadamer's arguments with twentieth-century thought extend beyond the work of his teacher. With subtle modifications in style and substance, resonances can also be found in seemingly remote perspectives— including the perspective of the early Frankfurt School as represented by Theodor Adorno. To some extent, Adorno's reflections always revolved around the relation between reason and reality, between rational (or metaphysical) construction and attentiveness to nature in the sense of a reconceived notion of "mimesis." These reflections reached their most mature form in his later writings, especially in *Negative Dialectics* and *Aesthetic Theory*. In the former text, the dark or problematic side of the "dialectic of enlightenment" was found in the relentless ascendancy of instrumental reason over nature, that is, in the modern project of the progressive scientific and technological domination or mastery of the world. As Adorno remarks critically, the modern primacy of reason (or Cartesian subjectivity) is only another form of the "Darwinian struggle for survival." The supremacy of reason aims at "the control and repression of nature for human purposes"; this aim is the panacea of the modern subject "which proclaims itself with Bacon as master of nature and with idealism as the creator of all things." As it happens, however, the Hegelian master-slave relation is operative here too, with the result that the presumed master becomes the target of repression and his ideal dominion turns into a mere "naturalism" (in the Darwinian sense). As an antidote to this dialectic, Adorno recommends not a naturalistic mimicry, but rather a new form of "mimesis" involving a reflective "opening up" of reason: "To retrieve the repressed mimesis, conceptual reason needs to embrace—without self-surrender—something mimetic in its own conduct. To this extent, the aesthetic moment is not extrinsic to philosophy." In more elaborate form, and with specific attention to modern and late-modern art, the same theme can be found in *Aesthetic Theory* where "mimesis" is invoked as a mode (not of nostalgia but) of resistance in the midst of industrial and commercialized society.[17]

Rather than pursuing further such resonances or affinities, it may be more appropriate at this point to return to Gadamer's work and explore its broader practical-philosophical significance, including its political implications. Some of these implications have been highlighted by Gadamer himself, in a manner deeply relevant to contemporary political theorizing. In *The Enigma of Health* he draws a clear parallel between health and the art of healing, on the one side, and the maintenance of human freedom, on the other. As he notes, modern medical science with its steadily more sophisticated forms of technical intervention is in our time increasingly the province of specialized experts—a development that conjures up the danger of "expertocracy" and thus the extension of the mastery of illness into a form of social control. Thus, he finds it important for laypersons to maintain an attitude of critical vigilance regarding "the social and political claims of the experts." Such vigilance, he writes, "defends the ideal of the free society," assuring citizens "that they will not be disenfranchised by the authority of experts." For Gadamer, the non- or anti-manipulative character of the art of healing also stands in the service of human freedom. For, what is demanded in such nontechnical treatment is a kind of "letting-be," a willingness to allow natural health to reassert itself. This in turn requires that the physician treat the patient in the "right way"—an attitude that extends beyond the medical realm. The demand in all human interactions, Gadamer comments, is that "we address the other person in the right way, that we do not force ourselves on them or compel them to accept something against their will." Differently phrased:

> What is important is to recognize the other in their otherness, as opposed, for example, to the tendency toward standardization promoted by modern technology, the autocratic control of education by school authorities, or the blind insistence on authority by a teacher or a father. Only by means of such recognition can we hope to provide genuine guidance, which helps the other to find their own, independent way. Treatment always also involves a certain granting of freedom.[18]

The defense of freedom against external manipulation or control is not restricted to the book on health, but is a recurrent theme in Gadamer's writings. Thus, an essay written at the time of *Truth and Method* vindicated a nondogmatic and (in a way) precognitive "naturalness" against the inroads of technical intervention and construction. Invoking Husserl's famous motto "To the things themselves," the essay found in that motto a transgressive or critical potential—despite Husserl's own metaphysical leanings. As Gadamer observed at the time, expressions like "to the things" (*zu den Sachen*) or "the nature of things" (*die Natur der Sache*) carry a polemical intent: namely, the "rejection of violent arbitrariness in our dealing with things," especially the resort to capricious "conjectures" or "constructions." Originally, the German term "*Sache*" designated a disputed "matter" under consideration, an issue placed in the middle between contending parties so as to protect it "against the domineering grasp of one party or the other." The appeal to "things" or the "nature of things" thus refers to an order removed from instrumental machination or control and intends to assure "the triumph of the living spirit of justice" (in the sense of fitting or appropriate judgment). Closely related, and perhaps even preferable, to the expression "the nature of things" is the phrase "the language of things"—which, in Gadamer's presentation, likewise has a critical or polemical accent. When employing this phrase, he writes, we acknowledge the fact that usually "we are not at all ready to hear things in their own being," but prefer instead to subject them to our calculus, to the "domination of nature through the rationality of science." Thus, in our modern and contemporary situation, the mentioned phrases signal an act of resistance and recollection: In speaking of a language of things "we remember what things really are, namely, not material that is used and consumed, not a tool that is manipulated and set aside, but rather something that has existence on its own and is 'not forced to do anything,' as Heidegger says."[19]

In concrete political terms, the appeal "to the things" (*zu den Sachen*) mounts a critical attack on a dominant feature of modern political life: the undisputed sway of ideologies seen as instrumental marching orders or blueprints. Ever since the time of Thomas Hobbes, modern politics has revolved around a central artifact (the "state") and around the continuous construction of political order by means of ideological strategies and designs. In *this* respect, there is not much difference between left-wing, middle-of-the-road, and right-wing ideologies—although, to be sure, some political platforms are more benign than others.[20] What is at issue here is only the extent to which political life is entirely subsumed under comprehensive formulas (whether market-liberal, socialist, or whatever). If we can give credence to Gadamer (as well as Adorno), such subsumption under strategic plans basically rebounds against human freedom—by streamlining society in a uniform mold, to the neglect of difference or otherness. In a clear and paradoxical way, this danger was illustrated by orthodox Marxism, which sought to engineer the transition to the "reign of freedom" through resort to party dictatorship—thereby ignoring the required "absoluteness" of freedom (in Hegel's sense). Critique of ideological politics—it is important to emphasize here—does not at all amount to a retreat from politics or a facile quietism (charges which are often leveled at it). On the contrary, abandonment or serious curtailment of technical formulas or blueprints allows politics to recover its "self-movement," that is, to reassert itself as a human praxis devoted not to overall control but to the cultivation of prudential judgment regarding what is just or "the right thing to do" under the circumstances. Leaving behind subject-centered metaphysics, such praxis forsakes mastery in favor of an attentiveness to the thing (*Sache*) at issue and to the recessed but not mute "language of things."[21]

In light of the ongoing process of globalization and the growing interpenetration of different cultural life-forms, Gadamer's concern with non-mastery and natural recovery finds support in several traditions that Western intellectuals in the past have tended to keep at bay. Thus, his attention to things and their nature or language reminds students of Asian thought of Mahayana Buddhism, and especially of the Buddhist effort (or non-effort) to gain access to the "suchness" of things (*tathata*). In the words of the Japanese Zen thinker Nishitani: "Hills and rivers are hills and rivers in *not* being [conceptualized as] hills and rivers, just as the self is self in not being the self. And yet it is only here that hills and rivers are real hills and rivers in their suchness, only here that the self is the real self in its suchness (*tathata*)." Similarly, Gadamer's turning away from manipulative or ideological politics in the direction of "natural" (but not naturalistic) praxis finds a parallel in Taoist thought, as articulated, for example, in these lines of the *Tao Te Ching*: "Those who would take over the earth / And shape it to their will / Never, I notice, succeed." Or those other lines: "A leader is best / When people barely know that he exists."[22] As previously indicated, Gadamer's turn toward natural praxis does not involve a lapse into apathy or quietism but rather the cultivation of practical judgment conducive to right and just conduct. In this respect, his work finds ample support in Confucianism with its emphasis on virtue ethics and on right or fitting behavior. As is well known, Confucian ethics is not "deontological" (or guided by abstractly universal maxims) but anchored in the demands of concrete relationships. Guided by these demands, one can ask questions like these: Can it ever be "naturally right" for parents to abuse or mistreat their children, or for children to abuse their parents? Can it ever be right for spouses to mistreat or harm each other? Conversely one can ask: Is it not "naturally right" for parents and children and for spouses to treat each other mutually with care and solicitude? Likewise, is it not right for citizens in a political community to treat each other with justice and respectful kindness?[23]

Without explicitly invoking these distant traditions, Gadamer's work in many ways seems saturated with the insights of Asian thought—which, of course, are not all that far removed from classical (and pre-Socratic) thought in the West. A prominent commonality or East-West bridge can be found in the accent on something like a cosmic balance and also in the association of right conduct with the pursuit of the "middle way"—an association which, as we know, characterizes both Mahayana Buddhism and Aristotle's *Nicomachean*

Ethics. Gadamer repeatedly stresses the importance of balance and the middle way, particularly in the domain of politics. His essay "From Word to Concept" emphatically denies that the central quality of a genuine politician resides in success-orientation and the pursuit of panaceas. Rather, what such a politician requires is "a distinctive gift, namely, a certain sensitivity for balance, for the many possibilities of equilibrating situations"—which in turn demands a qualitative measure (of fittingness). Projecting this sensitivity for balance onto the contemporary global scene, Gadamer reflects on the possibility of balancing or reconciling science and technology with the preservation of more natural or indigenous ways of life. Western modernity, we read in *The Enigma of Health*, has tended steadily to separate or distantiate humans from their natural habitat for the sake of Promethean mastery or control—a process which today increasingly shows its danger for global ecology and global cohabitation. In this situation, only a concordance and mutual learning among cultures can provide an antidote:

> A mantle of civilization, beneath which other developed and developing countries are almost hidden from view, arose in Europe and today covers the entire world. People's "exposed" condition, though true of all humankind, has been intensified in Western civilization to the point of endangering us all. We should consider it a universal responsibility of human beings to learn to turn this capacity for self-alienation—this permanent yearning for novel possibilities and new ventures—back in the direction of the vast, balance-sustaining rhythm of the natural order.[24]

NOTES

1. Hans-Georg Gadamer, *The Enigma of Health: The Art of Healing in a Scientific Age*, trans. Jason Gaiger and Nicholas Walker (Stanford: Stanford University Press, 1996), pp. 5-6, 38-39. Compare also the comment (p. 105): "Through modern science and its experimental methods we compel nature to offer up answers. But in doing so we inflict a form of torture on it."

2. Gadamer, *The Enigma of Health*, pp. 4, 17, 101 (translation slightly altered).

3. Gadamer, *The Enigma of Health*, pp. 32-33, 39.

4. Gadamer, *The Enigma of Health*, pp. vii-viii, 22, 89. As Gadamer adds (p. 89): "Medicine is the only science which ultimately does not make or produce anything. Rather it is one which must participate in the wonderful capacity of life to renew itself, to set itself all right . . . Recovery here does not only mean a return to the harmony of waking and sleeping, of metabolic change, of respiration and all the other vital functions involved in life which someone who has been sick must learn to coordinate once again. It also means meeting the challenge of finding a way back from the condition of social disruption which illness entails and of

taking up again one's work or occupation, the sphere in which we actually live our lives."

5. Gadamer, *The Enigma of Health*, pp. 107, 113-115, 130-131.

6. Gadamer, *The Enigma of Health*, pp. 36-37, 41-42, 115.

7. Gadamer, *The Enigma of Health*, pp. 98-99, 116, 132-135. In addition to *The Statesman*, Gadamer also refers to the *Republic* (Plato's "great utopia") where "the true part of the citizen in the ideal state is described in terms of health, as a harmony in which everything is in accord, in which even the fateful problem of governing and being governed is resolved through reciprocal agreement and mutual interaction" (p. 75).

8. Gadamer, *Truth and Method*, 2nd rev. ed., trans. Joel Weinsheimer and Donald G. Marshall (New York: Crossroad, 1989), pp. 3-5 (translation slightly altered). In making this point, Gadamer obviously relies on the distinction between "nomothetic" and "idiographic" sciences familiar from Heinrich Rickert and Wilhelm Windelband, though without sharing their preoccupation with methodology.

9. Gadamer, *Truth and Method*, pp. 11, 21-22.

10. Gadamer, *Truth and Method*, especially p. 519, note 26. Compare in this context also Gadamer's critique of a dogmatic and anti-hermeneutical "natural worldview" (as espoused, for example, by Karl Löwith), pp. 499-501, 532.

11. Gadamer, *Truth and Method*, p. 105. As he adds (p. 108): "Play is really limited to presenting itself; its mode of being is that of self-disclosure. Now self-disclosure is a universal ontological characteristic of nature."

12. Gadamer, *The Relevance of the Beautiful, and Other Essays*, trans. Nicholas Walker, ed. Robert Bernasconi (Cambridge: Cambridge University Press, 1986), pp. 83, 90-91, 99, 101, 103-104 (translation slightly altered). The two essays date respectively from 1965 and 1966.

13. Gadamer, "Wort und Bild—'so wahr, so seiend" (1992), in *Gadamer Lesebuch*, ed. Jean Grondin (Tübingen: Mohr-Siebeck, 1997), pp. 188-191, 193-194.

14. Gadamer, "Vom Wort zum Begriff" (1995), in *Gadamer Lesebuch*, pp. 104-105.

15. Heidegger, "Letter on Humanism," in *Martin Heidegger: Basic Writings*, pp. 193, 242. The letter also contains the famous phrase that thinking "lets being be" (p. 236). Heidegger moreover brings such thinking in connection with the search for "*das Heile*," meaning both the healthy and the "hale"—a subtlety which the English translation fails to notice (p. 237).

16. Heidegger, "The Origin of the Work of Art" (1936), in *Martin Heidegger: Basic Writings*, pp. 168-174; for the German text see "Der Ursprung des Kunstwerkes," in Heidegger, *Holzwege* (Frankfurt-Main: Klostermann, 1950), especially pp. 30-40. See also "Vom Wesen und Begriff der *Physis*; Aristotles' Physik B, 1" (1939), in Heidegger, *Wegmarken* (Frankfurt-Main: Klostermann, 1967), pp. 309-71 (on *physis* and art especially, p. 347). The latter essay also contains revealing comments on illness and health and on the contrast between the technology of modern medical science and the art of healing, pp. 325-327.

17. Adorno, *Negative Dialectics*, pp. 14-15, 179-180; and *Aesthetic Theory*, trans. C. Lenhardt, ed. Gretel Adorno and Rolf Tiedemann (London: Routledge and Kegan

Paul, 1984), especially pp. 453-455. On the relation between Adorno and Heidegger see my "Adorno and Heidegger" in *Between Freiburg and Frankfurt: Toward a Critical Ontology*, pp. 44-71.

18. Gadamer, *The Enigma of Health*, pp. 19, 109. The same collection contains an essay on "Authority and Critical Freedom" where Gadamer carefully distinguishes between proper authority and "authoritarianism" (pp. 117-124).

19. Gadamer, "The Nature of Things and the Language of Things" (1960), in his *Philosophical Hermeneutics*, trans. and ed. David E. Linge (Berkeley: University of California Press, 1977), pp. 69-72. As one should note, Gadamer differentiates the cited expressions again carefully from a simplistic and dogmatic "naturalism" or objectivism which undermines and erodes human freedom. Thus, countering the invocations of a superior divine reality (Gerhard Krüger) or of a humanly indifferent natural world (Karl Löwith), he asks whether these assaults on human "subjectivism" are not a very "dubious battle cry" which falls far short of the insights of classical metaphysics—to the extent that the latter transcended "the dualism of subjectivity and will, on the one hand, and object and being-in-itself, on the other, by conceiving their preexistent correspondence with each other" (p. 74). For a recent attempt to recover "nature's way," partly inspired by Gadamer and Heidegger, see Ute Guzzoni, *Über Natur; Aufzeichnungen unterwegs: Zu einem anderen Naturverhältnis* (Freiburg/ Munich: Alber, 1995).

20. Heidegger has often been taken to task for not sufficiently differentiating between modern ideologies, and especially for not giving modern "liberalism" its due. The above point is merely that in *one* respect (not in all respects) modern ideologies are similar. For a strong attack by Heidegger on modern politics as a politics wedded to mastery and "machination" (*Machenschaft*) see his recently published *Die Geschichte des Seyns*, especially pp. 46-50, 179-214.

21. As it seems to me, the "language of things" often operates most eloquently not in speech acts or argumentative discourses but in the suffering of the marginalized and oppressed. In recent political theory, the notion of a free and non-manipulative praxis was articulated especially by Hannah Arendt (despite a peculiar aversion to Aristotle) and in part by Michael Oakeshott. In a "non-Western" context, the above mode of praxis seems to resonate with the notion of *karma yoga* as articulated in the *Bhagavad Gita* and as exemplified in the life of Gandhi.

22. See *The Way of Life according to Lao Tzu*, pp. 46 (ch. 17) and 58 (ch. 29). As the text adds (p. 58): "The earth is like a vessel so sacred / That at the mere approach of the profane / It is marred / And when they reach out their fingers it is gone." Regarding Buddhism see Keiji Nishitani, *Religion and Nothingness*, pp. 159-160; also my essay "Heidegger and Zen Buddhism: A Salute to Keiji Nishitani" in *The Other Heidegger* (Ithaca, NY: Cornell University Press, 1993), pp. 200-226. The essay presents a comparison of the notions of "thing" and "nothing" in Heidegger and Nishitani.

23. In my reading of Confucianism I am deeply influenced by the work of Tu Wei-Ming, especially his *Confucian Thought: Selfhood as Creative Transformation* and *Humanity and Self-Cultivation: Essays in Confucian Thought* (Berkeley: Asian Humanities Press, 1979).

24. Gadamer, "Vom Wort zum Begriff," in *Gadamer Lesebuch*, p. 104, and *The Enigma of Health*, p. 85. As Gadamer adds in the latter text (p. 78): "Here lies my own deepest hope, or perhaps I should say dream: that from the shared inheritance which is gradually being built up for us from all the different cultures across the globe we might eventually learn how to recognize our mutual needs and to address our respective difficulties."

Chapter Nine

Borders or Horizons?
An Older Debate Revisited

What is the status of borders, boundaries, or demarcations? Do borders mandate separation and exclusion, or are they more like hyphens indicating a difficult kind of collusion, a correlation without sameness? Do they mean to keep the stranger out, or are they more like gestures honoring and welcoming the other's strangeness? In many ways, Western modernity is a high tide of borders and demarcations functioning as signs of exclusion. Politically, nation-states were divided from nation-states, Catholics from Protestants, ethnic loyalties from other ethnic loyalties—all in the name of autonomy and rigorous self-identity. In the philosophical domain, René Descartes drew sharp boundaries around the "thinking ego" (*ego cogitans*), in an effort to keep at bay all forms of nonmental otherness—including nature ("extended matter") and dubious assumptions impinging on mind's autonomy. The Enlightenment reinforced these boundaries by postulating a clear division between light and darkness, between reason and prejudice or tradition, and between revolution and all types of "old regimes." The most formidable demarcations as signs of exclusion were established by Kant's critical philosophy, with its insistence on the contrast between reason and sensation, between knowledge and faith, and between moral autonomy and nature (or natural causality). In Kant's own presentation, the reason-faith distinction was meant to grant broad room to religious belief or fideism. However, as other thinkers (including Hegel) noted, the same demarcation could also have the effect of rendering faith pointless and outmoded—which was precisely the conclusion drawn by later positivism.

There can be no doubt that boundaries—including the boundaries of Western modernity—can have beneficial effects, by protecting vulnerable forms of agency. In social settings marked by hierarchy and inequality, borders can serve as ramparts shielding the weak against the strong, the marginalized against hegemonic elites. Many of the achievements of modern liberal democracy—above all individual rights and liberties—are the result of careful border demarcations. It is equally clear, however, that borders can turn into prison fences and possibly into bastions of (external and internal) aggression. The latter result was dramatically demonstrated by events during the twentieth century when exclusionary aggression reached a climax of violence and destruction. The perils of this outcome were not entirely lost on contemporary observers and witnesses. At least partly in response to political events, some European philosophers began to revise the exclusionary role of borders—not in the direction of a "melting-pot" fusion but of their nuanced treatment as markers of both differentiation and contiguity.

This rethinking was evident in the motto of Husserl's phenomenology "to the things themselves"—a motto which boldly sought to regain access to the "thing-in-itself" (excluded by Kant) as an open horizon of inquiry. Even more resolutely, the same trajectory was pursued in Heidegger's philosophy, especially in his hyphenated formulations of human existence as "being-in-the-world" and "ecstatic" openness. The following pages seek to examine the status of borders and horizons in the respective works of Hans-Georg Gadamer and Jürgen Habermas. For this purpose, the focus is placed on the so-called Gadamer-Habermas debate initiated by the early Habermas—a debate that has been often reviewed, but rarely from this angle.[1] While the first section recapitulates some of Gadamer's teachings, chiefly with respect to a "universal hermeneutics," the second part reviews some of Habermas's critical rejoinders and initiatives aiming basically at a parceling of forms of human knowledge and the recovery of an objective "metatheory." In the concluding section, an effort is made to highlight the significance of the debate for the ongoing process of globalization and the possibility of a "dialogue of civilizations."

A UNIVERSAL HERMENEUTICS?

As is well known, Gadamer's *Truth and Method* sought to differentiate hermeneutics from a mere method or methodology—a method which necessarily distances the knower from the known, while specifying a path for the "subject" to grasp or come to know its "object." This concern with methodology was still prevalent in earlier forms of hermeneutics, including the "historicist" version of Wilhelm Dilthey who construed hermeneutical understanding after the model of a psychic-mental transfer whereby the interpreter would gain access to intended meaning-structures of the past. By following this path, the interpreter, in Dilthey's view, would gain "objective" knowledge of historical meanings—an objectivity paralleling (though radically different in kind from) the objectivity achieved in natural science. This narrowly methodological preoccupation was thrown into disarray by Heidegger's *Being and Time,* which insisted that interpreter and past meanings are both embroiled in an underlying temporal happening and that "understanding" is a basic feature of human existence as such (undercutting the distinction between human and natural sciences). With this insistence, Heidegger jeopardized and eroded the centrality of the Cartesian *ego cogitans* (as well as Kant's and Husserl's "transcendental consciousness") together with its radical demarcations from "external" nature, world, and fellow beings. As Gadamer comments, by renewing the "question of being" and by construing being as temporal, Heidegger "burst asunder the whole subjectivism of modern philosophy—and in fact, as was soon to appear, the whole set of questions asked by metaphysics which tended to define being as what is [objectively] present." By moving in this direction and by inaugurating a "hermeneutics of facticity," Heidegger "went beyond the concept of mind developed by classical idealism and the thematic of transcendental consciousness purified by phenomenological reduction."[2]

Given *Dasein's* embroilment in the world (as a temporal happening), understanding and interpreting cannot be a neutral method starting from scratch, but only an ongoing process of reinterpreting. Differently phrased: understanding always presupposes a preunderstanding before proceeding to a critique of meaning. This is the sense of the so-called hermeneutical circle which, as Gadamer observers, is not a vicious but a productive circle, an inevitable precondition of understanding as such. To center stage this circle, of course, does not equal an endorsement of arbitrary fancies or subjective constructions—which would mean a relapse into the problems of methodology. Rather, like human *Dasein* itself, understanding is a temporal process, involving an ongoing testing of preunderstandings against the demands of texts or historical events, that is, a dialogical-dialectical interchange between interpreter and *interpretandum.* In Gadmer's words: "All genuine interpretation must be on guard against arbitrary whims and the limitations imposed by imperceptible habits of thought"; for this purpose, it must "direct its gaze 'to the things themselves'" (in Husserl's formulation) and must steadfastly remain attentive to the thing or topic (*Sache*) "throughout all the distractions to which interpreters are prone to be subject." Seen from this angle, hermeneutics is not a mode of psychological empathy, nor is it a branch of subjective idealism; rather, it is part of *Dasein's* basic world involvement, of its radical openness or exposure to transformative learning experiences. As Gadamer adds: "Anyone trying to understand is exposed to distraction from preunderstandings or foremeanings (*Vor-Meinungen*) that are not borne out by the things themselves." Working out interpretive possibilities in order to have them "confirmed by the things" is the constant task of understanding: "There is no other objectivity here but the confirmation of foremeanings through the labor of 'working through' (*Ausarbeitung*)."[3]

As one should note, "foremeanings" or prejudgments in Gadamer's view can be modified and corrected, but never completely erased or eliminated (through a return to some kind of blank slate or *tabula rasa*). This is the gist of his much-discussed rehabilitation of "prejudice" (in the sense of prejudgment) and his critique of the radical "prejudice against prejudices" characterizing modern Enlightenment. For proponents of modern Enlightenment, reason is radically self-constituting and self-legitimatizing in that it grants legitimacy to nothing outside its jurisdiction. All unenlightened assumptions—including religious beliefs and cultural traditions—are basically suspect and discredited: they must either pass through the filter of reason, and hence become "rationalized," or else will be discarded as spurious or obsolete. By adopting this stance, rationalist Enlightenment reconfirms the stark demarcations of Cartesian philosophy: whatever exceeds the confines of the sovereign *cogito* must either be appropriated/assimilated, or else be excluded and controlled. What is missed in this approach is the possibility of a genuine learning experience through reason's exposure to what is unfamiliar or alien—including its own (prerational) prejudgments. To reopen this possibility was precisely the point of Heidegger's *Being and Time* with its emphasis on human finitude and the insertion of *Dasein* in world and temporal happenings (antedating rational constitution). From Heidegger's angle, Gadamer comments, reason is "not its own master but remains constantly dependent on circumstances in which it operates"; prominent among these circumstances is *Dasein's* "alienness" (*Fremdheit*) to itself. Seen in this light, he adds sharply, self-reflection (in the sense of rational self-constitution) is

> not primary and thus not an adequate basis for hermeneutics, because through it history is internalized or privatized once more. But in fact, history does not belong to us; we belong to it. . . . The focus of subjectivity [*cogito*] is a distorting mirror. The self-awareness of the individual is only a flickering in the circuits of historical life. That is why the prejudices of the individual, far more than his judgments, constitute the historical reality of his being.[4]

Given *Dasein's* insertion in temporality, the rehabilitation of prejudgments is closely linked with a valorization of "tradition" and of a certain "authority" exerted by texts or injunctions antedating reason's self-constitution. In adopting this approach—it is important to stress the point—Gadamer does not counsel a leap from autonomy into unfreedom, from reason into irrationalism. Basically, his hermeneutics seeks to undercut or problematize the rigid bifurcation between reason/freedom, on the one hand, and authority/tradition, on the other. As he notes, only from the vantage of an abstract rationalism could the notion of authority be viewed "as diametrically opposed to reason and freedom" and be equated with "blind obedience." In actuality, genuine authority for Gadamer is predicated not on a simple "abdication" of reason but rather on "an act of acknowledgement and knowledge": namely, on the uncoerced recognition that the views of a text or teacher can rightly lay a claim to our attention and hence deserve to be pondered carefully and seriously. The same considerations apply to the role of tradition. In view of *Dasein's* temporality, human relationship to the past for Gadamer is not characterized by a mode of radical "distancing or exodus from tradition"; differently phrased: *Dasein's* historical situatedness does not imply an "objectifying process" of detached analysis, but rather reflects the fact that tradition "addresses" *Dasein* which, in turn, "lets itself be *addressed* by tradition." Contrary to certain Enlightenment teachings, human "maturity" (*Mündigkeit*) does not signify a total self-mastery in the sense of a radical "liberation from all tradition." Here, again, one has to resist binary construals. Genuine tradition, for Gadamer, is not the "dead hand" of the past but a lived experience which involves "always an element of freedom"; as a process of transmission, preservation, and renewal, it implies "an act of reason, though an inconspicuous one." Once this is admitted, the "abstract antithesis" between tradition and historical knowledge needs to be discarded; the "effect" (*Wirkung*) of a living tradition and its reflective transmission must be seen as a dialectical continuity.[5]

Here a central future of Gadamerian hermeneutics comes into view: the dialogical-dialectical character of understanding and its embeddedness in an "effective" or effectively operative history (*Wirkungsgeschichte*). Hermeneutical understanding, in his account, does not mean an act of psychic empathy (a transposition of *ego* into *alter*), nor an act of assimilation (of *alter* and *ego*), but rather a process of reciprocal questioning at the intersection between self and other, between familiarity and strangeness (*Fremdheit*). Hermeneutics hence is basically marked by tension: for example, the tension between a traditional text's distance or strangeness and its familiarity as part of a tradition: "The true locus of hermeneutics is this in-between." This locus is also important for the role of prejudgments, namely by sorting out productive from unwarranted or misleading prejudices. In being open to strangeness or unfamiliarity, hermeneutical understanding allows itself to be addressed and to be "called into question"—which is "the first condition of hermeneutics." The same condition implies a questioning of initial, perhaps misleading "foremeanings" and their replacement by more productive judgments—which in turn become resources for continued questioning or in-

quiry. In Gadamer's words: "The essence of the *question* is to open up possibilities and keep them open. . . . Our own prejudices are properly brought
into play by being put at risk." Throughout this reciprocal questioning historical temporality manifests its effectiveness (*Wirkung*) by framing or struc-
turing the interchange, mainly by disclosing "the *right questions* to ask." The
same historical effectiveness also prevents closure or the final termination of
questioning. Here a Hegelian motif comes into play (though without recourse to "absoluteness"). As Gadamer notes, the task of philosophical
hermeneutics might be described as the effort "to retrace the path of Hegel's
'phenomenology of spirit' until we discover in all that is subjective the sub-
stantiality (*Substanzialität*) that guides it."[6]

Observations of this kind clearly underscore a main point of *Truth and
Method*: that hermeneutics is not merely a limited methodology, tailored to
specialized modes of inquiry, but rather a general philosophical perspective
relevant to the broad range of human experience (in both its theoretical and
practical dimensions). Given its extensive scope, hermeneutics can properly
be described as "universal"—although it is important to note the peculiar
character of its universality. As a participant in ongoing human experience,
hermeneutical understanding cannot claim the status of an abstract "metatheory," of a universal framework or schema under which particular events or
phenomena can be subsumed. In an emphatic manner, such a status is asserted by (variants of) modern philosophy of science, particularly by the
project of a "unified science" providing a comprehensive explanation of all
aspects of reality; in modified form, a similar ambition prevails in Kantian
and neo-Kantian types of rationalism as well as in versions of structural social analysis. In contrast to these schemas, hermeneutics has to pursue a
more subdued, and partially inductive, path; shunning metavistas, universalism in this case can only mean a particular openness and responsiveness: an
openness to the diverse horizons "addressing" or impinging on human understanding. This reticent kind of universalism was carefully elucidated by
Gadamer in the decade following *Truth and Method*. His essay "The Universality of the Hermeneutical Problem" (1966) pointedly invokes the Aristotelian model of inductive generalization (as discussed in *Posterior Analyt-
ics*). To illustrate the emergence of the general out of particulars, Aristotle
used the example of a fleeing and dispersed army, which somehow, without
unified superior command, comes to halt and take a stand again. "How,"
Gadamer queries,

does one arrive at a universal? How does it happen that words . . . have a general
meaning? . . . When is the principle present as a principle? Through what capacity? This question is in fact the question of the occurrence of the universal.[7]

In Gadamer's account, this "occurrence of the universal" stands in contrast to the stylized theories and metatheories which, in the modern context, oppose a detached spectator to an increasingly objectified universe. This spectatorial detachment is manifest in modern aesthetics where art and the arena of artistic experience tend to be "alienated into an object of aesthetic judgment" or taste. A similar detachment or alienation operates in modern historiography which tries to offer an objective account of all historical data, perhaps even a metatheory linking these data in an explanatory framework. Reduced to methodology, even hermeneutics sometimes parades as a neutral "science" of understanding in which substantive contents are alienated into objective targets of analysis. In opposition to these theoretical and metatheoretical pretensions, Gadamer invokes the notion of "hermeneutical experience" which—far from being a synonym for subjective egocentrism—points to the open-ended or "horizonal" character of human understanding. Replicating themes from *Truth and Method*, his essay insists on the "secondary" status of aesthetic judgment vis-à-vis the "immediate truth-claim" of art, that is, the challenge or address issuing from the artwork itself. As he writes, in a near-poetic vein, "our sensitive-spiritual existence is an aesthetic resonance chamber resonating with the voices that are constantly reaching us, preceding all explicit aesthetic judgment." History is a similar resonance chamber, in that the past is always illuminated by present and future hopes, showing (in Heidegger's terms) the "primacy of futurity for possible recollection or retention." In these and other ways, hermeneutical experience reveals itself not as a closed circuit but as a gateway opening up to new visions, including dimensions of alterity (*Fremdheit*): "The nature of hermeneutical experience is not that something is outside and desires admission. Rather, we are claimed by something and precisely by means of it we are opened up for the new, the different, the true."[8]

In Gadamer's presentation, hermeneutical experience denotes a primary mode of embeddedness (prior to theoretization), a mode that is preeminently displayed in language as the matrix of human being-in-the-world (or, with Heidegger, as the "house of Being"). As he states forcefully: "Language is the fundamental *modus operandi* of our being-in-the-world and the all-embracing form of the constitution of the world" (which is not a subjective-intentional production). Along the same lines, he speaks of the "linguistic constitution of the world," adding that it presents itself as "historically effected consciousness (*wirkungsgeschichtliches Bewusstsein*) that provides an initial schematization for all our possibilities of knowing." What is important to note here is that, just like experience, language for Gadamer is not a prison house but again a gateway to infinite explorations. "While we live wholly within a language," he emphasizes, "the fact that we do so does not constitute linguistic relativism because there is absolutely no captivity within a language—not even within our native language." The latter aspect is demonstrated by our ability to learn foreign languages and by the experience on distant journeys when we manage to "master a foreign idiom to some extent." What Gadamer opposes here is the axiom of the "incommensurability" of language games— an axiom fashionable in some skeptical and/or deconstructive quarters and often associated with the claim of radical cultural relativism. The axiom is clearly incompatible with hermeneutics that steers a difficult course between abstract (metatheoretical) universalism and a debilitating particularism. Here is an eloquent passage that deserves to be lifted up:

> Any language in which we live is infinite in this sense [of opening up vistas], and it is completely mistaken to infer that reason is fragmented because there are different languages. Just the opposite is the case. Precisely through our finitude, the particularity of our being, which is evident even in the variety of languages, the infinite dialogue is opened in the direction of the truth that we are.[9]

The crucial and even primordial character of language for human being-in-the-world was examined roughly at the same time in another essay titled "Man and Language" (1966). In that context Gadamer noted first of all a certain "lag" of philosophical reflection: the fact that Western philosophy traditionally has not placed language at the center of its considerations. This situation changed only slowly during the Enlightenment period when Herder and von Humboldt began to construe human "nature" as basically linguistic; however, even then that nature tended to be seen largely in terms of "consciousness" and subjectivity. Only more recently has the depth-quality of language come into view. "For it is part of the nature of language," Gadamer states, "that it has a completely unfathomable unconsciousness of itself." This means that—rather than being merely a handy tool or utensil—language challenges and addresses us in complex ways. Although we can "theorize" about language, raising it to an object of scientific analysis, the problem is that "we can never really do this completely." For, all thinking about language is already once again "drawn back into language"; and this "residing of our thinking in language" is precisely "the profound enigma that language presents to thought." In his essay, Gadamer highlighted three main features of language that are crucial for hermeneutics. The first feature is the "essential self-forgetfulness" of language in that the focal concerns of linguistic science— such as grammar and syntax—are not at all "conscious to living speaking." The second aspect is the basic "I-lessness" or non-egocentric character of language, the fact that language comes to life in dialogue—which, in turn, is not just an intentionally controlled exchange but rather exhibits the quality of a "play" (*Spiel*). For, when participants are carried along by dialogue, it is no longer their will or intention that is governing but rather the topic (*Sache*) it-self which "plays them into each other." The last feature is the "universality of language" which is not a delimited realm of discourse or of the "sayable" over against which "other realms of the unsayable" might be positioned. Like hermeneutical experience, language and dialogical saying have "an inner in-finity and no end."[10]

HABERMAS AND SCIENTIFIC METATHEORY

As articulated in these and related writings, Gadamer's philosophical hermeneutics clearly signaled a broadscale attack on the "unified science" program (promoted by logical positivism); in doing so, it also mounted a challenge to the self-conception of the social sciences which, during this pe-riod, were increasingly coming under the sway of positivist or narrowly em-piricist paradigms. In a nuanced and carefully calibrated way, the latter chal-lenge was taken up by Jürgen Habermas whose dual role as philosopher and sociologist nearly predestined him to the task. Barely a year after "Man and Language," Habermas published an extensive review of Gadamer's *Truth and Method*, a review which moved from an initial endorsement of key Gadamer-ian insights through a crescendo of reservations to the formulation of a criti-cal counter-model along social-scientific (or social-theoretical) lines. Among the positive elements of Gadamer's perspective, the review focused first of all on the role of language or "linguisticality" (*Sprachlichkeit*) seen as the shared matrix of understanding. In order to break through the barriers of particular grammars, Habermas noted, it was not necessary to abscond into the kind of metalanguage favored by structural linguistics (and logical empiricism). Rather, to preserve the "unity of reason" in the multiplicity of languages, or-dinary language itself furnishes the needed resources, in the sense that every ordinary grammar provides the possibility "to transcend the language it de-termines," that is, "to translate from and into other languages." Following Gadamer it was hence legitimate to say that "we are never locked into a sin-gle grammar" and that the idea of a "monadology" of language games was il-lusory. In opposition to this mistaken idea, it was important to affirm (with Gadamer) that the first grammar we learn to master already puts us in a posi-tion "to step out of it and to interpret what is foreign, to make comprehensi-ble what initially is incomprehensible, to assimilate in our words what at first escapes them."[11]

Habermas in this context explicitly referred to Hegel's "dialectic of the limit"—where "limit" denotes both boundary and linkage. As he observed, this ambivalence of "limit" was adequately captured in Gadamer's hermeneutics, and especially in the notion of "hermeneutic experience" seen as the corrective through which reason, though language-based, escapes the "spell" (or prison house) of a given grammar. Wedded to the task of translation, hermeneutics appropriately mistrusts any relinquishment or "mediatizing" of ordinary language; refusing the exit route into metalanguage, it makes use instead of the "tendency to self-transgression" embedded in ordinary linguistic practices. Hence, without denying its linguistic "incarnation," reason can also cleanse itself of the "dross" of a linguistic particularity—namely, by "passing over into another" (through translation). At this point, the Hegelian idea of "limit" shades over into the hermeneutical notion of "horizon" which is always open-ended and transgressive. In Habermas's words: "Horizons are open, and they shift; we enter into them and they in turn move with us." Contrary to Wittgenstein's "monadological" conception, ordinary languages are not tightly closed circuits but rather open-ended life-forms endowed with a "horizonal" quality linking them with what is other or alien (*Fremdheit*). Reiterating central Gadamerian teachings, the review stated:

> Proper to the grammar of a language game is not only that it defines a form of life but that it defines a life-form as one's own over against others that are foreign. Because every word that is articulated in a language is a totality, the horizon of a language also encompasses that which it is not—it discloses itself as particular among particulars. For this reason, the 'limits' of the world that it defines are not irrevocable: the dialectical confrontation of what is one's own with what is foreign leads, for the most part imperceptibly, to revisions.[12]

In Habermas's account, the horizonal quality is operative not only laterally between different language communities, but also temporally between generations and historical epochs. In this connection, "horizon" refers to the complex interlacing of temporalities, and translation shades over into the notion of "tradition" (*Überlieferung*). In contrast to reductive learning models, learning a language does not merely involve a rigid process of socialization, but also an initiation into the interpretation and even creative transformation of linguistic rules—rules which are designed "to overcome, but *thereby also to express*, distance." Seen from this angle, interpretation is a mode of "application"—but with a difference; in Gadamerian terms, language performance implies an application of linguistic rules that, in turn, "further develops these rules historically." Differently phrased: language application is a practical act or a form of participatory *praxis*—which stands in sharp opposition to the metastance of an external observer, and also to the mere implementation of technical rules or formulas. In Habermas's words, technical rules are "abstractly general" and can be compared to theoretical statements "whose conditions of application are expressed in general terms"; in this case, it is possible to "subsume cases under something abstractly general." The situation is different with practical, including linguistic, rules. For here, generality shapes the particular "only to the degree to which it is itself first concretized by this particularity"; only in this manner does the general gain "intersubjective recognition." The review acknowledges at this point the connection between Gadamerian hermeneutics and Aristotelian teachings, especially Aristotle's notions of *praxis* and practical (ethical-political) knowledge (*phronesis*). For both Gadamer and Aristotle, we read, language performance and related activities are "components of a life-form (*bios*)"; and the latter is always "a social form of life that is developed through communicative action."[13]

In elaborating on the participatory aspect of language, Habermas also comments on the difference between hermeneutics and "objective" or obectifying methodologies—including the methods (previously discussed) of "aesthetic consciousness" and "historical (or historicist) consciousness." Regarding the latter, he focuses first of all on historicist versions of hermeneutics as championed by Schleiermacher and Dilthey—whom he charges with "aestheticizing history" while "anaesthetizing historical reflection." Against this defect, he notes, "Gadamer brings to bear, subtly but relentlessly, Hegel's insight that the restitution of past life is possible only to the extent that it is a reconstruction of the present out of its past." A similar defect afflicts phenomenological and linguistic approaches in sociology—which tend to "move to the side of historicism"; unwilling to embrace hermeneutical insights, they "succumb to objectivism," since they claim for the phenomological observer and the language analyst "a purely theoretical [spectatorial] attitude." In this respect, Gadamer's "first-rate critique of the objectivistic self-understanding of the cultural sciences (*Geisteswissenschaftten*)" appears right on target. In a more circuitous way, the same critique also applies to Arthur Danto's construal of historiography in terms of narrative or narratology. According to Habermas, Danto was quite correct in debunking the concept of an "ideal chronicler" who would be able to describe historical events by using a "temporally neutral observation language"; for such a language would exclude the very interpretation "that alone makes possible the comprehension of an observed event as an historical event." What vitiated Danto's approach, however, was his attempt to exclude the interpreter's practical engagements from his historical narrative. From a hermeneutical angle, the historian's work is only "the last rung on a ladder of interpretations" whose first rung is the reference system of the historian that, in principle, cannot be independent of his/her "horizon of expectations." More sharply phrased: the historian cannot grasp anything that he knows of history "independently of the framework of his own life-praxis (*Lebenspraxis*)."[14]

In light of this sensitive and appreciative reading of Gadamer's work, the review's conclusion is bound to come as a surprise. Although preceded by reservations cautiously inserted into the exegesis, the concluding argument somewhat abruptly shifts gears in the direction of a more social-scientific (and objectifying) mode of analysis. Without directly abandoning hermeneutics, Habermas decides to restrict its scope to a compartmentalized domain among others—a division accomplished no longer under hermeneutical-participatory but under theoretical (or metatheoretical) auspices. As a result, the fluidly open-ended or "horizonal" quality of hermeneutics gives way to theoretically stipulated forms of inquiry; as a corollary, the Hegelian "dialectic of the limit" makes room for delimiting boundaries (more along Kantian lines). Despite an admission that hermeneutics cannot be assigned one-sidedly "either to theory/reason or to experience," the review finds in Gadamer's work a deficit of rational theory—a topic which Hegel could address "with greater legitimacy." Despite the earlier recognition of the role of distance and strangeness (*Fremdheit*) in hermeneutics, Habermas now stresses a more rigorous or disciplined type of exodus or alienation: "A controlled distantiation (*Verfremdung*) can raise understanding from prescientific experience to the rank of a reflective procedure"—which is the way in which its insights "enter into the social sciences." The defensible critique of spectatorial objectivism, from this angle, cannot justify the suspension of that "methodological distantiation of the object" which is the hallmark of science. At this point, the accents of Gadamer's title are resolutely shifted from "truth" to "method," making the former in large part a derivative result of the latter. In Habermas's words: "The confrontation of 'truth' and 'method' should not have misled Gadamer to oppose hermeneutic experience abstractly to methodological knowledge." The legitimate resistance to positivist scientism, in any event, brings "no dispensation from the business of methodology as such."[15]

The defense of method (vis-à-vis "truth") is paralleled in the review by the vindication of reason over "prejudice" and of emancipatory freedom over "tradition." In Habermas's account, the rational appropriation of the past "breaks up the nature-like (*naturwüchsige*) substance of tradition and alters the position of the subject within it." In modernity, this breaking-up has been powerfully promoted by science and scientific reflection through which the fabric of tradition has been "profoundly altered." These and related developments have shifted the balance between tradition and reason and also between authority and reason—something Gadamer fails to see because he does not appreciate "the power of reflection that is developed in understanding" and that "shakes the dogmatism of life practices." Bypassing the nuanced distinction between tenable and untenable "prejudgments," Habermas now charges Gadamer with an incipient antirationalism and with the "rehabilitation of prejudice as such"—adding that "Gadamer is motivated by the conservatism of that first generation, by the impulse of a Burke that has not yet [fully] turned against the rationalism of the eighteenth century." Countering questions or critical queries addressed at the Enlightenment "project," Habermas in this context champions rational self-reflection as the gateway to complete rational transparency and hence also to human freedom or emancipation. Reason or reflection, in his account, acts as a kind of solvent or detergent cleansing the "dross" of the past; once exposed to this solvent, preunderstanding "can no longer function as a prejudice." As Habermas adds, celebrating the legacy of Kant and Fichte:

> Gadamer's prejudice for the rights of prejudices certified by tradition denies the power of reflection. The latter proves itself, however, in being able to reject the claim of tradition. Reflection dissolves 'substantiality' because it not only confirms, but also breaks up, dogmatic forces. Authority and knowledge do not converge. . . . This experience of reflection is the unforgettable legacy bequeathed to us by German Idealism from the spirit of the eighteenth century.[16]

As one should note, Habermas's celebration here does not cover idealist reflection *in toto*, but only a kind of formal or metareflection (minus Hegel's "objective" and "absolute spirit"). Parceled off from the domain of prereflective experience, this metareflection in turn allows the parceling out or compartmentalization of domains of methodological knowledge or inquiry. As Habermas observes, reflection today can no longer "comprehend itself as absolute spirit"; in the wake of the "linguistic turn," language has come to function as a sort of limited or "contingent absolute." Hence, Hegel's notion of experience contracts into the awareness of a happening in which "the conditions of rationality change" depending on types of inquiry. Seen from this angle, hermeneutical understanding no longer exhibits the "horizonal" quality claimed by Gadamer and must content itself with a more restricted scope. For Habermas, Gadamer's approach is "not objective enough" because it does not recognize the external forces impinging on understanding, that is, the "walls" or "boundaries" against which it comes up "from the inside." Despite its status as a social matrix, language is "evidently dependent" also on objectively analyzable social processes: most prominently the processes of labor and domination. By "social labor" Habermas means a broad spectrum of activities ranging from economic production to the instrumental designs of science and technology, activities ultimately rooted in the "anthropologically deep-seated vantage point of technical mastery." A similar impact is wielded by social power and domination that distort language into ideological manipulation. As the review concludes, the linguistic matrix of society is part of a complex that is "also constituted by the constraint of reality": more specifically by the "constraint of outer nature animating procedures for technical mastery" and the "constraint of inner nature reflected in the repressive character of social power relations." Operating "behind the back of language," these forces reveal society as an "objective framework" that is "constituted jointly by language, labor, and domination."[17]

Although startling in the context of the review, Habermas's concluding arguments could not come as a complete surprise to readers of his own evolving opus which, precisely at that time, was revolving around the problem of types of knowledge and their "constitution" in prereflective experience. Already two years prior to the review, Habermas had presented his inaugural lecture in Frankfurt on the topic "Knowledge and Human Interests"—an address that, in lapidary style, contained the main seminal ideals subsequently elaborated in book form (under the same title). Although richly nuanced and replete with complex historical allusions, the address advanced mainly two points: first, the need to reconnect knowledge or reason with prereflective experience; and secondly, the importance of compartmentalizing modes of knowledge in three rubrics. Both points were basically meant as corrective antidotes to positivism. According to Habermas, one of positivism's misleading claims was the neutral detachment of science from life contexts. Partly following in Husserl's footsteps, his address sought to uncover a deep-seated or "quasitranscendental" framework of human reason: the framework of cognitive or "knowledge-guiding interests." As he wrote, for three categories of inquiry one can demonstrate "a specific connection between logical-methodological rules and knowledge-constitutive interests"—a demonstration that is the task of a "critical philosophy of science escaping the snares of positivism." The other corrective to positivist scientism was the compartmentalization of knowledge into three domains: the "empirical-analytical sciences," the "historical-hermeneutics sciences," and the "critique of ideology" (governed respectively by a "technical," a "practical," and an "emancipatory" interest). Among the three types, the highest form of rational transparency was provided by self-reflection operative in ideology critique. In the words of the lecture:

> The specific viewpoints from which, with transcendental necessity, we apprehend reality ground three categories of possible knowledge: informations that expand our power of technical control; interpretations that make possible action orientation in the context of shared traditions; and analyses that free consciousness from its dependence on hypostatized powers. These viewpoints originate in the interest structure of a species which is naturally tied to distinctive media of socialization: labor (work), language, and power. . . . The emancipatory interest aims at the pursuit of reflection as such . . . ; hence, in self-reflection knowledge and interest are one.[18]

HERMENEUTICS AND POLITICAL PRAXIS

This is not the occasion to recapitulate in detail the debate that ensued from Habermas's theoretical intervention. Here it must suffice to highlight some salient points and broader implications. Basically, the texts reviewed above pinpointed a contrast of philosophical positions, a kind of parting of ways which subsequent discussions and elaborations only managed to reinforce (despite occasional accommodations); in a sense, they laid the groundwork for sharply divergent trajectories only partially mitigated by a shared commitment to dialogue or communication. For his part, Gadamer immediately recognized the challenge and promptly responded in a series of essays. A major point taken up in response was the issue of the "horizonal" (or universalizing) quality of hermeneutics, as opposed to its narrow, "methodical" compartmentalization. As Gadamer reiterated, hermeneutical understanding is not a confined mode of inquiry but rather a distinctive mark of human "being-in-the-world" in all its dimensions. His own "philosophical hermeneutics" hence was not meant to inaugurate a special methodology, but rather to thematize the pervasive significance of understanding in all types or modalities of human experience. It is in this sense that hermeneutics can properly lay claim to a universal (or horizonal) scope because it discloses "the universality of human linguisticality as a limitless medium that carries *everything* within it . . . because everything (in the world and out of it) is embraced in the realm of 'understanding' and understandability in which we move." The term "everything" here includes even modern science because it is the matrix of understandings (or preunderstandings) which generates the questions addressed to science.[19]

Given the scope of this matrix, Gadamer could not possibly consent to Habermas's compartmentalizing strategy. One important feature of this strategy was the separation of methodological inquiry from prereflective understanding or—more broadly stated—of reason from tradition (or life-world). As Gadamer noted, this separation or division involved a "prior decision of greatest significance": by extricating itself entirely from tradition, methodology removed itself very far from the customary ambience of human understanding "with all its bridge building and recovery of the best in the past." As an antidote to this breach, his response advanced the thesis—crucial both philosophically and socially—that "the thing which hermeneutics teaches us is to see through the dogmatism of asserting an opposition or separation between the ongoing, prereflective 'tradition' and the reflective appropriation of it." Gadamer at this point brought this assertion in contact with the sort of positivist objectivism which "critical theory" supposedly challenged. In his words: "Behind the claim [of separation] stands a dogmatic objectivism that distorts the very concept of hermeneutical reflection itself." From the angle of this objectivism, understanding is construed no longer in relationship to "the hermeneutical situation and the constant operativeness of history (*Wirkungsgeschichte*)," but in such a way as to imply that the observer "does not enter at all into the hermeneutical event" (preferring instead the role of spectator or the "view from nowhere"). Habermas's contention that this retreat or distantiation was the necessary consequence of modern science—or even the "priceless heritage of German idealism"—neglected the human and social costs of the process. For: "What kind of understanding is achieved through 'controlled alienation'? Is it not likely to be an alienated understanding"—and possibly no understanding at all?[20]

The latter comments were relevant particularly to the tripartition of types of inquiry (as outlined in "Knowledge and Human Interests"). For Gadamer, this partitioning rested on a basic misconception of hermeneutics: namely, its misconstrual as a narrowly cultural, mental, or "idealist" enterprise opposed to a "real" world outside. As *Truth and Method* repeatedly insisted, however, self stands always in relation to nonself, the familiar in relation to the alien or foreign (*Fremdheit*), in a manner undercutting inside/outside binaries and also the bifurcation between understanding, on the one hand, and labor and power, on the other. Does hermeneutics, Gadamer asks, "really take its bearings from a limiting concept of idealized interaction between understood motives and deliberate actions," or does it not also pertain to meanings which are "not actually intended"? In the latter case, why should the so-called real factors (of labor and power) lie "outside the realm of hermeneutics"? From the hermeneutical vantage properly understood, he added, it is "absolutely absurd to regard the concrete factors of work and politics as hovering outside the scope of hermeneutics." Regarding the "critique of ideology" and especially the claimed "coincidence" of reason and emancipatory interest, Gadamer chided its triumphalist hyperbole, manifest in the absorption of interest into reason and the resulting radical ascendancy of "enlightenment" over traditional life practices. In his pointed rejoinder: "I cannot accept the assertion that reason and authority/tradition are abstract antitheses, as the emancipatory Enlightenment claimed. . . . In my view, this antithesis is a mistake fraught with ominous consequences: rational reflection here is granted a false power, and the true dependencies involved are misjudged on the basis of a fallacious idealism."[21]

On Habermas's part, the rejoinder triggered a rethinking of some disputed issues—but without jeopardizing the privilege accorded to method (and metatheory). Among the points advanced by Gadamer, Habermas accepted mainly the critique of the merger or coincidence of reason and life practice—a notion he jettisoned in favor of further compartmentalization. As he admitted, the relation between knowledge and interest had been too narrowly construed in terms of "knowledge-constitution," a construal that needed to give way to a sharper distinction between the origin or "genesis" of knowledge claims and their general "validity." To mark this division, the notion of rational "discourse" was now introduced to designate a formalized mode of communication in which prereflective life practice is bracketed (or "virtualized") in order to permit rigorous testing of arguments. Corresponding to the previous tripartition (labor, interactive language, and critique of power), three types of validity claims were specially highlighted: the claims to cognitive "truth," moral "rightness," and personal "truthfulness." Still more importantly, the notion of critical "self-reflection" was further internalized or subjectified, thus making room for a more detached and "objective" metareflection termed "rational reconstruction" designed to uncover anonymous rule mechanisms and competences governing human thought and practices in general.[22] In quick succession, the reconstructive model was applied both to the genetic or "diachronic" development of human societies and to the "synchronic" analysis of rule systems underlying universal language performance. Habermas's *Legitimation Crisis* (1973) offered a broad reconstructive sketch of social evolution, relying chiefly on the twin engines of progressive social differentiation and rationalization. Differentiation in this context signaled the growing separation between formalized "system" and "life-world," where "system" embraced the domains of the economy (labor) and the state (power), while life-world denoted interactive processes (undergoing the steady pull of rationalization). In turn, the reconstruction of speech performance led to the theory of a "universal pragmatics" (first presented in 1976), a theory according to which speakers necessarily relate to three different "worlds": the "objective world" of external nature through "constative" speech acts, the "social (norm-regulated) world" through "regulative" speech acts, and the "subjective world" through "avowals" or "expressive" acts—while relying on language itself as means or medium of communication.[23]

Habermas's penchant for border drawing and compartmentalization was continued and even intensified in subsequent writings—of which only brief glimpses can be offered here. His magnum opus, *The Theory of Communicative Action* (1981), transferred the partitioning of "worlds" and speech acts to the domain of action theory, a transfer that yielded the stipulation of four main sociological concepts of action correlated with three basic types of formal "worlds" (plus the life-world). As before, the latter included the "objective world" defined as "the totality of entities about which true statements are possible"; the "social world" seen as "the totality of all legitimately regulated interpersonal relations"; and the "subjective world" as "the totality of the experiences to which a speaker/actor has privileged access." The corresponding types of action were "teleological" (and/or "strategic") action involving relations with external reality (and subject to the criteria of truth and/or efficacy); "norm-regulated" action involving relations mainly with society (criterion: rightness); and "dramaturgical" action pertaining mainly to the expression of inner dispositions (criterion: truthfulness). As a fourth type, "communicative" action was said to bring into play the "linguistic medium" reflecting an actor's relation to "the world a such." More recently, similar forms of partitioning have emerged in Habermas's moral, political, and legal theories. In the field of political theory, in particular, his notion of "deliberative" or "procedural" democracy maintains the early triad of labor, interaction, and power—now under the system- (or meta-) theoretical rubrics of economy, civil society, and public administration (or "state"). As we read in *Between Facts and Norms*: the procedural model of democracy "respects the boundaries between 'state' and 'society' but distinguishes civil society, as the social basis of autonomous public spheres, from both the economic system and public administration." Accordingly, this model requires a "realignment in the relative importance of the three resources from which modern societies satisfy their need for integration and steering: money, administration, and [social] solidarity."[24]

As can readily be seen, in these and related writings the contrast marking the initial encounter was steadily deepened—with both theoretical and practical consequences. Philosophically, Habermas's evolving trajectory involved a progressive sidelining or marginalization of hermeneutics, its reduction to at best a subsidiary role in the midst of complex, mutually delimited compartments. What was lost in this reduction was basically the "horizonal" or border-crossing quality of hermeneutics: the readiness of understanding to be "addressed" and possibly be transformed by multiple domains of experience, including the domain of the other or alien (*Fremdheit*). This loss was particularly evident in the compartmentalization of "worlds"—the segregation of three formal worlds juxtaposed to the life-world—a segregation which undercut the key notion of human "being-in-the-world," thereby jeopardizing the possibility of coherent self-understanding (and perhaps the very meaning of *Dasein* itself). In addition to its problematic effects on human "being," the same partitioning carries significant implications for the "worldliness" of human life: namely, by distancing "nature" into a radically external reality amenable to technical mastery and control or else to the productive forces of modern industry (labor). Despite repeated complaints about the modern ascendancy of "instrumental rationality," Habermas's segregating strategy bars any hermeneutical transition or border crossing between human endeavors and nature (especially when the latter is seen in the Greek sense of *physis*). To this extent, his work is scarcely sensitive to contemporary ecological concerns, especially to the urgent need to curb technological mastery and industrial production for the sake of a more sustainable ecospace for humanity. A similar reduction is manifest in the stylizing of psychic life into a "subjective world" of self-expression, a move curtailing prereflective moorings in favor of a progressively rational self-transparency.[25]

In sidelining hermeneutics, Habermas's trajectory also steadily weakened or eroded its linkage with *praxis* or practical philosophy in Aristotle's sense—whose legacy, in modified form, was preserved and continued in Gadamer's work. In this respect, Habermas's bracketing of ordinary life practices in favor of formalized discourses and rational reconstructions was bound to exact a price. Compared with formal validity claims and anonymous rule structures, concrete life practices were liable to slide into the backwaters of unexamined traditions or, worse yet, into the cauldron of irrational impulses and atavistic desires. The same peril inhered in Habermas's extensive borrowing from sociological "system theory" with its spectatorial (or metatheoretical) biases. By acknowledging the need for "system integration" and maintenance, this borrowing jeopardized the very notion of a "legitimation crisis"—whose chances were liable to be thwarted by superior system imperatives (geared to efficacy and administrative control). In a particularly patent manner, the peril persists in Habermas's recent legal and political theorizing, especially in his model of deliberative democracy. Wedged between the subsystems of "money" and "administration," practical "solidarity" in the social life-world seems to have little room to unfold and thrive. In fact, the extensive homage paid to economic, technical, and bureaucratic expertise tends to undercut the significance of political participation and practical engagement—thus corroborating the long-standing retreat or atrophy of the "public sphere" in modern politics. At the very least, greater attention would have to be given in the model to hermeneutical-political bridge building, especially to the need to reintegrate expert knowledge into the ordinary language of practical political life.[26]

Closely linked with the retreat of *praxis* is the danger posed to dialogue and communication—especially in our rapidly globalizing age. What is urgently needed in this context is an open-ended, "horizonal" dialogue supportive of intercivilizational learning and practical engagement. This prospect is thwarted both by a retreat into narrow particularism and a leap into spectatorial metatheory. Although the dangers of the former are manifest, the drawbacks of the latter are often ignored. As Gadamer insists, however, both particularism and metatheory are equally non-conducive to hermeneutical learning. From the vantage of metatheory—including formal metacommunication—ordinary languages and life practices are prone to be distanced and objectified, only to be subsumed as instances under universal categories. (Alternatively, life practices are stylized as separate "worlds" without mediating connections). In Gadamer's view, the leap into metatheory has always been a particularly Western or "Occidental" temptation, encouraging the pretense of a "superior" standpoint. As opposed to concrete or "effective" reflection, he notes, objectifying metareflection has been the hallmark of the "Occidental linguistic tradition"—a paradigm that is now being globalized, thus establishing "the grounds for the planetary civilization of tomorrow." To counter the defects of this paradigm, Gadamer persistently counsels the return to lived practices, and especially the cultivation of engaged dialogue across borders or boundaries. Only such cultivation can engender a genuine social "solidarity"—the term understood not in the sense of a constraining or exclusivist communitarianism, but in that of a nurturing and mutually liberating democratic engagement. To conclude with a "vintage" Gadamerian passage:

> And so, in answer to the question: What is practice? I would like to sum up: Practice is conducting oneself and acting in solidarity. Solidarity, however, is the condition and basis of social reason (or reasoning). There is a saying of Heraclitus, the "weeping" philosopher: The *logos* is common to all, but people behave as if each had a private reason. Does this have to remain this way?[27]

NOTES

1. For some discussions of the debate see Dieter Misgeld, "Critical Theory and Hermeneutics: The Debate between Habermas and Gadamer," in *On Critical Theory*, ed. John O'Neill (New York: Seabury Press, 1976), pp. 164-183; Paul Ricoeur, "Hermeneutics and Critique of Ideology," in *Paul Ricoeur: Hermeneutics and the Human Sciences*, ed. John B. Thompson (Cambridge, UK: Cambridge University Press, 1981), pp. 63-100; also my "Life-World and Critique," in *Between Freiburg and Frankfurt: Toward a Critical Ontology*, pp. 13-24.

2. Gadamer, *Truth and Method*, pp. 257-258. As he adds (p. 259): Understanding for Heidegger is "not the resigned ideal of human experience adopted in the old age of the spirit, as with Dilthey; nor is it, as with Husserl, a last methodological ideal of philosophy in contrast to the naiveté of unreflective life; it is, on the contrary, the *original form of the realization of Dasein*, which is being-in-the-world."

3. Gadamer, *Truth and Method*, pp. 266-67 (translation slightly altered).

4. Gadamer, *Truth and Method*, pp. 272, 276-277 (translation slightly altered). Despite these sharp comments, one cannot deny that Gadamer sometimes blunts the edge of his argument by resorting to very conventional vocabulary (such as "historical consciousness" or "historically effective consciousness") and by substituting often very "ontic" descriptions for Heidegger's ontological account. On some of these points see my "Hermeneutics and Deconstruction: Gadamer and Derrida in Dialogue," in Dallmayr, *Critical Encounters* (Notre Dame: IN: University of Notre Dame Press, 1987), pp. 130-158.

5. Gadamer, *Truth and Method*, pp. 277-282. Regarding the rehabilitation of "authority" compare also Hannah Arendt, "What is Authority?" in *Between Past and Future: Six Exercises in Political Thought* (Cleveland, OH: World Publishing Co., 1963), pp. 91-141, especially her comment (p. 106) that "authority implies an obedience in which men retain their freedom."

6. Gadamer, *Truth and Method*, pp. 295, 298-299, 301-302. Elaborating on the last point Gadamer adds (p. 302): "All self-knowledge arises from what is historically pre-given—what with Hegel we call 'substance,' because it underlies all subjective intentions and actions and hence both prescribes and limits every possibility for understanding any tradition whatsoever in its historical alterity (*Andersheit*)."

7. Gadamer, "The Universality of the Hermeneutical Problem," in *Philosophical Hermeneutics*, trans. and ed. David E. Linge (Berkeley: University of California Press, 1976), p. 14.

8. Gadamer, "The Universality of the Hermeneutical Problem," pp. 4-9.

9. Gadamer, "The Universality of the Hermeneutical Problem," pp. 3, 13, 15-16. The last sentence points to a complex notion of "truth," transgressing correspondence or adequation in the direction of an ontological mode of disclosure or *aletheia*. Compare in this respect Gadamer, "Was ist Wahrheit?" in *Kleine Schriften I: Philosophie, Hermeneutik* (Tübingen: Mohr, 1967), pp. 46-58.

10. Gadamer, "Man and Language," in *Philosophical Hermeneutics*, pp. 60-62, 64-67. In stressing the sayable, Gadamer does not question the correlation of the "said" and "unsaid" (p. 67): "Nothing that is said has its truth simply in itself, but refers instead backward and forward to what is unsaid."

11. Jürgen Habermas, "A Review of Gadamer's *Truth and Method*," in *Understanding and Social Inquiry*, ed. Fred Dallmayr and Thomas A. McCarthy (Notre Dame, IN: University of Notre Dame Press, 1977), p. 335. The review was first published in German in *Philosophische Rundschau* in 1967, and was subsequently incorporated into Habermas, *Zur Logik der Sozialwissenschaften* (Frankfurt-Main: Suhrkamp, 1970), pp. 251-290. For an English version of the latter study see *On the Logic of the Social Sciences*, trans. Shierry Weber Nicholson and Jerry A. Stark (Cambridge, MA: MIT Press, 1989).

12. Habermas, "A Review," pp. 336, 338. As he adds (p. 342): "Gadamer uses the image of the horizon to capture the basic hermeneutic character of every concrete language—far from having a closed boundary, each concrete language can in principle incorporate what is linguistically foreign and at first incomprehensible."

13. Ibid., pp. 339-340, 353-354.

14. Habermas, "A Review," pp. 344, 346-348, 350. The reference is to Arthur C. Danto, *Analytical Philosophy of History* (Cambridge: Cambridge University Press, 1965).

15. Habermas, "A Review," pp. 354-356. In this context, Habermas targets the influence of Heidegger, especially Heideggerian "ontology," as responsible for Gadamer's privileging of "truth" over "method."

16. Habermas, "A Review," pp. 356-358.

17. Habermas, "A Review," pp. 359-361.

18. Habermas, "Knowledge and Human Interests: A General Perspective," in *Knowledge and Human Interests*, trans. Jeremy J. Shapiro (Boston: Beacon Press, 1971), pp. 308, 313-314. For the German text of the lecture "Erkenntnis und Interesse" see Habermas, *Technik und Wissenschaft als "Ideologie"* (Frankfurt-Main: Suhrkamp, 1968), pp. 146-168. The book *Erkenntnis und Interesse* was first published in 1968, also by Suhrkamp.

19. Gadamer, "On the Scope and Function of Hermeneutical Reflection" (1967), in *Philosophical Hermeneutics*, pp. 18, 25-26.

20. Gadamer, "On the Scope and Function," pp. 26-29.

21. Gadamer, "On the Scope and Function," pp. 30-31, 33.

22. For some of these arguments, see Habermas "A Postscript to *Knowledge and Human Interests*," *Philosophy of the Social Sciences* 3 (1975): pp. 157-189; and "The Hermeneutic Claim to Universality," in *Contemporary Hermeneutics: Hermeneutics as Method, Philosophy and Critique*, ed. Josef Bleicher (London: Routledge & Kegan Paul, 1980), pp. 181-211.

23. Habermas, *Legitimation Crisis*, trans. Thomas McCarthy (Boston: Beacon Press, 1975), pp. 1-17; "What is Universal Pragmatics?" in Habermas, *Communication and the Evolution of Society*, trans. Thomas McCarthy (Boston: Beacon Press, 1979), pp. 1-68.

24. Habermas, *Between Facts and Norms: Contributions to a Discourse Theory of Law and Democracy*, trans. William Rehg (Cambridge, MA: MIT Press, 1996), p. 299. See also his *The Theory of Communicative Action*, vol. I: *Reason and the Rationalization of Society*, trans. Thomas McCarthy (Boston: Beacon Press, 1984), pp. 84-94.

25. Following *Knowledge and Human Interests*, Habermas turned increasingly away from Freudian psychoanalysis in the direction of developmental psychology, especially the model of cognitive and moral development as articulated by Jean Piaget and Lawrence Kohlberg. See, e.g., his "Moral Development and Ego Identity," in *Communication and the Evolution of Society*, pp. 69-94, and "Lawrence Kohlberg and Neo-Aristotelianism," in *Justification and Application: Remarks on Discourse Ethics*, trans. Ciaran P. Cronin (Cambridge, MA: MIT Press, 1994), pp. 113-132. In Habermas's normative theory, hermeneutical ethics is precariously wedged between a "pragmatic" and a properly "moral" use of practical reason; in the specific domain of "moral discourse," hermeneutical judgment (*phronesis*) is allotted a subsidiary role in the field of "application." See *Justification and Application*, pp. 5-6, 13-14, 37-38.

26. The importance of such reintegration was still stressed in some of Habermas's early writings, especially *Toward a Rational Society: Student Protest, Science and Politics*, trans. Jeremy J. Shapiro (Boston: Beacon Press, 1970), and *The Structural Transformation of the Public Sphere*, trans. Thomas Burger and Frederick G. Lawrence (Cambridge, MA: MIT Press, 1989). More recently, however, the integrative capacity of both language and philosophy has been greatly curtailed, with language shrinking into a means or "medium" of communication, and philosophy mainly into a "stand-in" for scientific-theoretical knowledge. See in this respect Habermas,

"Does Philosophy Still Have a Purpose?" in *Philosophical-Political Profiles*, trans. Frederick G. Lawrence (Cambridge, MA: MIT Press, 1983), pp. 1-19; and "Philosophy as Stand-In and Interpreter," in *Moral Consciousness and Communicative Action*, trans. Christian Lenhardt and Shierry Weber Nicholson (Cambridge, MA: MIT Press, 1990), pp. 1-20; also my "Habermas and Rationality," in *Between Freiburg and Frankfurt*, pp. 132-159.

27. Gadamer, "What is Practice?" in *Reason in the Age of Science*, p. 87; "On the Scope and Function," in *Philosophical Hermeneutics*, p. 25.

Chapter Ten

Empire and Faith: Sacred Non-Sovereignty

The nations shall see and be ashamed of all their might.

Micha 7:16

In recent times, theology has turned its attention to narrative. In the view of leading practitioners, sacred scripture offers not so much a doctrine or system of ideas as rather a treasure chest of stories capable of transforming lives. Here is one such story. After having been captured or apprehended, Jesus was first taken to the high priest and then to Pontius Pilate who, in line with Roman custom, began to interrogate him—albeit in a half-hearted manner. One question that seemed to intrigue Pilate was the alleged authority or power of Jesus. He asked bluntly: "Are you the king of the Jews?"—to which Jesus answered with a counterquestion (according to John 18:34): "Do you say this of your own accord, or did others say this about me?" In the three synoptic Gospels the answer is more concise and perhaps more telling (Matthew 27:11, Mark 15:2, Luke 23:3): "You have said so"—which might be rendered as: "These are your words not mine" or "This is your way of speaking not mine." Unsurprisingly, Pilate was not satisfied with this response and kept pressuring Jesus on the issue. At this point, Jesus was willing to elaborate a bit more and said (again according to John 18:36): "My 'kingship' is not of this world. If my 'kingship' were of this world, my servants would fight that I might not be handed over to the Jews; but my 'kingship' is not from the world." Taking this answer as a kind of admission, Pilate shot back: "So then you are a king?" To which Jesus gave this memorable reply (John 18:37): "You say that I am a king [or this king-talk is your kind of talking]. But I was born for one thing, and for this I have come into the world: namely, to bear witness to the truth."

199

As we know, the biblical story continues and leads the reader ultimately and ineluctably to a somber ending. It will be necessary at a later point to return to the ending of the story. At this juncture, however, it seems advisable to stop and reflect briefly on the meaning of the story recounted so far. First we may wish to glance at the questioner and his possible motives. As a provincial governor appointed by imperial Rome, it seems reasonable to assume that Pilate was primarily preoccupied with political power and governance; from this angle, Jesus' religious faith or status was for him prone to be a matter of sublime indifference (his interrogation at no point showed any interest in the topic). If Jesus was indeed a king—as some people apparently asserted—then this claim was clearly a cause of apprehension: politically understood, kingship constituted a challenge to the power or *"potestas"* of the governor and ultimately a challenge to the supreme power or *"suprema potestas"* of the emperor in Rome—something which later came to be articulated as "sovereignty." No matter how puzzled or irritated he may have been by the answers he received, these political points were quite clear in Pilate's mind. In modern or contemporary terminology, we might describe him as a devotee of *realpolitk*—and from the angle of *realpolitik* only power, especially supreme power, counts.

As the story shows, Pilate—in order to reduce his confusion—was tempted to interpret Jesus' replies precisely in terms of his own familiar political framework. And in this respect, Pilate is not alone. As it happens, his interpretation has been a perennial temptation hovering like a shadow over the history of Christianity (or what some theologians now call "Christendom"). When Jesus stated: "My 'kingdom' is not of this world" or "from this world," Pilate immediately jumped to the conclusion: "So you are a king"—perhaps not here and now at this place, but somewhere else, at another place. It is unlikely that Pilate's mind was able to move beyond a realist, geopolitical perspective: if Jesus' "kingdom" was not right here in Judaea, it was probably next door, in some other province—and as such still a potential danger to Rome's *suprema potestas*. Without departing entirely from Pilate's geopolitics of place, more metaphysically inclined readers have interpreted Jesus' statement as postulating "another world" behind this world, another spiritual kingdom behind the worldly kingdom. According to this metaphysical reading— which reverberates powerfully throughout the ensuing "Christian" centuries—there are basically "two worlds," a spiritual or immaterial one and a worldly or material one; as a corollary, there are two kinds of supreme power: the supreme power or sovereign kingship of God, and the *suprema potestas* or sovereignty of worldly rulers. In the view of metaphysical theologians, the two worlds and types of power exist side by side, but ultimately are—or should be—related in the mode of subordination: the worldly power responding or being subordinated to divine power—just like a provincial governor (say Pontius Pilate) was subordinated to imperial Rome.

It was the fault not of Pilate but of his metaphysical successors that Christian religion became embroiled in power plays, in the endless competition for supreme power or sovereignty. Throughout the Christian Middle Ages, Europe was in the grip of intense and nearly interminable struggles between worldly (or temporal) and spiritual (or ecclesiastic) power-holders, with each side claiming to hold the ultimate trump card: the ability to depose and humiliate the other. Whatever damage this contest may have inflicted on "worldly" politics, the price exacted from religious faith was higher. By being sucked into power plays, the metaphysical distinction between "this world" and the "other world," between temporal and spiritual realms was leveled into a Pilate-style geopolitics—with the result that the presumed omnipotence of God became nearly indistinguishable from the might of a Genghis Khan. In the memorable words of Merleau-Ponty, God was assigned the position of an "absurd emperor of the world."[1] Even after the collapse of the medieval empire, the geopolitical streamlining of religion persisted. Following the horrendous experiences of the religious wars, Europe in the Peace of Westphalia settled on a formula which joined temporal and spiritual power in the hands of a territorial ruler (*cuius regio eius religio*)—a formula which approximated, at least in part, the caesaropapist arrangement prevalent for a long time in Eastern Christianity. From this time forward, the main energies of churches and religious believers in the West were invested in the struggle to loosen again the juncture of spiritual and temporal realms—a struggle carried on chiefly under the banner of religious freedom or freedom of religious belief. Aided and abetted by the Enlightenment and other progressive modern tendencies, this struggle for religious freedom was largely successful—but it again exacted a price. In its effort to extricate itself from public-worldly affairs, religious faith increasingly retreated into inwardness or allowed itself to be "privatized." Yet, as a purely private affair, the encounter between Jesus and Pilate, recounted above, becomes pointless or a matter of taste. Under secular-liberal auspices, faith basically becomes an individual pastime—perhaps nobler and "higher" than other pastimes, but not substantially different from playing golf or watching video games.

No doubt, Western Christianity through the centuries has seen resolute attempts to counteract the co-optation and domestication of religious faith by "worldly" rulers or potentates. In fact, both worldly co-optation and private complacency have been the repeated target of religious resistance or countermovements—movements sometimes fueled by revolutionary and even millenarian zeal. Students of history will recall the intermittent upsurge of radical antiauthoritarian sects during the Middle Ages, and also the more effective uprisings of Puritans, Levellers, Diggers, and "*Schwärmer*" during the early part of modernity. In terms of their intrinsic logic, movements of this kind are basically *anti*-movements predicated on radical negation: anti-political, antigovernmental, anti-church, and even anti-world. In lieu of worldly *potestas*, they postulate the annihilation of *potestas*, in lieu of hierarchy, some form of anarchy. If one pushes their logic to the extreme, one ultimately arrives at a radical dualism, not far removed from a gnostic Manichaeanism: a dualism opposing a purely spiritual realm inhabited by God and his saints to the corrupt "this-worldly" realm ultimately governed by an evil demiurge and his potentates. In the eyes of gnostic millenarians, this dualistic scheme vindicates the project of a radical eschatology or global conflagration: the utter destruction of "this" world with all its evil ways (including politics) leading to the apocalyptic triumph of God and his millenarian (though antipolitical) militants.[2] Even when not carried to this extreme, the spirit of gnostic Manicheism still hovers behind metaphysical construals of "two worlds" seemingly exiting from geopolitics.

As the example of millenarianism shows, radical antipolitics still is a form of politics, though operating in the mode of denial; like every radical negation or antithesis, antipolitics remains linked to what it denies or rejects. Viewed from the angle of power or *potestas*, one might say that radical anti-sovereignty still pays tribute to the idea of sovereignty (now construed as negative power or power of destruction). Glancing back at the encounter of Jesus and Pilate, one can readily see that Jesus was not antipolitical in any millenarian sense. At no point during the interrogation does Jesus threaten the destruction of imperial Rome or its provincial governance in Judaea, or the destruction of political life per se. According to many historians of the period, Jesus was probably quite familiar with the sect of Essenes and their gnostic-dualistic beliefs; but nowhere in his ministry or during his trial does he resort to their millenarian rhetoric. As indicated before, he does suggest to Pilate the possibility that armies of "servants" could come to his rescue—yet he immediately adds that this was not going to happen simply because his "kingdom" (if the term was at all applicable) was not a kingdom of that kind, his rulership not the rule of a worldly potentate. When he was brought before Pilate, one of the specific charges leveled against Jesus by his accusers was that he was "perverting" the people, forbidding them "to give tribute to Caesar" in light of his own, alternative kingship (Luke 23:2). Yet, the falsity of this charge must have been evident to Pilate and other Roman authorities who, no doubt, had kept watch of his public teachings precisely on this issue. They probably were familiar with one particular episode in which Jesus' enemies had tried to lure him into a trap, in the presence of the "Herodians" (who were sycophants of Rome). "Tell us then," his enemies asked him, "is it lawful to pay taxes to Caesar, or not?" Aware of their scheming design, Jesus urged them to produce a piece of money, and when they had done so, he pointed to the coin's surface asking: "Whose likeness and inscription is this?" And when they had responded "Caesar's," he told them plainly and without equivocation: "Render therefore to Caesar the things that are Caesar's, and to God the things that are God's" (Matthew 15:17-21).

What this episode reveals is that Jesus at no point aimed to establish a counter regime to the prevailing political regime, nor an alternative *suprema potestas* to the *potestas* of the provincial governor or imperial Rome. This does not mean that Jesus' life and ministry did not represent a genuine alternative to prevailing politics, but the alternative was predicated neither on competition nor on negation or destruction, but on transformation. Differently phrased: his ministry was designed not to trump the world (by establishing a worldly superpower), nor to destroy or eradicate this world (along millenarian lines), but rather to salvage and redeem the world—redeem it through truth and divine grace. In political terms, his ministry inaugurated neither a super-politics nor an antipolitics, but rather an "other" kind of politics—what might be called a politics of sacred or redemptive non-sovereignty. The notion of an "other" kind of politics seems to collide with a widespread (liberal) view that faith is entirely a private matter. This view, however, is contestable. That religion for Jesus was more than a private idiosyncrasy is evident from the public character of his life and ministry. As he said to the high priest: "I have spoken openly to the world . . . (and) have said nothing in secret" (John 18:20). One of the things he had spoken about publicly was his conception of worldly rulership and community life. As reported in Mark's Gospel, two of Jesus' disciples once came to him asking him to be able to share in God's sovereignty or supreme power (namely, by sitting "one at your right hand and one at your left, in your glory"). Rebuking them, Jesus taught them about non-sovereignty (Mark 10:37-44):

> You know that those who are supposed to rule over the gentiles lord it over them, and their great men exercise power over them. But it shall not be so among you; but whoever would be great among you must be your servant, and whoever would be first among you must be slave of all.

One of the tragedies of Christianity is that Jesus' teachings about non-sovereignty have fallen for so many centuries mostly on deaf ears. Even today, the hankering for sovereignty has not subsided—even among otherwise religious people. One of the standard accusations leveled by religious "fundamentalists" against democratic rule is that democracy challenges or undermines the absolute power or "sovereignty of God."[3] Fortunately, the situation is no longer devoid of encouraging initiatives. Among theologians (both Christian and non-Christian), the upsurge of "liberation theology" has put a dent into traditional preoccupations with *suprema potestas* (both in temporal and spiritual domains). Among contemporary political theorists, major strides toward a deconstruction of "sovereignty" have been undertaken, especially by Hannah Arendt and Jean Bethke Elshtain. As Hannah Arendt has pointedly written, human freedom and responsibility are incompatible with *suprema potestas* and hence, to salvage these goods, "it is precisely sovereignty that they [people] must renounce"—a view which has been further developed and fleshed out by Elshtain, especially in *New Wine and Old Bottles*.[4] Similar initiatives can be found in the works of recent and contemporary philosophers (sometimes under "postmodern" auspices). Thus, when Claude Lefort writes that, in modern democracy, the locus of ultimate power becomes "an empty place," he does not simply refer to a vacuum or a negative anti-sovereignty, but to another kind of politics or another way of conceiving political rule—a conception not too far removed from the "other" mode of politics often invoked by Jacques Derrida. One of the most significant interventions in this debate has been made by Martin Heidegger, a philosopher not often credited with political insight. In several of this treatises dating from the 1930s, Heidegger formulated the idea of a "power-free" realm (*das Machtlose*), a realm equally far removed from *suprema potestas* and from the negation of *potestas* or impotence.[5]

Let us put philosophy aside here, however, and return to our initial story. We have left Jesus standing before a puzzled and increasingly bewildered Pilate. As far as this prisoner was concerned, Pilate must have felt completely out of his depth: he did not comprehend the main charges brought against him, and those he did understand were patently false or unsubstantiated. Repeatedly he made an effort to get the charges dropped and to wash his hands of the entire affair; but to no avail. Under growing pressure from the accusers, Pilate finally relented and grudgingly pronounced his sentence. From this moment on, the story quickly gathered momentum and hurried to its bitter conclusion. What particularly must have annoyed or irritated Pilate was the fact that, at the moment when he sentenced Jesus, he also was induced or compelled to set another prisoner free. That prisoner's name was Barrabas—and he was "a murderer and an insurrectionist" (Mark 15:7, Luke 23:19). Setting this man free must have greatly irked Pilate, because the insurrection was against his own rule and the *suprema potestas* of Rome. While he did not comprehend the crime committed by Jesus, the situation in the case of Barrabas was crystal clear. As a Roman governor involved all his life in *realpolitik*, he felt comfortably on familiar ground with Barrabas. Together with his fellow insurrectionists, Barrabas operated on the customary ground of *realpolitik* and geopolitical conflict. His aim was basically to replace one power by another power, to substitute the power of the insurrectionists for the *potestas* of Rome. And there was a clear and well-known punishment for insurrection.

By that time, however, things had taken their course and were basically out of Pilate's hands. What followed was the beating and flagellation of Jesus and then the road to Calvary. In the end, however, Pilate managed to take revenge—a peculiar revenge unexpected by the accusers. When Jesus was nailed to and hoisted up on the cross, Pilate had an inscription placed over his head that read: "Jesus of Nazareth, king of the Jews." And in order to make sure that passersby could in fact read the message, he had the sentence written in three languages: Hebrew, Latin, and Greek (John 19:19-20). At this point the accusers had second thoughts about their accusations—a key charge being Jesus' counter-kingship against Rome—and urged Pilate to change the inscription so that it would read not "king of the Jews" but "this man claimed to be king of the Jews." But at this juncture, Pilate proved to be stubborn: as a hard-boiled Roman politician he had no taste for esoteric double-talk. Having given in too much earlier, he now stood his ground firmly saying: "What I have written I have written (*Quod scripsi scripsi*)" (John 19:21-22).

At this moment, Pilate—unwittingly and probably against his intentions—became a participant and a witness in a much larger salvation history. The words he had written (perhaps out of spite) reflected a wisdom that great philosophers might envy. So, at the very end, Jesus was after all proclaimed a "king." But what kind of a king? Surely not a sovereign potentate, not the kind of mighty overlord that one finds among the gentiles whose rulers "lord it over them." A king nailed to a cross and seemingly devoid of all power or *potestas*—except for the power of sacredness. But then, this is what Jesus had stated at the very beginning of his interrogation when he said that he was born and came into the world for one purpose alone: "to bear witness to the truth"—which is a truth not of empire but of grace and redemption.

NOTES

1. Merleau-Ponty, *In Praise of Philosophy*, p. 47.

2. On millenarianism see especially Michael Walzer, *The Revolution of the Saints: A Study in the Origin of Radical Politics* (Cambridge, MA: Harvard University Press, 1965); also Howard Hotson, *Christian Millennarianisms: From the Early Church to Waco* (London: Hurst & Co., 2000).

3. For a discussion of this charge, especially in the context of Islamic fundamentalism, see Roxanne L. Euben, *Enemy in the Mirror: Islamic Fundamentalism and the Limits of Modern Rationalism* (Princeton: Princeton University Press, 1999), pp. 49–92; also my "Islam: Friend or Enemy?" *International Studies Review*. 3 (2001): pp. 171-174.

4. See Hannah Arendt, "What is Freedom?" in *Between Past and Future*, pp. 164-165; Jean Bethke Elshtain, *New Wine and Old Bottles: International Politics and*

Ethical Discourse (Notre Dame, IN: University of Notre Dame Press, 1998), especially chapter 1, pp. 6-24 ("Sovereignty at Century's End"). Compare also Daniel Ergester, *Divine Sovereignty: The Origins of Modern State Power* (DeKalb, IL: Northern Illinois University Press, 2001).

5. See Claude Lefort, *Democracy and Political Theory*, trans. David Macey (Minneapolis, MN: University of Minnesota Press, 1988), pp. 17-19; Derrida, *The Other Heading: Reflections on Today's Europe*, pp. 76-78; Heidegger, *Besinnung*, pp. 189-191. Compare also my "Resisting Totalizing Uniformity: Martin Heidegger on *Macht* and *Machenschaft*," in *Achieving Our World: Toward a Global and Plural Democracy* (Lanham, MD: Rowman & Littlefield, 2001), pp. 189-209.

APPENDIX

Appendix A

The Dignity of Difference:
A Salute to Jonathan Sacks

In the teeth of its modern despisers, religion has made a comeback in our time—for good or ill. Too often, the negative side is in the limelight: what Gilles Kepel has called the "revenge of God" on inspection usually turns out to be the ill will and vengefulness of religious communities and their leaders. The litany of contemporary religious clashes—or conflicts in good part spawned by religious motives—is long and depressing: Christians pitted against Muslims in Africa and the Balkans; Jews against Palestinians in the Near East; Hindus against Muslims in India and Kashmir; Hindus against Buddhists in Sri Lanka—not to forget the old feud between Catholics and Protestants in Northern Ireland. In this situation it is uplifting and refreshing to encounter a religious leader, like Jonathan Sacks, vigorously defending interfaith harmony and goodwill. Sacks is not an agnostic or cultured despiser claiming a stance high above the fray. He is a deeply religious and even "orthodox" Jew (in fact, the Chief Rabbi of the United Hebrew Congregations of Britain and the Commonwealth); for this very reason, he is able to tackle and illuminate festering issues from the inside of religious belief—something agnostics are never able to do. Not long ago, in a spirited and eminently sage text called *The Dignity of Difference*, he issued a plea to members of all faiths (as well as nonbelievers) to cultivate mutual goodwill and thus to "avoid the clash of civilizations." As he notes in the opening pages: the world's religions "have a significant potential role in conflict resolution and not merely, as many continue to believe, in conflict creation." To reach this potential, something seemingly paradoxical is required: a deep religiosity open to the "dignity" of the other—in such a way that "the more passionately we feel our religious commitments, the more space we make for those not like us."[1]

The prologue clearly sets forth the spirit animating the entire text. As an antidote to religious and civilization clashes, Sacks counsels a broad-based dialogue or "conversation" of humankind—a conversation not limited to the exchange of information or propositions, but operating on a deeper existential level, with participants freely "speaking [their] fears, listening to the fears of others, and in that sharing of vulnerabilities discovering a genesis of hope." Carried on at this level, religious faith is bound to enter the existential dialogue—because faith addresses itself to humankind's most wrenching agonies as well as to its most intense yearnings and aspirations. Karl Marx had described religion as "the sigh of the oppressed creature, the feeling of a heartless world, the soul of soulless conditions." Far from contributing to human oppression and misery, Sacks insists, religious leaders today have to take this description to heart: they should "speak the silent cry of those who today suffer from want, hunger, disease, powerlessness, and lack of freedom." In our time of globalization, human agonies are intensified by dislocation, loss of identity, and loss of place. It is precisely here that Sacks detects the great significance of Judaism because of its long existence on the cusp of globalism/localism. "The prophets of ancient Israel," he writes, "were the first to think globally, to conceive of a God transcending place and national boundaries, and of humanity as a single moral community." At the same time, Judaism had to wrestle with the reality of global dispersion, an experience which forced Jews to ponder how to preserve their singularity in the midst of a global universality, how to maintain their distinctive faith in relation to a multitude of beliefs. In a bold formulation, Sacks maintains that the heart of (Jewish) monotheism is not what it has traditionally been taken to be: "one God, therefore one faith, one truth, one way." Instead, its core is "that unity creates diversity" and that "the glory of the created world is its astonishing multiplicity." This is what he means by "the dignity of difference."[2]

Unfortunately, the envisaged dialogue of humankind is under siege today. Under the combined impact of consumerism, emotivism, and corporate globalism, conversation is in fact "dying" and with it "our chances of civic, let alone global, peace." Propelled by consumerism and emotivism, wants and desires are forcefully advanced—but not discussed, negotiated, or transformed. In turn, corporate globalism promotes the sway of a uniform mold of practices throughout the world, disdainful of differences. In Sacks's view, Western history has moved through a sequence of universalizing systems or regimes, ranging from ancient Greece and Rome via medieval Christianity and Islam to the Enlightenment. Wedded to "grand narratives," all these systems tended to sweep away local customs, ancient cultures, and different ways of doing things. Today, a new universal regime holds sway: corporate globalism (or global capitalism), anchored in the market, the media, and multinational corporations. Again, the emphasis is on uniformity, now on a global scale; and again, what is chiefly endangered are "all things local, traditional, and particular" (akin to the threatened biodiversity in the realm of nature). Channeled by this new regime, the entire world is in the process of becoming "one giant satisfaction-producing machine" (what Heidegger might have called *Gestell*). Behind the sequence of regimes, Sacks perceives a deeper metaphysical principle at work: the principle of unitary holism that he traces ultimately to Plato and Socrates. "It is time," he writes provocatively, "that we exorcised Plato's ghost, clearly and unequivocally." Although there may indeed be "moral universals"—and Sacks is far from rejecting them—they exist only or mainly "to create space for cultural and religious difference." This is precisely the space needed for genuine conversation:

> We must learn the art of conversation, from which truth emerges—not, as in Socratic dialogues, by the refutation of falsehood but from the quite different process of letting our world be enlarged by the presence of others who think, act, and interpret reality in ways radically different from our own. We must attend to the particular, not just the universal.[3]

The relation between unity and difference is pursued further in a chapter specifically subtitled "Exorcising Plato's Ghost." Again, Sacks notes the sequence of universal (or imperial) regimes in Western history, a sequence now culminating in globalization and the emergence of a universal culture spanning the globe. Although they may have "brought about great good" (by taming tribalism), he comments, such universal regimes also "have done immense harm" (by squashing distinctness). In order to counteract this Western trajectory, the text postulates "nothing less than a paradigm shift" in our understanding of the world: a shift away from traditional Platonism in the direction of a greater appreciation of worldly concreteness. What is called "Plato's ghost" in this context is the idea (developed in the *Republic*) that "the true essence of things is not matter but form, ideas, not their concrete embodiment in the world of the senses"—differently stated: the notion that "truth (reality, the essence of things) is universal," while "particularity (the world of the senses and the passions) is the source of conflict, prejudice, error and war." Although familiar from Nietzsche and much post-Nietzschean literature, the critique of Platonism here acquires a new and surprising salience by its connection with religious faith—and especially a reinterpretation of the core meaning of Judaism. For Sacks, Judaism inaugurated a completely novel correlation of universalism and particularism—in such a way that "the Bible represents the great anti-Platonic narrative in Western civilization." While, after the great flood, God (through Noah) established a universal covenant with all humanity, this universalism soon decayed in the attempt (symbolized by the tower of Babel) to "impose a man-made unity" on diversity; in response, God made a new covenant with Abraham, thus instituting Judaism as a "particularist monotheism." While the "God of Abraham" may be the God of all peoples, the specific "faith of Abraham" is not the faith of all humanity. Thus, through the Abrahamic covenant, Sacks boldly asserts, God commanded the Jews "to be different *in order to teach humanity the dignity of difference.*" Implicit in this account is the distinction between God and religion, between the radical transcendence of God and the inevitable diversity of particular religious faiths: "*God is God of all humanity, but no single faith is or should be the faith of all humanity.*"[4]

In addition to its religious salience, Sacks's account is eminently relevant to contemporary philosophical discussions of ethics and epistemology. Picking up some cues from Michael Walzer, he distinguishes between "thin" and "think" forms of ethics, between "context-free" and concretely contextualized forms of moral reasoning—placing the accent squarely on the latter modality. On the one hand, he writes, we are members of "the universal human family and thus of the (Noahide) covenant with all mankind," a covenant stipulating universal rights and liberties. On the other hand, however, we are part of "a 'thick' or context-bound morality (represented, in Judaism, by the Abrahamic and Mosaic covenants)" according to which we have concrete loyalties and obligations to family and friends as well as to members of the wider society. The important thing here is to get one's priorities straight, for moral universality is "not something we learn by being universal but by being particular." Generally speaking, there is for Sacks "no road to human solidarity that does not begin with moral particularity." Hence, we learn to love humanity not by embracing abstract principles but "by loving specific human beings. There is no shortcut." With regard to epistemology and especially the question of "truth," Sacks forges a difficult path between absolutism and relativism, between total knowledge and ignorance—a path that in many ways is reminiscent of Gandhi and his "experiments with truth." "For life to be livable," he asserts, "truth on earth cannot be what it is in heaven"—where it may be Platonic, eternal, and radiant. On the ground where people live, truth is bound to be "multiple and partial," with fragments being scattered everywhere. Basically, each person, culture, and language has, or can have, part of it; but "none has it all." Truth from this angle is a challenge and a stimulus to conversation—in line with a passage from Mishnah that says: "Who is wise? One who learns from all people."[5]

As one should note well, attention to particularity and situated concreteness here does not equal a retreat into parochialism or a myopic "culturalism" averse to transformative change; above all, no concession is made to fundamentalist intransigence. Embedded in all cultural and religious contexts, in Sacks's account, is a radical call to justice and truth—a call emanating ultimately from the "God of Abraham" and the Noahide covenant. The core of the Hebrew Bible, in his view, is not a series of abstract commandments but the exhortation *"Shema Israel"*—where *shema* means "to hear, to understand and to respond, to *listen* in the fullest range of senses." As he adds: "I believe that God is summoning us to a new act of listening" today, beyond traditional confinements and insidious defenses of the status quo. Faced with the injustices and inequities of the contemporary world, the text issues a stirring call for "listening" which deserves to be cited in full. What is significant about contemporary religious movements, we read, is

> precisely the fact that they represent protests against, rather than accommodations to late modernity. They are expressions of a deep dismay at some of the side effects of global capitalism: its inequities, its consumerism and exploitation, its failure to address widespread poverty and disease, its juggernaut insensitivity to local traditions and cultures, and the spiritual poverty that can go hand in hand with material wealth. It is religion not so much in its modern but in its countermodern sense that has won adherents in today's world, and it is here that the struggle for tolerance, coexistence and nonviolence must be fought.[6]

As one can see, religious faith is invoked here not as a bulwark for political or economic privileges, nor as a mere adjunct of "modernism" (where it would lose its "salt"), but as a source of ferment and contestation. In the midst of the contemporary malaise, the religious *shema*, in its timely urgency, harbors a "narrative of hope," a promise of social justice and renewal. This narrative carries important implications in many domains, ranging from economics to education, civil society, and ecology. Although appreciating the role of free economic choices, and opposing the centralized control of the means of production, Sacks is by no means willing to glorify the liberal market economy. Together with George Soros he challenges "market fundamentalism"—the idea that we can leave the market to its own devices—with a firm "We cannot." As he notes, global capitalism today is a system of "immense power," a system whose social effects in terms of maldistribution constitute "a scar on the face of humanity." Entering into specifics, Sacks reports that the average North American today consumes "five times more than a Mexican, ten times more than a Chinese, thirty times more than an Indian." While nearly one-fourth of the world's population lives beneath the poverty line, almost one billion people are malnourished and without access to medical care.[7] Relying again on religious resources, Sacks invokes the biblical notion of *"tzedakah,"* meaning a mode of distributive justice where justice and charity are combined. In terms of the biblical tradition, he writes, a free society cannot be built on *"mishpat"* or a procedural rule of law alone; it also—and crucially—requires the practice of *tzedakah* or the just distribution of resources in light of a substantive conception of the common good. Above all, *tzedakah* guarantees not only individual freedom but a collective or people's freedom enacted in a shared political space or public sphere: "A society in which the few prosper but the many starve, in which some but not all have access to good education, health care, and other essential amenities, is not a place of liberty."[8]

Next to a certain level of economic well-being, exercise of public freedom requires a high degree of literacy which derives from education. In a chapter filled with historical insights, *The Dignity of Difference* offers a perceptive overview of the evolutionary development of humankind seen as a "learning species." In Sacks's account, the evolution of humankind depended in crucial ways on modes of communication and societal learning. While the birth of writing was a condition of the possibility of ancient "cosmological" societies, the invention of the alphabet in "proto-Sinaitic" scripts heralded a profound transformation of older hieratic or hierarchical forms of social order: "For the first time, the entire universe of communicable knowledge was reduced to a symbol-set between twenty and thirty letters, small enough to be mastered, at least in principle, by everyone." The next breakthrough came with the invention of printing, which challenged the privilege of clerical knowledge and potentially democratized education. In our own time, the ongoing information revolution heralds the prospect of global democracy and a global public sphere—a prospect, however, which is severely hampered by social and economic inequalities (evident in the fact that, of the world's children, 113 million are still unable to go to school and that some 88 countries will not achieve primary education for all by 2015).[9] Hence, for education to perform its proper role as a cornerstone of free public life, modern civil society as a whole needs to be reconstituted or reconstructed—away from a mere assemblage of shopping malls and corporate complexes in the direction of a revitalization of "civic spaces" supported by shared loyalties. Here again, the biblical tradition provides assistance with its notion of "covenantal" relationships. For Sacks, what is urgently needed today are "covenants as well as contracts; meanings as well as preferences; loyalties, not just temporary associations for mutual gain."[10]

The advantage of covenants is that they promote not only procedural fairness but also shared ethical commitments nurtured through sustained conversations about the meaning of the "good life." Beyond this inter-human engagement, covenants also restore another kind of bonding: that between humans and nature, civilization and ecology—a bonding undermined by the modern drive for technological mastery. Challenging devotees of unlimited "modernization," Sacks states that modernity (in the Western sense) was meant to be "the triumphal march of a single cluster of ideas"—above all the ideas of market exchange, science, and technology. With the help of these guideposts, the entire world was expected to become "one giant satisfaction-producing machine delivering ever-larger yields of that measure-of-all-things, called 'progress.'" Countering this panacea, he reminds readers of the limits of ecological sustainability—limits which require a radical shift of perspective: "We do not, severally or collectively, own nature but instead hold it in trust on behalf of those who will come after us. We are guests and guardians on earth." Once again, the Jewish biblical tradition provides antidotes to the modern assault on nature. In terms of that tradition, humans are able to work the land for six days, but on the seventh day "we symbolically abdicate that power." In this manner, the Sabbath is "a weekly reminder of the integrity of nature and the boundaries of human striving." In the same way, the so-called *chukkim* statutes of the Bible require humans to respect the integrity of nature and not to destroy the viability of diverse forms of plant and animal life. Finally (and perhaps most importantly), there is the tradition of prayer which counsels us "to make a blessing, as Jews do, over everything we eat or drink to remind ourselves of God's ownership of the world."[11]

The present pages can only convey selective glimpses of the rich insights contained in *The Dignity of Difference*. Nor is there adequate room here for the airing of possible qualms and reservations. In the spirit of conversation, let me just suggest the possibility of another reading of the Platonic legacy where Plato is seen more as a dialogical than an "essentialist" thinker. In the same spirit, one might wish for a more extended discussion of correctives to the ills of corporate capitalism, beyond the confines of *tzedakah*. These and related qualms, however, pale into nothingness before the humane-spiritual depth of Sacks's text. Where else can one find a religious leader exhorting fellow believers not only to show distant respect for other religions but "to do an act of service or kindness to someone or some group of another faith or ethnicity—to extend a hand of help, in other words, *across* the boundaries of difference and thus to communities outward instead of inward"? Where else can one find a religious leader endorsing the famous words of Isaiah: "Blessed be Egypt my people, Assyria my handiwork, and Israel my inheritance" (Isaiah 19:25)? Taken seriously, these words would transform the present world of interethnic and religious mayhem; they would certainly transform and tame the conflict presently raging in the Middle East. As Sacks makes it clear, implicit in these words is a more-than-contractual, namely, a covenantal view of human relationships. Perhaps the most important and stirring message of his text is the call for a global covenant—what he calls a "covenant of hope" involving the attempt to create a "partnership without dominance or submission." To be sure, this covenant is not going to happen by itself, but requires openness to the great "*shema*" of our time, the global summons (as Sacks writes)

to see in the human other a trace of the divine Other. . . . to see the divine presence in the face of the stranger; to heed the cry of those who are disempowered in this age of unprecedented powers; who are hungry and poor and ignorant and uneducated, whose human potential is being denied the chance to be expressed. . . . We are not gods; but we are summoned . . . to do His work of love and justice and compassion and peace.[12]

NOTES

1. Sacks, *The Dignity of Difference*, pp. viii, xi.

2. Sacks, *The Dignity of Difference*, pp. 2, 11-13, 20-21. In an intriguing formulation (p. 13) he calls the Jews "the world's first global people."

3. Sacks, *The Dignity of Difference*, pp. 3, 20, 22-23. In this context (p. 22), Sacks offers some thoughtful and perceptive comments on Western modernity: "To a remarkable degree, modernity was meant to be a single cluster of interrelated ideas. Its model was science, its discourse reason shorn of the accretion of tradition. Via market exchange and the division of labor it would generate wealth. Through industrialization and technology it would conquer nature. By utilitarian calculation it would maximize happiness." Countering this trajectory he adds: "The world is not a single machine. It is a complex, interactive ecology in which diversity—biological, personal, cultural, and religious—is of the essence."

4. Sacks, *The Dignity of Difference*, pp. 47-49, 51-53, 55. As he adds (p. 56): "The God of the Hebrew Bible is not a Platonist, loving the abstract form of humanity. He is a particularist, loving each of his children for what they are: Isaac *and* Ishmael, Jacob *and* Esau, Israel *and* the nations, choosing one for a particular destiny, to be sure, but blessing the others, each in their own way."

5. Sacks, *The Dignity of Difference*, pp. 57-58, 64-65. As can readily be seen, Sacks's account of ethics differs sharply from the Enlightenment interpretation of Judaism as a system of abstract moral and legal principles (an interpretation propounded at the time by Jews and non-Jews alike). Compare in this context Michael Walzer, *Thick and Thin: Moral Argument at Home and Abroad* (Notre Dame: University of Notre Dame Press, 1994); and M. K. Gandhi, *An Autobiography: The Story of My Experiments with Truth*, trans. Mahadev Desai (Ahmedabad: Navajivan, 1927).

6. Sacks, *The Dignity of Difference*, pp. 18-19.

7. Sacks, *The Dignity of Difference*, pp. 15, 19, 28-29, 88. As he adds (p. 29): "By the end of the millennium, the top fifth of the world's population had 86 percent of the world's GDP while the bottom fifth had just 1 percent. The assets of the world's three richest billionaires were more than the combined wealth of the 600 million inhabitants of the least developed countries. . . . In the United States in the past twenty years, 97 percent of the increase in income has gone to the top 20 percent of families, while the bottom fifth have seen a 44 per cent reduction in earnings." These figures are amply supported by the annual Human Development Reports issued by the United Nations. See also the additional data provided by Sacks on pp. 106-108.

8. Sacks, *The Dignity of Difference*, pp. 113-116. Intriguingly, Sacks compares *tzedakah* with Amartya Sen's concept of "development as freedom." See Sen, *Development as Freedom* (New York: Anchor Books, 2000). Sacks (p. 114) also brings

tzedakah in connection with a "trusteeship" conception of economic property which in many ways resembles the views of Gandhi. Compare on this point Thomas Pantham, "Beyond Liberal Democracy: Thinking with Mahatma Gandhi," in *Political Thought in Modern India,* ed. Thomas Pantham and Kenneth L. Deutsch (New Delhi: Sage Pub., 1986), pp. 329-330.

9. Sacks, *The Dignity of Difference,* p. 136. As he states emphatically (p. 141): "No other single intervention [apart from education] offers greater prospects of enhancing economic opportunities for everyone, and for moving us forward in the long, hard journey to universal human dignity."

10. Sacks, *The Dignity of Difference,* p. 157.

11. Sacks, *The Dignity of Difference,* pp. 16, 22, 167, 171. As Sacks adds (p. 171): "Prayer, ritual, and narrative are ways we shape what Tocqueville called 'habits of the heart.'"

12. Sacks, *The Dignity of Difference,* pp. viii, 202, 204, 208. Regarding the present conflict in the Middle East, Sacks writes (p. 189): "Yet there can be little doubt that a solution exists: a division of the land into two states, roughly coinciding with existing centers of population, an agreement about Jerusalem and holy sites so that each has access to places important to them, joint supervision of shared resources such as water, and an international accord about the future of displaced refugees."

Appendix B

Religion and Rationality: Continuity in the Frankfurt School

This is a time to take stock, especially for intellectuals on the (traditional) Left. The end of the Cold War and the demise of the Soviet Union have brought to the fore two major conflicting tendencies: on the one hand, the upsurge of religious faith in many parts of the world, sometimes in the guise of a dogmatic fundamentalism; on the other hand, the triumphant rise of liberalism—now in the form of capitalist neoliberalism—as a corollary of globalization. These developments have a peculiar bearing on the Frankfurt School, which by now spans at least two generations. While many members of the first generation were sympathetic to religion (though not to any kind of dogmatism) in the form of a subdued Jewish messianism, the basic initial impulse of the School—as an "Institute of Social Research"—was the critical analysis of late capitalism and bourgeois-liberal society. These tendencies were greatly altered during the second generation. Under the guidance of Jürgen Habermas, "critical theory" has shown little interest in religious faith, preferring instead to champion a purely rational discourse (inspired in part by neo-Kantianism and linguistic philosophy). At the same time, again under Habermas's influence, critical theory has steadily moved closer to political liberalism, to the point that the distinction from Rawlsian proceduralism sometimes appears as a mere nuance. Small wonder that many observers have detected a gulf separating the two generations. Eduardo Mendieta's book seeks to counteract and correct this perception. In his view, the second generation of the Frankfurt School has "without equivocation" continued the agenda of the first. With regard to religion, a central thesis of his book is that Habermas's work "is not correctly characterized by the image of a temporal rupture between an early positive and a later negative appraisal of the role of religion."[1]

The essays collected in *Religion and Rationality* are meant to "constitute evidence" (p. 14) of Mendieta's claim of undisrupted continuity. As it happens, several of the selected essays date from the earlier period of Habermas's career—prior to his full "linguistic turn" to discourse theory—when he was still relatively close to first-generation thinkers; and while chapters taken from a later period—including a recent interview with Mendieta—mitigate the harsher connotations of "temporal rupture," they can hardly be said to provide evidence of a smooth continuity. The impression of discontinuity is confirmed even by Mendieta's own (otherwise informative) "Introduction" to the volume. Here one finds first of all a sensitive discussion of the religious leanings of the first generation, especially of its "Jewish utopian messianism"—in which Mendieta detects four main ingredients (p. 4): restorative-anamnestic, utopian, apocalyptic, and messianic. Aspects of this outlook are illustrated in the writings of Bloch, Benjamin, Horkheimer, and Adorno. In the case of Horkheimer, reference is made (pp. 5, 7) to his appeal to "an entirely Other" (*ein ganz Anderes*), his yearning for something "wholly other" and "absolutely unrepresentable" through which the injustices of history could be redeemed. Similar motifs are found in the writings of Adorno (pp. 8-9), especially in his treatment of the otherness of the Other as "irreplaceable and unrepresentable singularity," and his refusal to accept "the assimilation of the singular into the concept" (without dismissing concepts as such). Mendieta also quotes Adorno's statement: "If religion is accepted for the sake of something other than its own truth content, then it undermines itself," and his addendum (in *Negative Dialectics*) that attempts to capture the Other immanently always put otherness "in jeopardy." What was common to most first-generation thinkers was the assumption (p. 11) that religion remains a reservoir "of humanity's most deeply felt injustices and yearned for dreams of reconciliation."

Seen against this background, the following discussion devoted to Habermas gives the impression of a sea change—despite Mendieta's assurance (p. 11) that the notion of an antireligious bias is "misleading."[2] Rather than explicating this assurance, the Introduction turns to Habermas's pronounced social-scientific endeavors, especially his embrace of a mode of "functionalism" (inspired by Parsons and Luhmann) and his elaboration of evolutionary models of social and individual development. In large part, as Mendieta observes (p. 14), these endeavors were prompted by "dissatisfaction" with the first generation's treatment of rationality, and especially its refusal to take seriously Weber's thesis of progressive societal "rationalization," secularization, and disenchantment. Borrowing from Weber and functionalists, Habermas at this point developed a comprehensive theory of social life, comprising "system" and "life-world" dimensions and moving through the stages of archaic, primitive, traditional, and modern societies. From a social-scientific vantage, religion fulfills basically an immanent societal "function" whose

meaning changes over time. Habermas comes close to this view in his statement (p. 18) that "the idea of God is transformed [*aufgehoben*] into the concept of a *Logos* that determines the community of believers and the real life
context of a self-emancipating society" and in the notion that "God is the
name for the substance that gives coherence, unity, and thickness to the life-
world." Mendieta also elaborates on Habermas's "linguistic turn," especially
his formulation of a "discourse morality" and a "universal pragmatics" of
speech acts (totalizing all modes of linguistic interaction). Crucial in this context is the thesis of the progressive "linguistification of the sacred," the latter
seen as the "catalyst of modernity." Religion at this point remains relevant
(only) to the extent that it can be translated or assimilated into discursive language. Illustrative here are Habermas's assertion (in *The Theory of Communicative Action*) that "the aura of rapture and terror that emanates from the sacred, the spellbinding power of the holy, is sublimated into the
binding/bonding force of criticizable validity claims," and his parallel statement that "only a morality, set communicatively aflow and developed into a
discourse ethics, can replace the authority of the sacred" (p. 24).

At the end of this overview, Mendieta reaffirms his conviction of continuity, stating (p. 24) that, while "certainly a secularist," Habermas is by no
means an "anti-religion *philosophe*." The point here, however, is not being for
or against religion, but whether there are sufficient antennae to respect the
difference, and respective integrity, of reason and faith, discursive validity
and redemptive hope. In a functionalist (or quasi-functionalist) systems theory assigning a place or role to everything under the sun, where can there still
be room for the "wholly other" and "absolutely unrepresentable" invoked by
Horkheimer? Likewise, in a theory of universal pragmatics comprehending
all possible speech acts, where can there still be room for any language be-
side that of discursive validity claims? Moreover, in a conception of linguistic intersubjectivity construed (with Mead) as "ego-alter ego" relation, is
there still a loophole left for the Other as "irreplaceable and unrepresentable
singularity" in Adorno's sense? As Mendieta points out (p. 12), Habermas repeatedly acknowledges the debt owed by Enlightenment and modernity to the
Judeo-Christian legacy. But this can be read as a simple developmental
scheme. Here the "linguistification" thesis needs to be pondered. Does the
thesis mean that, before discourse theory, religion or the sacred lacked language and was "speechless" (p. 28)? But then how were its teachings trans-
mitted? Or does the thesis mean that, in modernity, religion will be sublimated or absorbed without a rest in discursive rationality? In this connection,
how is one to read Habermas's statement (in *Postmetaphysical Thinking*): "As
long as no better words for what religion can say are found in the medium of
rational discourse, it [communicative reason] will even coexist abstemiously

with the former"? Does this leave to religion only the options of absorption (into rationality) or exclusion?[3] Does faith always have to "accommodate itself" (p. 150) and bend to modern reason, and never the other way around? But how does this respect their differential integrity? More specifically, given the fact that "universal" pragmatics is necessarily timeless, holding good at all times and places, how can it allow for the distinct temporality of salvation history and the redemptive hope for a messianic future animating the early Frankfurt School?

Limitations of space do not permit a detailed review of all the essays assembled in the volume. For present purposes I restrict myself to a few brief comments. Readers interested in Jewish thought may find most appealing the first and the last of the selected essays where Habermas displays his more sensitive-empathetic qualities. The first is titled "The German Idealism of the Jewish Philosophers" and ranges broadly (and insightfully) from Buber and Rosenzweig via Cohen and the Marburg School to Cassirer, Bloch, and Benjamin. The last deals with Habermas's friend Gershom Scholem and his search for "the other of history in history" (a search focused on Isaak Luria, Sabbatai Sevi, and the kabbalistic tradition). As distinguished from this amicable treatment, the other chapters tend to accentuate more the tensional/conflictual nexus between reason and faith or Athens and Jerusalem. Thus, an essay "On the Difficulty of Saying No" illustrates, in Mendieta's words (p. 25), the "relationship between rationalization and mythological or religious world views, in which the latter must submit to the transformative criticism enacted by the former." Another chapter titled "Transcendence from Within, Transcendence in this World" goes back to a conference held in Chicago on "Habermas and Public Theology" (in 1988). There, responding to theologians and nontheologians, and defending "methodical atheism" as the only acceptable option for "postmetaphysical" philosophy, Habermas asserts among other things (p. 76) that "whoever puts forth a truth claim today must, nevertheless, translate experiences that have their home in religious discourse into the language of a scientific expert culture" (or at least into the language of discourse theory). He also questions (p. 81) whether the "*superadditum*" of religion is required if we "endeavor to act according to moral commands."[4] Another essay titled "Israel or Athens" deals with the Judeo-Christian theology of Johannes Baptist Metz, and especially with the latter's notions of "anamnesis" and a "polycentric world church." There, while appreciating some of Metz's leanings, Habermas comes to the defense of Athens, arguing (pp. 133, 136) that "profane reason must remain skeptical about the mystical causality of a recollection inspired by the history of salvation" and that "the idea of a polycentric church depends in turn on insights of the European Enlightenment and its political philosophy."[5]

Perhaps the distance separating Habermas from the first generation of Frankfurt thinkers is most clearly illustrated in an essay devoted to the work of Michael Theunissen and entitled "Communicative Freedom and Negative Theology." As it happens, Theunissen's writings—under Christian auspices and with a focus on Hegel transformed by Kierkegaard—recapture in many ways the Jewish religious aspirations of that first generation. As Habermas acknowledges (p. 113), Theunissen maintains trust in "an eschatological turning of the world" and tries to show philosophically "why profane hope must be anchored in eschatological hope." To buttress this view, Theunissen transforms Hegelian subjectivity into a Kierkegaardian "unrepresentable singularity," and Hegel's lateral conception of intersubjectivity into a much more open-ended, vertical relation to radical otherness. In Habermas's words (p. 116), "he is convinced that every interpersonal relation is embedded in a relation to the radically Other, which precedes the relation to the concrete Other" and which "embodies an absolute freedom"—a conception that "can be traced back to elements of Jewish and Protestant mysticism." In this perspective, God as the "radically Other" is present in human history "in the form of a promise, the 'anticipatory' present of a fulfilled future," which alone can redeem human suffering and despair. Countering this outlook, Habermas brings to bear a battery of considerations: first of all the "anthropological fact" (p. 122) of human self-maintenance (despite despair); and secondly the Kantian notion of apriori conditions of possibility (saying that "the mode of successfully being a self can only be employed in a *hypothetical* way in the transcendental clarification of its conditions of possibility"—on which basis "faith could only be justified in functional terms"). Finally, the essay chides Theunissen for ignoring the basic tenets of formal or universal pragmatics, which "all subjects must accept insofar as they orient their action towards validity claims at all" and which alone "can provide the normative basis for a critical theory of society" (p. 118).[6] Regarding Theunissen's trust in "a transcendence irrupting into history" and his attempt to provide arguments supporting this trust, Habermas concludes (p. 123): "I am unable to accept these reasons."

My task here is not to arbitrate between Athens and Jerusalem or to judge the respective merits of rational-philosophical and religious-theological arguments. My point here is simply to cast doubt on Mendieta's claim of a smooth, uninterrupted continuity between the two generations of the Frankfurt School. This doubt is further reinforced by developments in another arena for which Habermas has shown little sympathy: French philosophy, especially in its deconstructive variant. As it seems to me, many of the motifs of the first generation—appeals to eschatology and a "radically Other"—have resurfaced in recent decades in the writings of French Jewish and Christian thinkers, from Levinas to Derrida and Marion. Habermas's essays make no reference to Levinas, and his comments on Derrida are almost uniformly dismissive. Have motifs of the first generation thus emigrated from Frankfurt into new terrains? Whatever the answer here may be, the concern is that other issues may likewise have traveled elsewhere. I mentioned at the beginning the progressive accommodation of "critical theory" to American liberalism—a trend acquiring ominous portents under the auspices of a globalized neoliberalism. To Habermas's credit, there are passages in Mendieta's book showing awareness of these portents, as when, in the essay on Metz (p. 130), he castigates "the barbaric reverse side of its own mirror" which Western Enlightenment has ignored for too long and which has encouraged the rise of "the stifling power of a capitalistic world civilization, which assimilates alien cultures and abandons its own traditions to oblivion."[7] However, in the later interview with Mendieta, we learn (p. 153) that the current state of the world is really "without any clearly recognizable alternative" and that "there is no reasonable exit-option left to us from a capitalist world society today." Although deploring the "unjust distribution of good fortune in the world," redress for this situation belongs for Habermas to politics and economics, "not in the cupboard of morality, let alone moral theory" (p. 166). As he reiterates, the "burning issue of a just global order" is basically a "political" (that is, a tactical or strategic) problem, and "not a question for moral theory" or discourse ethics. Does this mean that the poor and marginalized populations of the Third and Fourth World can no longer expect intellectual and ethical support for their plight from Frankfurt? In this case, the rupture between the two generations would indeed seem unbridgeable.

NOTES

1. See Jürgen Habermas, *Religion and Rationality: Essays on Reason, God, and Modernity*, ed. Eduardo Mendieta (Cambridge, MA: MIT Press, 2002), pp. 2, 12. As Mendieta adds plaintively (p. 13): "The debates about whether Habermas's turn toward the philosophy of language (analytic philosophy), the appropriation of certain motifs from Weber's functionalism and Luhmann's systems theory, and his severe criticism of Adorno and Horkheimer have transformed him into an apostate, have had the unfortunate consequence of eclipsing the ways in which Habermas's thought has indeed inherited the spirit of the first generation of the Frankfurt School." (Page numbers in the above text refer to this book.)

2. This assurance forms a kind of *cantus firmus* of the Introduction. Thus, we read (p. 12) that Habermas "has without equivocation continued the interdisciplinary research agenda that informed the Frankfurt School's Critical Theory"; and a bit later (p. 14) that Habermas "remains true to the spirit of Horkheimer's and

Adorno's critique of religion in his criticism of their own negative theology." Unfortunately, the meaning of both "negative theology" and of its critical negation remains unclear.

3. In a later context, in the interview with Mendieta, Habermas remarks more cautiously (p. 164): "It would be the worst kind of intellectualism to expect that philosophy's 'way of translation' could completely appropriate the forms of experience preserved in religious language" (which seems to indicate that religion was not quite speechless before linguistification).

4. Habermas in this context (pp. 88-91) also comments on some of my own critical views offered at the same conference—an exchange whose understandings and (mutual) misunderstandings it would be too laborious (and self-serving) to disentangle at this point.

5. As Habermas adds (p. 137): "In this domain, therefore, it is the philosophical spirit of political enlightenment which lends theology the concepts with which to make sense of moves towards a polycentric world church. I say this without any intention of scoring points." But, of course, points are continuously scored.

6. From the perspective of formal pragmatics, Theunissen's focus on the "radically Other" is quickly stripped of its unrepresentable quality and placed into the first person-second person box provided by formal-pragmatic theory (pp. 124-125). Habermas also castigates Theunissen's "polemic" against the formalism of Kantian moralism and his preference for substantive ethics (pp. 123-124). Relying again on his discourse model, he holds that moral theory focuses on universal moral principles whereas ethics deals (merely) with "the successful achievement of selfhood" and "an unspoiled life" in a particularistic context. However, a long line of ethical thinking (dating back to Aristotle) argues that ethics properly speaking deals precisely with efforts of self-transformation or self-overcoming, that is, the overcoming of particularistic self-enclosure. On the other hand, the meaning of "universal principles" depends crucially on criteria or frames of significance, criteria that are typically provided by ethical contexts (thus undermining Habermas's priority scheme).

7. In a similar vein, he states in the later interview with Mendieta (p. 154): "Surely, the West still maintains a privileged access to the resources of power, wealth, and knowledge in our world. . . . Thus, the West, molded by the Judeo-Christian tradition, must reflect on one of its greatest cultural achievements: the capacity for decentering one's own perspectives, self-reflection, and a self-critical distancing from one's own traditions. The West must abstain from any non-discursive means, must be only one voice among many, in the hermeneutical conversation between cultures. In a word: overcoming Eurocentrism demands that the West make proper use of its own cognitive resources."

Appendix C

Nomolatry and Fidelity:
A Response to Charles Taylor

Recently, Charles Taylor wrote an essay titled "The Danger of Moralism."[1] I have been asked to comment on Taylor's essay; I feel honored both because of the author and his chosen theme. In my view, Taylor is one of the few contemporary philosophers who, without being petulant, writes against the grain of prevalent intellectual prejudices, that is, "against the self-images of our age" (to borrow the phrase from one of Alastair MacIntyre's early books). At a time when all academic disciplines were increasingly patterned on the model of the natural sciences, he reminded his colleagues in the humanities and social sciences of a different standard of inquiry: that of the interpretive understanding of meaning—a standard depending on participant engagement rather than neutral observation. At a time when the legacy of Hegel was shunted aside by devotees of logical rigor, he almost single-handedly rescued from oblivion this philosopher of "spirit" (whose notion of *Geist* was not very far removed from the trinitarian spirit). Above all, at a time when agnosticism and indifference or even hostility to religion are *de rigeur* in much of academia, he never stopped to inject into his writings a certain mode of faithfulness or fidelity—a faithfulness to something unconditional, something that cannot be grasped or instrumentally manipulated and which, despite its oblivion, never stops to call on us.

Taylor's essay takes aim at a central feature of modern Western life: the fascination with rules and regulations, with attempts at harnessing or controlling all human conduct by fixed codes of behavior. The fascination can be traced back in the West at least as far as the Roman Stoics; but it has become particularly virulent in the modern era. Taylor speaks in this context of "code fetishism" and "nomolatry." In the domain of philosophy, this fetishism manifests itself in the effort of major thinkers to reduce ethical life to a codified set of moral rules, that is, to a morality "defined in terms of obligatory and forbidden actions" and "generated from a single source or principle." In the social and political domain, modernity has given rise to the codified and bureaucratically administered rule-of-law state distinguished by the "legal entrenchment of certain fundamental principles of our society" and by the progressive legalization and "constitutionalization" of social relations (including the enactment of charters of rights and civil codes). Taylor perceives danger in this pervasive legalism and codified moralism: especially the danger of a crucial foreshortening of perspectives and human possibilities. First of all, in terms of perspectives, code fetishism tends to "forget the background which makes sense of any code," the awareness (still present in earlier times) that "any code can only hold in a larger order which transcends the code." More importantly, nomolatry forgets that rules and norms cannot operate in a vacuum, that is, in the absence of ethically motivated and nurtured people. The ethical life of people, however (Taylor reminds us), proceeds not on one, but at least on two levels: a "horizontal" level or dimension in which we have to find "the point of resolution" or fair adjustment between two or more parties; and a "vertical" level or dimension opening up the possibility of genuine human transformation, the possibility that "by rising higher" we find a new plane for the relations between all parties.

Such transformation can happen in ordinary human interactions; but it is most visibly displayed in such public venues as the Truth and Reconciliation Commission in South Africa. In the case of the latter proceedings, Taylor notes, the aim was not primarily punishment (an eye for an eye), but rather the search for a settlement which would lead to reconciliation and hence to the possibility of parties "living together on a new footing." Such reconciliation is not alien to Christian faith; in fact, it constitutes one of its central motives. "Christian faith," Taylor writes, "can never be decanted into a fixed code," because "it always places our actions in two dimensions, one of right action, and also an eschatological dimension," that is, a horizon of hope and promise. Unfortunately, Christian hope has also been affected by the creeping nomolatry of the modern age—which means, in this case, the tendency to "normalize" faith by leveling it horizontally into the comfortable format of a "reasonable religion." Under the impact of this tendency, Christianity becomes part of the "civilized order of polite society," a social arrangement dedicated to the "mutual benefit among rights-bearing individuals." From here it is only a short step to the disappearance of verticality: "It takes only a burst of confidence in procedural reason (never in short supply in modern culture) to believe that [human relations] can be arbitrated finally and decisively by a rationally derived code" (governed by rational validity claims). What this "foreshortened vision" puts out of sight is the possibility of transformation, including that of a "sharing communion" of vertical ascent. What it also puts out of sight is a certain recollection of darkness or "*memoria crucis*": a memory of the mystery of "world-healing through suffering."

As a respondent to Taylor's essay I am expected to raise a number of critical queries or objections. However, being in basic agreement with his central point I find myself in a quandary; all I can come up with are some minor reservations or qualms. One such reservation concerns an overabundance of content. The essay presents a multiplicity of intellectual trajectories, a dense array of polemical contestations "as the nova expands." The entire discussion is eminently scholarly and learned—but perhaps a bit too learned for the intended *periagogé*. Faced with this complex intellectual scenario, readers may be induced to admire the historical scholarship—rather than being moved an inch from their spot. One particular aspect of the narrative strikes me as unfortunate: the association of the Protestant Reformation with code morality or the attempt of "inculcating disciplines." In my own view, the time for confessional recriminations is long past; moreover, a religious movement stressing the centrality of grace or faith seems an unlikely breeding ground for codified rigidity (witness the Pietist sects mentioned in the essay). At some junctures, the essay could gain from the further clarification of salient issues. One such issue is the distinction between code morality and properly ethical life. The point here is surely not the complete abolition of all codes or normative rules, but rather a specification of priorities: that codes make sense or are viable only against the backdrop of a vibrant ethical life, and not the other way around. Another issue concerns the relation between "horizontal" and "vertical" dimensions of human conduct. Taylor's essay sometimes seems to suggest that the two dimensions are radically separate or can be neatly distinguished from each other. As he surely knows, such a suggestion is not really plausible on religious, especially Christian, grounds—as long as we take seriously the words reported in Matthew's Gospel (Matthew 25:40): "Truly, I say to you: as you did it to one of the least of these my brethren, you did it to me."

Rather than critiquing Taylor's arguments I prefer to augment and strengthen them by alluding to some additional resources (both biblical and philosophical). In my view, his priority scheme is amply supported by the Gospels, especially some sayings reported in the Gospel of John. There, at the end of the last supper, Jesus speaks to his disciples, telling them about the meaning of his entire ministry. Among other things he says (John 14:15): "If you love me, you will keep my commandments." Notice that he does not say: if you keep my commandments, you will come to love me. Rather, love—the ethos of loving devotion—comes first, and only then can rules make sense and take hold. This point is corroborated by some other words Jesus spoke at the same time, especially by the principal plea addressed to his disciples, namely, "that you love one another" and that "even as I have loved you, you also love one another." As he further added (perhaps to avoid any misunderstanding): "By this all men will know that you are my disciples, if you have love for one another" (John 13:34-35). To be sure, with these sayings Jesus merely underscored and further illuminated the basic meaning of Judaism and of Jewish faith from early times. For, all the Jewish laws and regulations, recorded in Deuteronomy and elsewhere, are empty and arbitrary rules without the great *"Shema Israel"* (Hear, o Israel) that Moses pronounced at the same time when he announced the Ten Commandments. What was Israel supposed to hear or be attentive to? In view of God's unmatched sacredness, the *Shema* pleaded that "you shall love the Lord your God with all your heart, and with all your soul and with all your might." As an expression of this intimate love, the people were asked to carry God's words as a "sign" on their hands and as "frontlets" between their eyes (Deuteronomy 6:4-8). To underscore that the commandments were not merely coercive edicts, Moses reminded the people that they were "not too hard for you, neither far off." For God's word, he said, is not simply up in heaven or beyond the sea. Rather, "the word is near you; it is in your mouth and in your heart, so that you can do it" (Deuteronomy 30:11-14).

In his essay, Taylor speaks as a Christian, but also as a philosopher. So perhaps I should augment his argument also a bit on the philosophical side. Among prominent recent philosophers, Taylor's view of priorities is supported above all by Martin Heidegger (whose name is invoked briefly in the essay, together with numerous novelists and poets). As is well known, the German philosopher departed from the traditional conception of human nature as "rational animal" (*animal rationale*), especially because of an apprehension that "rationality" might be too conducive to a certain cleverness in rule-making and nomolatry. In lieu of this traditional conception, his work highlighted as a crucial feature of human life the quality of "care" (*Sorge*), a quality whose range extends from anxious worry to careful solicitude and caring love. In a number of places, Heidegger also addressed the "perils of moralism," especially the penchant for code fetishism in moral theory. As he writes in his "Letter on Humanism," the prevailing social disarray understandably fosters a desire for "binding rules and directives" capable of guiding human conduct. And "who could disregard this predicament?" Yet, although we may wish to safeguard existing norms for the sake of maintaining a tenuous social order, the problem disclosed in the predicament goes deeper: pointing to the need to recover the underlying premises or preconditions of ethical life. The Letter at this point draws attention to a recorded saying of

Heraclitus consisting of only three words: "*ethos anthropo daimon.*" Heidegger translates "ethos" as dwelling place, abode, or place of human dwelling—which yields this translation of the entire fragment: "Human beings dwell, in their very humanity (or their ethical life), in the nearness of god (*daimon*)." The Letter goes on to tell a story about Heraclitus, as reported by Aristotle. According to the story, a group of Greek tourists went out (perhaps by bus) in search of the philosopher, hoping to come upon him while he was "thinking." On arrival, they find him warming himself by a stove. When they were about to leave disappointedly, Heraclitus motioned them to come closer with these memorable words: "Even here [at this inconspicuous place] gods are present."[2]

Heidegger's views resonate with those of another major recent philosopher, a French thinker unjustifiably neglected today (and perhaps even closer to Taylor in spirit): Gabriel Marcel. Roughly contemporary with Heidegger, Marcel was preeminently a thinker of wayfaring and pilgrimage. His numerous diaries are testimony of a life lived as a continuous quest, in search of transformation and spiritual ascent (which may well coincide with a descent on the social ladder). Like Taylor, he was apprehensive of the bent toward rationalization and codification in modern life, detecting in this bent the danger of formalism and detached moralism. What he feared above all in the cult of rationalism was "a gradual secularization of reason, a functional treatment tending more and more to reduce reason to a series of technical operations" while obscuring the "properly sacral quality" human life. Again like Taylor, he deplored the normalizing or leveling bent implicit in modern contractual egalitarianism, a bent stifling the possibility of vertical movement, including the transformative ascent offered by friendship and love. As opposed to the self-centered character of contractual equality, he wrote at one point, "fraternity is essentially heterocentric" proclaiming: "you are my brother, I recognize you as such," and because you are my brother, "I rejoice not only in anything good which may happen to you but also in acknowledging the ways in which you are superior to me." In the same text, we find these lines that Taylor (I believe) might appreciate:

> We are entitled to suppose that we are grossly deceived by appearances in our hypostasis when we treat as independent, circumscribed reality what may be only the emergence of some measureless kingdom whose submerged regions and underwater ramifications can be sighted only accidentally and by sudden illuminations. Might not the very fact of living, in the full sense we give the word when we speak of our own life, of human life, imply for one who would go to the heart of the matter, the existence of a metaphysical Atlantis, unexplorable by definition, but whose presence actually gives our own experience its dimension, its value, and its mysterious quality?[3]

One of Marcel's most inspiring texts is a book called *Homo Viator: Introduction to a Metaphysics of Hope*. The title already discloses the author's central concern with voyaging or peregrination. Among other things, the book contains an essay on "Obedience and Fidelity"—a theme not far removed from Taylor's discussion of moralism. The essay contrasts obedience, construed as submission to a code morality or fixed rules, with fidelity, seen as a properly ethical (and heterocentric) life. For Marcel, fidelity means a life "no longer degraded, alienated, or prostituted, but lived in all the fullness of its true significance." As he notes, obedience is basically the "virtue of the child" who submits to prevailing regulations; regardless of whether rules are externally dictated or self-generated, the duty exacted by obedience "does not fundamentally and necessarily involve the being of him who obeys." By contrast, fidelity involves a genuine bonding of oneself, an unconstrained and unconditional loyalty and faithfulness. In Marcel's words, fidelity "cannot be separated from the idea of an oath; this means that it implies the consciousness of something sacred." As an unconstrained bonding, fidelity cannot be prescribed or "humanly exacted, any more than love or life." In such a domain, he says, "prescriptions cannot go beyond the *as if* (*comme si*), and only deal with (external) behavior." In fact, being undomesticated and creative, fidelity like liberty itself "infinitely transcends the limits of what can be prescribed." In its creative urgency, fidelity ultimately is transformative, disclosing the potential of an inner ascent. And it is in this way that an ethics centered on fidelity is "irresistibly led to become attached to what is more than human, to a desire for the unconditional which is the very mark of the absolute in us."[4]

The same book contains two essays dealing with the poet Rainer Maria Rilke. In these essays Rilke (a hero also of my own youth) is presented as "a witness to the spiritual"—to be sure, a poetic and unorthodox witness. Marcel's discussion makes clear, among other things, the vast distance separating genuine faithfulness or fidelity from any kind of religious triumphalism. In his essay, Taylor repeatedly uses the word "God"—no doubt, without any hidden political agenda. Still, believers today have to be extremely cautious or careful in using this word, observing something approximating the "prohibition of images." As it seems to me, great reticence and parsimony of language is demanded of believers at a time when God's name is invoked routinely and obscenely by political rulers in their pursuit of imperialist agendas, wholesale slaughter, and possibly nuclear holocaust. In a diary fragment dating from October 1900 and quoted approvingly by Marcel, Rilke writes: "I was speaking of him in a low voice." And in a letter to Ilse Jahr dating from February of 1923, he reports about a journey to Russia, saying: "Then, Russia opened out for me and gave me the brotherliness and darkness of God, in whom alone there is fellowship. That was how I named him then, the God who has dawned upon me, and I lived long in the antechamber of his name, on my knees." And he continues: As the tangible or ephemeral slips away, "instead of possession one learns the relativity of things, and there arises a namelessness that must begin again with God if it is to become perfect and without deceit."[5]

Rilke's reticence does not signify aloofness or a lack of transformative fidelity. As he writes in one of his notebooks: "Perhaps a sort of ordination has been conferred upon me, perhaps others having become strangers to me, it has befallen me sometimes to approach a man with solemnity, as though I had access to him by a golden gate."[6] The gate he is referring to here, I believe, is the gate to the promised city, a place always anticipated by lovers in their conduct. For, in approaching a beloved person, do lovers not sometimes feel like standing on sacred ground? Nor does reticence denote an absence of vertical intensity. Listen to these lines from Rilke's "Book of Pilgrimage":

> Put out my eyes; I can see thee.
> Stop up my ears; I can hear thee.
> And without feet I can go to thee,
> and without a mouth I can still call upon thee.
> Tear off my arms, and I shall yet seize thee
> with my heart as with a hand.

But note well: the "thee" he is invoking here is not a big and mighty overlord, an accomplice of imperial rulers and powerful armies. Here are some additional lines from the "Book of Hours," lines reflecting a profound shyness and saturated distantly with *memoria crucis*:

> But thou art the most profoundly needy,
> The beggar with concealed face.
> Thou art the great rose of poverty,
> The eternal transformation
> of gold into sunlight.

> (*Du aber bist der tiefste Mittellose,*
> *Der Bettler mit verborgenem Gesicht.*
> *Du bist der Armut grosse Rose,*
> *die ewige Metamorphose*
> *des Goldes in das Sonnenlicht.*)[7]

NOTES

1. See Charles Taylor, "The Danger of Moralism," in *Theology and Public Philosophy,* ed. Kenneth L. Grasso and Jean Bethke Elshtain (Chicago: Eerdman, 2005), forthcoming.

2. Heidegger, "Letter on Humanism," in *Martin Heidegger: Basic Writings,* pp. 231-234.

3. Gabriel Marcel, "Human Dignity," in *Existential Phenomenology and Political Theory: A Reader,* ed. Hwa Yol Jung (Chicago: Henry Regnery, 1972), pp. 307-312.

4. Gabriel, Marcel, "Obedience and Fidelity," in *Homo Viator: Introduction to a Metaphysic of Hope,* trans. Emma Craufurd (New York: Harper and Row, 1962), pp. 125-127, 132-134.

5. Gabriel , Marcel, "Rilke: A Witness to the Spiritual (I and II)," in *Homo Viator,* pp. 219, 242. The quotation in the letter is taken from Rainer Maria Rilke, *Selected Letters,* trans. R. F. C. Hall (London: Macmillan, 1947) p. 373.

6. Rilke, *Briefe und Tagebücher* (Leipzig: Insel Verlag, 1951), p. 370; as quoted in *Homo Viator,* p. 219. Marcel at another point (p. 217) speaks of Rilke's "passion for distance and for spaces," noting: "But it must immediately be added that in his case this passion itself is joined with his devotion to intimacy"—an intimacy which "did not exclude distance, but demanded it."

7. Marcel, *Homo Viator,* pp. 227, 233. The verses are Craufurd's translation of Marcel's own translation from the German. For the German text see Rilke, *Das Stundenbuch* (Leigzig: Insel Verlag, 1959), and for another English translation, Rilke, *The Book of Hours: Prayers to a Lowly God,* trans. Annemarie S. Kidder (Evanston, IL: Northwestern University Press, 2001).

Index

Abe, Masao, 129
absolutism, 212; global, 59
activism, 82
Adivasis, 85
Adorno, Theodor W., 5–6, 10, 19–20, 24, 26–27, 34–39, 44–49, 125, 168, 170, 219–20
aesthetics, 182
affectivity, 3, 7
Agamben, Giorgio, 21–22
agnosticism, 10, 225
Alexander the Great, 60, 66
al-Jabiri, Mohammed, 130
Althusser, Louis, 128
amateurism, 99–100
Ambedkar, Bhim Rao, 130
analectics, 46
anti-Americanism, 104
anti-essentialism, 103
anti-metaphysics, 20
anti-politics, 202
anti-rationalism, 187
application, 185
appropriation, 162, 164
Arendt, Hannah, 174n21, 196n5, 204
Ariyaratne, A. T., 130
Aristotle, 3, 12n2, 14, 33, 39, 60–61, 67–69, 75n34, 120, 163–67, 171, 181, 186, 194, 224n6, 229

art, 164–67, 182; of healing, 163
artifact, 156
assimilation, 180, 219
Auerbach, Erich, 109
Augustine, St., 137
authority, 41–44, 179–80, 187–88

Bacon, Francis, 33–38, 101, 148, 168
Balfour, Lord, 101
Barber, Benjamin, 57–59, 70
Barsamian, David, 83
Barthes, Roland, 28, 128
Beck, Ulrich, 8, 116, 131–32
behaviorism, 25
Benda, Julien, 81, 96–97
benevolence, 61–62; civilizational, 62
Benjamin, Walter, 4, 10, 13, 23, 79, 98, 219, 221
Bergson, Henri, 129
Besinnung, 42
Bhargava, Rajeev, 139, 143, 149, 151–52
Bildung, 163
Blake, William, 105
Bloch, Ernst, 219, 221
body, 31n26
Boyle, Francis, 71n1
Brzezinski, Zbigniew, 57
Buber, Martin, 221

About the Author

Fred Dallmayr is Packay J. Dee Professor in the departments of philosophy and political science at the University of Notre Dame. He holds a Doctor of Law degree from the University of Munich (1955) and a Ph.D. in political science from Duke University (1960). He has been a visiting professor at Hamburg University in Germany and at the New School for Social Research in New York, and a Fellow at Nuffield College in Oxford. He has been teaching at Notre Dame University since 1978. During 1991-92 he was in India on a Fulbright research grant. Some of his recent publications are: *Between Freiburg And Frankfurt* (1991); *The Other Heidegger* (1993); *Beyond Orientalism: Essays On Cross-Cultural Encounter* (1996; Japanese translation 2001); *Alternative Visions: Paths In The Global Village* (1998: Persian translation 2005); *Achieving Our World: Toward A Global And Plural Democracy* (2001); *Dialogue Among Civilizations: Some Exemplary Voices* (2002; Italian translation forthcoming); *Hegel: Modernity And Politics* (new ed. 2002); and *Peace Talks–Who Will Listen?* (2004).